Eric Lewis

The Video Art of Sylvia Safdie

McGill-Queen's University Press

Montreal & Kingston · London · Ithaca

ISBN 978-0-7735-4169-6 (cloth)
ISBN 978-0-7735-8900-1 (ePDF)
ISBN 978-0-7735-8901-8 (ePUB)

Legal deposit second quarter 2013
Bibliothèque nationale du Québec

Printed in Canada on acid-free paper.

McGill-Queen's University Press acknowledges the support of the Canada Council for the Arts for our publishing program. We also acknowledge the financial support of the Government of Canada through the Canada Book Fund for our publishing activities.

Library and Archives Canada Cataloguing in Publication

Lewis, Eric, 1961-
      The video art of Sylvia Safdie / Eric Lewis.

Includes videography.
ISBN 978-0-7735-4169-6 (cloth).-- ISBN 978-0-7735-8900-1 (ePDF).—
ISBN 978-0-7735-8901-8 (ePUB).

      1. Safdie, Sylvia, 1942- --Criticism and interpretation.
2. Video art--Québec (Province)--Montréal. I. Safdie, Sylvia,
1942- II. Title. III. Title: Sylvia Safdie.

N6549.S23L49 2013   709.2   C2013-900420-3

THE VIDEO ART OF SYLVIA SAFDIE

Contents

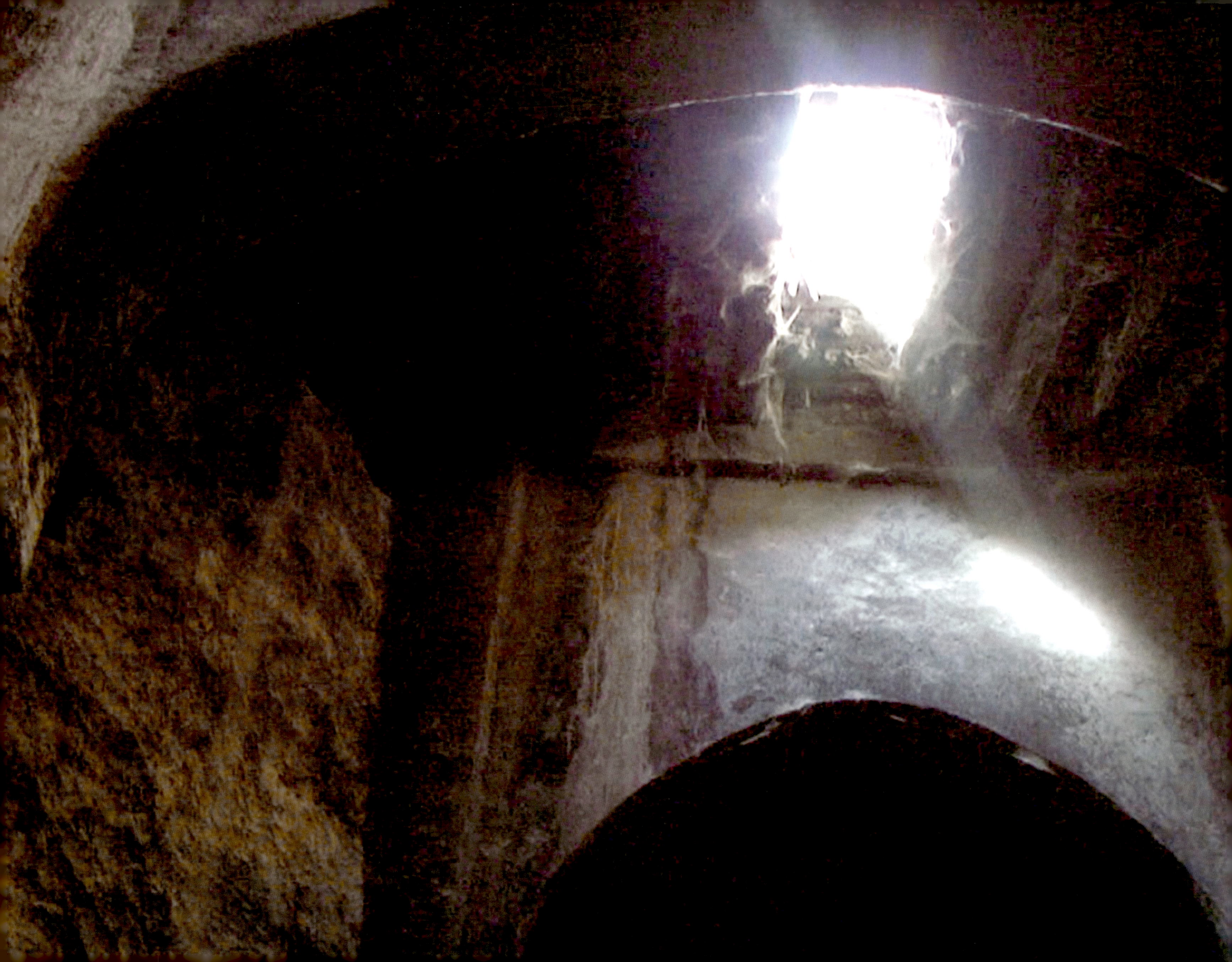

THE VIDEO ART OF SYLVIA SAFDIE

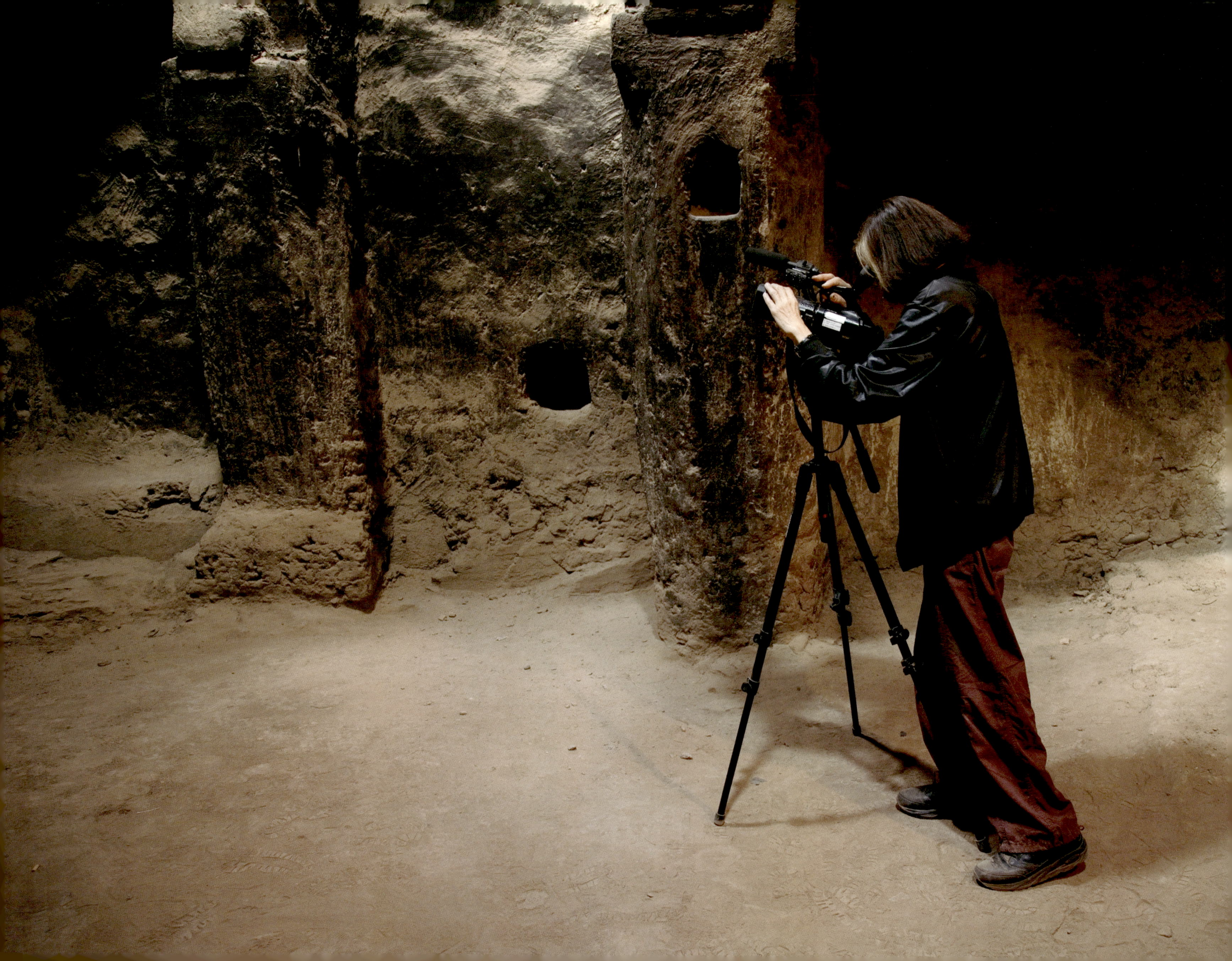

Introduction

Eric Lewis

The Video Art of Sylvia Safdie explores the most recent medium that this prolific artist has chosen to explore and situates her video work within her broader artistic career. Safdie's works in painting, drawing, and sculpture are meditations on the convergence of place, time, and memory. The themes of temporality and transformation run deeply throughout her work, especially in relation to the human form and its connections and correspondences with the natural world. Indeed, much of her art invokes the human body either directly or abstractly. Bodies, or parts of bodies, are presented in a state of transformation and flux, emerging from or disappearing into natural backgrounds of earth, water, or stone. Even absent bodies often make their presence felt. Her works frequently employ raw materials from the earth – soil, stone, metal, wood, and oil – used with little or no alteration, implying that an imprint is left on the natural world by every act of creation.

Safdie's video art, begun in 2001, can be seen as a natural extension of her work in painting, drawing, and sculpture. The metaphors and metamorphoses suggested by her previous work in these static media (such as a focus on cycles of natural change, and using natural elements as placeholders for human bodies) are played out in many of her videos, which become a moving canvas on which to explore ideas of space and time, stasis and movement, embodiment and nature. Her use of a fixed camera framing a moving subject – whether it is a bird hovering in flight, water running over stones, or dust moving in a column of light – captures ordinary movements and processes within nature that acquire heightened meaning and significance from the artist's unwavering attention. The transition to video has also allowed Safdie to experiment with sound in her work and, crucially, with the interaction between sound and

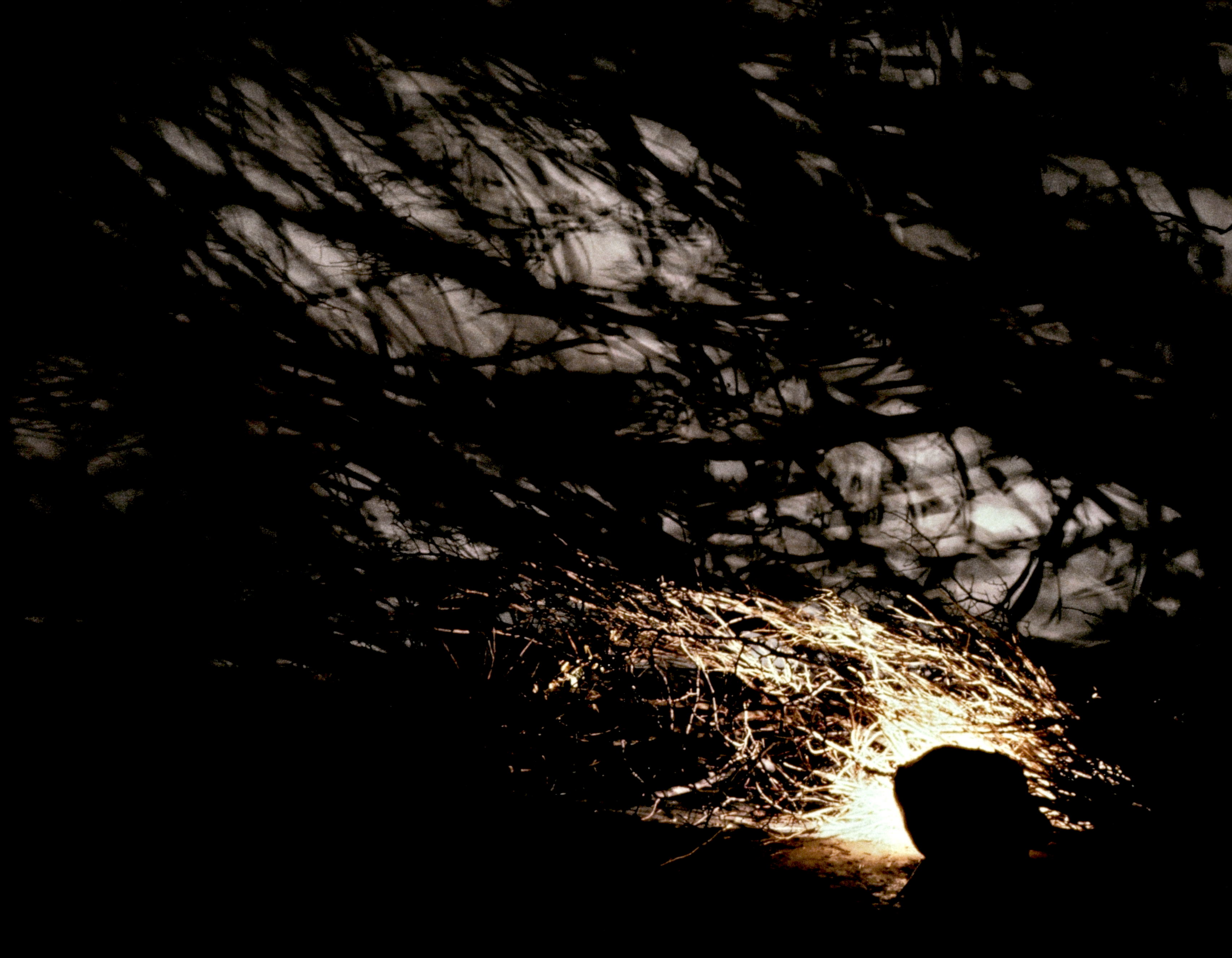

image. Collaborating with improvisational artists such as Malcolm Goldstein, David Prentice, Lori Freedman, Joe McPhee, and John Heward, she has explored the interplay between image and sound, and between body and breath, adopting an approach to video art that may itself be identified as improvisational in so far as it is highly dialogical, intentional, transformative, and attentive to process.

Born in Aley, Lebanon in 1942, Sylvia Safdie spent her early years in Israel before moving to Montreal at the age of eleven. Her Middle Eastern Jewish heritage and her Israeli childhood provided a particular set of memories and experiences that she has drawn upon throughout her artistic career. As a child, Safdie would play for hours on the beaches near Haifa, an Israeli port city, building sand sculptures. She describes how she was mesmerized by the fragility of the sand castles, how they would be gradually eroded and then erased by the encroaching waves.[1] Her interest in the passage of time, the process of transformation, and the environmental traces left behind by people and lost objects would become major themes in her oeuvre. The natural materials that she played with on the beach at Haifa – sand (crushed stone), water, and the marks of absent bodies etched in the sand – would become the canvas and materials of her later work. In these same years, Safdie became an avid collector of rocks, stones, bones, and pieces of wood, all of which she hid in a cave near her home on the slopes of Mount Carmel. Here she would hoard and classify the natural ephemera, grouping and regrouping them by shape, size, colour, type, and place of origin, conscious that each one signaled the existence of another place from which it had been found. This curatorial impulse, which has the effect of both documenting and transforming the objects collected, has continued throughout her career. Two notable examples are her installations: one (*Extensions*, 2002) is of samples of earth gathered from around the globe; another (*Feet*, 1977) is a remarkable collection of foot-shaped rocks. In these ways, Safdie's childhood memories found expression in her artistic practices and became a way of exploring the sense of displacement she felt after leaving Israel while still a girl. Much of her art bears the traces of absent agents, whether they are lost or displaced individuals, communities, environments, or cultures. But although they are now absent, their presence remains. It is not as if they never were. This idea of the "presence of absence" and of how "absent presences" leave traces of their former selves and live on in altered forms permeates Safdie's work and is uniquely revealed in her video art.

In 1981 Safdie travelled to Morocco for the first time. In a remote shrine, long visited by women seeking a divine blessing for an unborn child, she discovered a collection of cult objects left by mothers-to-be. These scraps of clothing and pieces of scroll, which served as memory traces of the mothers and children, inspired Safdie to experiment in her work with the representation of human bodies. In her paintings from this period, such as *Wayside Shrine* (1982) and *ADAD* (1983) – in which human forms are composed of scraps of sticks and scroll, or emerge from roughly etched markings resembling neolithic cave paintings – the human and the natural, person

1. All biographical details are culled from numerous interviews with Sylvia Safdie by the author conducted in 2011 and 2012.

Tzel (1990), installation at the Extention Gallery
Branches, graphite, light bulbs, plaster
Photograph: Sylvia Safdie

and environment, merge in ways that her later video work would vividly explore. On a later trip in 1994, Safdie explored the traces of the once vibrant Jewish communities in the Atlas and Anti-Atlas mountains and discovered an abandoned Jewish cemetery that whispered the absent-presence of the departed community. Newly sprung trees and plants grew over and around the old tombstones, creating a complex mingling of the natural environment and the human-marked environment. Later she would look back on this scene as an inspiration for many of her subsequent works.

Between these first visits to Morocco and the filming of her video works there in 2009, Safdie began artistically experimenting with light and the effects of reflection and refraction. Installations such as *Keren no. 1* (1994), *Assaf* (1994), *Kever* (1994), and the early *Tezel* (1990), which incorporate artifacts from the Moroccan cemetery and the many foot-shaped rocks she collected throughout her travels, are particularly attentive to the casting of shadows and the movement of light over textured surfaces. Safdie was concerned with the roles that shadow and light and play in marking the passage of time and with the ability of light to both reveal (enlighten) and obscure (dazzle or blind). Playing with the movement of light and the effect of shadow was a natural bridge to the use of video. To shoot video is to capture light. The manipulation of luminosity characteristic of her video work was presaged by these striking light installations.

Safdie's concerns with transformation, with the traces that people and the natural environment leave on each other, with the absent present, and with memory and loss, combined with her installation work focusing on the properties of light, converge in her remarkable Auschwitz video series (*Pond/Auschwitz I–III* [74–76], *Reflection/Auschwitz I–III* [77–79], *Web/Auschwitz Series I* [80.1–80.4]). These works are discussed and visually rendered in the pages that follow.

◼

Any book that attempts to visually document artwork faces a host of issues involving ideas of representation and depiction. Illustrations in books, whether they are adaptations of photos, drawings, sketches, or other technologically mediated forms of reproduction, can never perfectly reproduce the artwork they represent. This is hardly a profound observation – since antiquity, the differences between reproductions/representations and what they reproduce or represent has informed the study of mimesis in general and the mimetic arts in particular. Differences of scale, media, perspective, colour, and surroundings, among others, ground such discrepancies. Illustrated books on art choose either to attempt to mask such differences or to foreground them in order to serve assorted critical and documentary purposes.

Given the centuries of practice and theory on how to reproduce art, it came as a surprise to us to learn that there were neither commonly accepted methods for the book-form presentation of video art, nor many examples from which to draw guidance. Although books and catalogues have been written about video art and video artists, the illustrations tend to be low-quality screen-captures that provide only a vague idea of the subject matter and the visual content of the videos. The reasons for the poor book-form reproductions of the medium are due to the very nature of video art. Works within this medium often lack narrative structure, dialogue, and actors. Many video artworks are interactive or may involve multiple screens. Few cinemagraphic conventions are followed. The medium of video differs from conventional film and has different qualities. Video art's relatively low production cost allows for a more artist-driven approach. Its precise history, emerging from the Fluxus movement and related mid-1960s avant-garde art practices, responds to a different history of criticism and consumption than either cinema or television.

Video is, in a sense, a performance art because it unfolds in time. As a result, books about video art tend to treat illustrations in a similar style as books about theatre – a photo placed here and there to enliven the accompanying text. No one believes that the photos in a book about a play are a stand-in for watching the play, or even that they allow one to know what it is like to experience the performance. This book is perhaps an immodest attempt to do just that – to illustrate Safdie's videos in such a way that the viewer gets a sense of what it is like to watch the video. Safdie's approach to video art makes this possible because her background as a painter and sculptor results in video images that have a painterly quality, a sense of which we hope is captured by the images reproduced here. Moreover, there are many affinities among her work in assorted media, which unify her oeuvre and which the video images will help us demonstrate.

Sylvia Safdie's long career as a painter, sculptor, and installation artist made it clear from the beginning that the images in this book, and this book as a whole, had to serve two masters. It needed to both document the breadth and history of Safdie's video art and be an art object in its own right. Safdie was not interested in offering her assistance to a project that was simply a catalogue of her video art. We hope to have produced a beautiful book, and a book that gives one *a feel* of what it is like to watch Safdie's videos. The images are not intended to jog one's memory into recalling past experiences with the video works. Rather they are intended to induce a totally distinct experience in the viewer, one with essential aesthetic content that relates to experiencing the video but does not attempt to reproduce that experience. While the images shown here are *of* the videos they should not be considered discrete parts of such videos (as in, "this image is frame number X at temporal point Y"), but instead should be thought of as being *about* the videos. For each video documented here this required us to come to a nuanced understanding of what the video was about, what it was trying to express, and through which visual and sonic means it achieved its expression. We then strove to represent these understandings with either a single image or a series of images, even if these images do not always correspond in an obvious way to the appearance of the video itself. Some examples of this divergence are *Lori* [41], *Rajasthan (Red)* [39], or *Late Afternoon Raga* [40], all shown in the pages below.

One difficulty posed by the representation of video artwork arose as soon as we began the process of choosing images and considering layouts. When reproducing artwork in a book it is standard to compare the appearance of the illustrations with the art objects themselves. Does the colour match? Are the spatial relations represented appropriately? Is the image in focus? When this process involves an art object such as a sculpture or painting, it is relatively easy to make these comparisons since there is an established original for comparison. But with video there is not a similarly established original that permits comparison. What we call "the video" necessarily includes the media through which the artwork is presented, including the device that plays the video and the monitor that displays it. Initially we were very concerned with matching the colours of our images with the colours in the video, but we soon found ourselves asking, "What are we comparing the colour of this image with?" How a video looks on one monitor is different from how it looks on another, and how it appears in one format is different from how it appears in another. Similar issues arise with the choice of monitor size and dimension, as well as more technical features of video screen performance. Images reproduced in a book are perceptible in so far as they reflect light; light is an added element whose features may vary and thereby alter how the images appear. But video images are perceptible because they emit light – light in which the properties are controlled by the video data and the screen itself. The difference between reflecting light and emitting light profoundly affects the way in which images are both illuminated and luminous. Safdie's videos consciously play with the luminous nature of video, something that cannot be directly captured by images in a book. We therefore chose not simply to produce screen-captures of video stills (something akin to a photograph of a video screen), but extracted and manipulated the digital data that constitutes the DNA of video, altering as necessary the data's qualities of saturation, brightness, and transparency. In this sense we did not reproduce the video images as they might be seen on a certain screen as part of a certain computer system, but *recreated* an image that we felt best captured the aesthetic of the video. None of the images that follow are screen-captures, all are created images.

For these and other reasons, there is no standard way that video looks, nor is there necessarily *a* way that the artist wants it to look. The final visual presentation is mediated by a host of technologies, each of which affects what the video looks like, however subtly. Herein lies a paradox of a book on video art – the images must be true to the video, but there is no such thing as *the* video. We then started looking for consistency between the illustrations and sought colours, textures, and shapes that created compelling images in their own right. As we moved further away from mimesis, we came to realize that our decisions needed to be far less journalistic and far more artistic.

There are other features of video in general, and of Safdie's videos in particular, that helped to determine our choice of images and their layout. One might think that the natural way to present video in printed form would be through a series of frames in a fixed temporal sequence – say, a series of six images spaced five seconds apart, corresponding to thirty seconds of a video. Such a method draws inspiration from strip animation's presentation of narrative in a cellular fashion and may be seen as an attempt to simplify the density of information found in the video. For several reasons such methods proved ineffective in presenting Safdie's videos. First, such methods work best when they intend to trigger the memory of a video sequence that a viewer has already seen. Seeing a representative sequence of images from the video will prompt recollection: "Ah yes, this is when the cowboy enters the bar, turns left, then right, and shoots the piano player." A viewer moves from image to video via memory. But what if someone has not seen the video and is more interested in the experience of watching the video than in its content? Presenting a fixed sequence of frames is unlikely to produce an experience akin to that of watching the video itself; the experience will be utterly different with respect to expressiveness, aesthetic interest, and content. As a result, we searched for images and sequences that might affect the viewer in ways similar to that of the video itself. We wanted to move from video to image, not vice versa and to present images that the videos themselves suggest as their correlates. We were not mining for memories but building experiences afresh. Just as a painted portrait needs to be of aesthetic interest even to those who are unfamiliar with the subject of the portrait, we needed images that stood on their own as aesthetic objects.

The second reason a series of frames would not adequately represent Safdie's work concerns the precise methods she uses to produce her videos. Many of the video works carefully layer and superimpose a number of distinct videos, where the opacities, transparencies, and arrangement of each often move and change through the course of the video. A moment of a particular video that, when viewed in real time, would seem to be a representative screen-capture may be unsuitable when viewed as a single frame. Such a moment might include the transition of two distinct videos from foreground to background, and thus would create a confused and indistinct image. What the eye sees in sequence in a video is a fiction produced by the video itself and is not the same as viewing a series of photos. This effect is well known, but it may surprise viewers of Safdie's videos

to learn just how technically complex many of them are, since they appear so naturalistic. This is a product of Safdie's painterly approach to video production, which will be discussed later in more detail. She hides the technology behind her images as an artist may hide brushstrokes. Even when the subjects of her videos are clearly imaginary – bodies emerging out of rocks, for example – the treatment is so natural that the viewer receives the images without question. These videos are visual equivalents of magic realist writing – both mask the magic by creating a world where the exceptional seems unexceptional.

The third reason concerns the intimate relationship between sound and image in many of the videos, as Safdie has worked closely with a number of important improvisational musicians in creating her video works. More than just providing an interesting soundtrack, the improvisations interact with the video images, forming a highly deliberate and unified multi-media artwork. It is not going too far to argue that Safdie improvises with her musical partners, allowing images to dialogically relate to the music. The importance of the visual-audio dimension in many of these videos challenged us further still to capture something of the rhythm, pulse, texture, and tone of the accompanying music. The images presented here are not only abstract representations of the videos' visual appearance, but of their sounds as well.

■

The more than 200 images derived from thirty videos found in the following pages are supplemented by two interpretative essays exploring different aspects of Safdie's video art. The first essay, by Eleanor Stubley, entitled "Sylvia Safdie's Bodies: Portrait of a Hand at Work," explores representations of the body in Safdie's videos. In describing her fascination with the human form, Safdie has noted: "Our bodies are in constant motion as the gestures we make disappear and evaporate within seconds, one into the next," yet these movements carry us through the world and "connect us to our pasts and to our futures." As Stubley observes, Safdie finds motion in the slightest gestures, and even in the still positions, of a drummer and his drum, a figure in sleep, and a body in meditation. Her overlay of bodies with images of water and stone suggests the tension between movement and stasis, fluidity and fixity, but these properties are not immutable as sometimes it is the waters that are unchanging and the stone that transforms. Where some videos encompass the entire body, others frame a single part such as the head, the hand, or the foot. Although the wholeness of the body is always implied, viewers are invited to contemplate each part of the body as a repository of different memories. In her video work Safdie has deployed her camera to explore the representability of the body, although as Stubley notes, what the videos and video installations essentially build upon is "the seductive allure of the living." As such, what we see is the poetic expansion of the notion of "body" to include all that it touches and with which it resonates.

In the second essay, "Breathing Sound – Sounding Breath: The Video Art of Sylvia Safdie," I explore the importance of breath in the development of her early video art and its importance to her treatment of the themes of vitality, embodiment, and the cycles of life. Safdie's focus on breath, as both a hallmark of life and the source of the most human of sounds, presages her explorations with improvised sound in her later video work. I also discuss Safdie's deliberate interplay of sound and image, which approaches a creative dialogue, and the role and function of improvisation in her creative process.

The book concludes with a complete videography documenting Safdie's video art up to July 2012. Excerpts of many of the videos represented and discussed in this book are available for viewing on the artist's web site, www.sylviasafdie.com. The e-book edition of this volume includes a modest selection of embedded video files to provide examples of her video work.

The creation of this book was very much a collective enterprise and involved more than its share of improvisation. Lauren Diez d'Aux was instrumental in getting the project off the ground, conducting many interviews with Sylvia Safdie, undertaking background research, and providing many of the descriptions used in the videography. It was she who realized that a book such as this was possible, and without her work and insight it would never have come to be. Safdie's video editor and assistant, Patrick Andrew Boivin, spent many, many hours working with the videos in order to produce the magnificent images. He has the eye of an artist and the technical genius of an engineer. He worked closely with Yvan Tétreault, who created the lay-out and design of the book and experimented with countless ways of representing Safdie's video art on the printed page. Were it not for his subtle understanding of the challenges we faced in producing a book that both documents Safdie's video art and attempts to capture a measure of its artistic achievements, this book would be of far less interest than we hope it is. Sylvia Safdie herself gave us complete access to her video library, shared with us stories behind the creation of many of these videos, and lent us her eye at many stages of this book's production. Her interest and advice helped make this book a pleasure to create. We wish to thank the Scott Griffin Foundation for their generous support of this project. Finally, I have benefited from the careful and thoughtful assistance of the editorial and production departments at McGill-Queen's University Press, which immediately saw the potential of this enterprise and worked to overcome the various hurdles to publication. In particular, Kyla Madden was instrumental in seeing this book to fruition, while the meticulous work of Ryan Van Huijstee far transcended mere copy-editing.

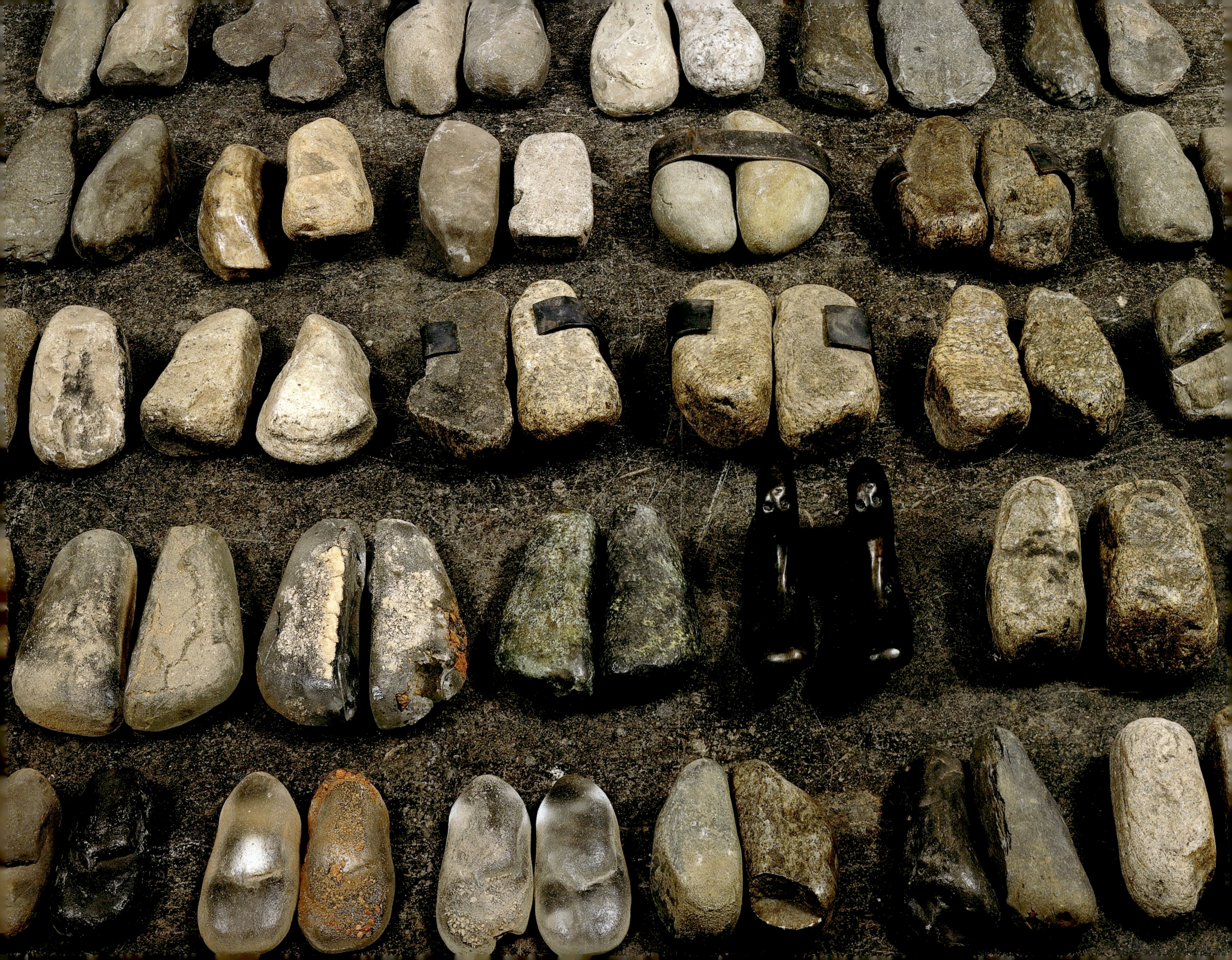

Sylvia Safdie's Bodies: Portrait of a Hand at Work

Eleanor V. Stubley

The wonder that is the essence of art … begins with movement.

Paul Valéry, Notebooks, *volume 2*

Many locate the heart of Sylvia Safdie's art in her penchant for gathering objects and the ways in which she twists, turns, and bends them to both reveal and renew the flux of the world.[1] The centrality of the body in her expression has received less discussion. The body initially appears through the flat, two-dimensional language of the stick figure, where its image becomes a playground for exploring the transformative power of the artist's own gesture. With the paint fabricated from an elemental mixture of earth and oil, the *Earth Marks* and *Notations* (as Safdie calls them) articulate the textured nature of the body and its primacy as the medium of our worldly interactions. Her sculptures (*Heads*, *Feet*, *Vases*, *Earths*, *Sefer*) use the objective materiality of stones, fossils, and other natural objects to explore the

dimensionality of the body and the ways in which it occupies space across time and place. These works often represent multiple bodies to illustrate how life is replenished and renewed through individual bodies as well as the transformational potential of the body itself as material substance. Her videos and video installations extend this exploration from the perspective of the body's gestures as they unfold through the temporal and spatial language of film as a multi-sensory medium that involves both sight and sound.

Where Safdie's paintings and sculptures typically present the traces of a body that once was, or the illusion of a body that might be, her videos and video installations build on the seductive allure of the living. For Safdie, the allure of the living begins with the individuality of her subjects who range in age from the young to the old, from the strong to the infirm, from the famous to the unknown. The allure

1. Irina Zantovskà Murray, *The Inventories of Inventions* (Galerie d'art Leonard and Bina Ellen), 2003.

Feet (1992–), installation in the artist's studio (detail).
Photograph: Richard Max Tremblay

Notations p. 192, 1997
Earth, oil, and graphite on mylar. 43 x 35.5 cm

Notations p. 390, 2002
Earth, oil, and graphite on mylar. 43 x 35.5 cm

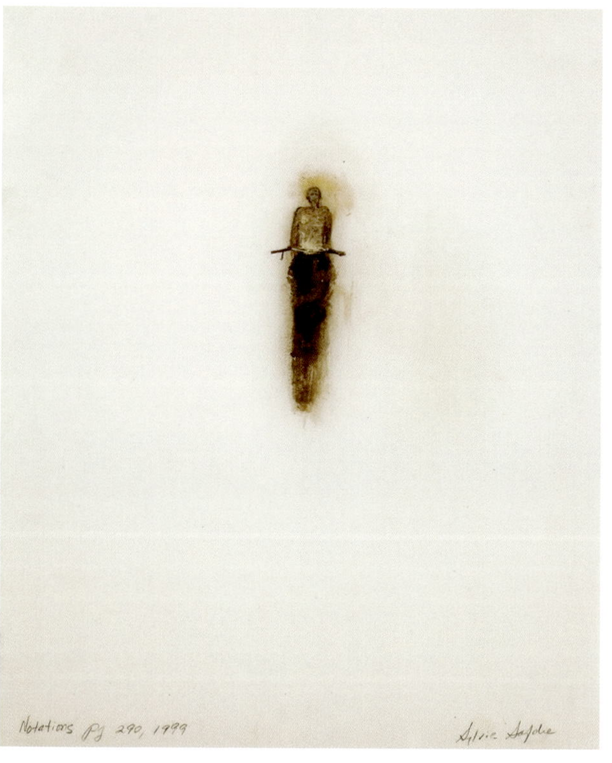

Notations p. 290, 1999
Earth, oil, and graphite on mylar. 43 x 35.5 cm

ultimately hangs on the ways in which her subjects' gestures seem to animate and give life at moments of great vulnerability. "Life is movement," Safdie notes, "movement is life." "Our bodies are in constant motion" [as] "the gestures we make disappear and evaporate within seconds," one into the other.[2] Yet, as the movements through which we situate ourselves in the world, "they are the lifelines" that "connect us to our pasts and to our futures."[3] In some instances, the vulnerability shown in her videos is a function of the subject's age and the preciousness of the moment at which the camera caught his or her image. In other instances, the vulnerability stems from the ways in which Safdie combines images in the editing process using various light, framing, shadow, and other layering techniques to convey the instability and flux of the unfolding moment as an evolving present and the fragility of all life as it marches inexorably towards death.

This allure is often enhanced by a camera technique that focuses attention on the minute detail of an evolving gesture from unusual and unexpected sightlines that are close to the body. The technique leads Safdie to find movement in postures and positions of stillness such as the torso that grounds a drummer and his drum, the inward reflection of a meditative body, and the figure deep in sleep, seemingly caught in some in-between place where life hangs in the balance. It also often endows the viewing of a video work with a sense of intimacy, while simultaneously magnifying the evolving gesture to give it a magical, almost larger-than-life quality. For example, in *Gladys:*

A Life (2005) [19] we are so transfixed by the life-giving powers of an evolving smile as it erases the fine lines of a face wizened by time, that when the video begins again (as many of her works do) we find ourselves lingering in the presentness of the moment and savouring its unfolding again and again, as if each time was the first time.

Just as often, though, the magic is associated with the mystery and sensuality of that which typically cannot be seen – namely the feel or experience of the body as a body becoming, a body felt internally as a body that is constantly evolving with its surroundings. A case in point is Safdie's portrait of a stonecutter (*Stone Cutter*, 2003 [9] and *Foot*, 2003 [10]) where the gestures of a single foot and a single hand are each projected onto its own screen. The constant motion of each is in and of itself spellbinding, both for the quickness of the motion and the way in which it conveys a continual re-forming and re-positioning of foot and hand in response to the stone as the stonecutter cuts into it. Safdie, however, has also cloaked the installation in a mantle of silence that draws our attention to the inter-connectedness of foot and hand. While the corporeal essence of the stonecutter as a recognizable identity has seemingly disappeared into the empty space between the two screens, that space is also alive with the throb of their synchronicity. And, in the marked absence of the sounds of a nail contacting stone and a foot shifting in the sand, we not only see this sense of internal cohesiveness or inner attunement, we sensually feel it from our own vantage point within the empty space as the kinesthetic essence of the body Henri Bergson describes as pure rhythm.[4]

2. Sylvia Safdie, "Note about *Figures and Ground II*", www.sylviasafdie.com/video/2009/index.htm.
3. Ibid.

4. Henri Bergson, *Time and Free Will: An Essay on the Immediate Data of Consciousness*, trans. F.L. Pogson (London: George Allen and Unwin, 1910).

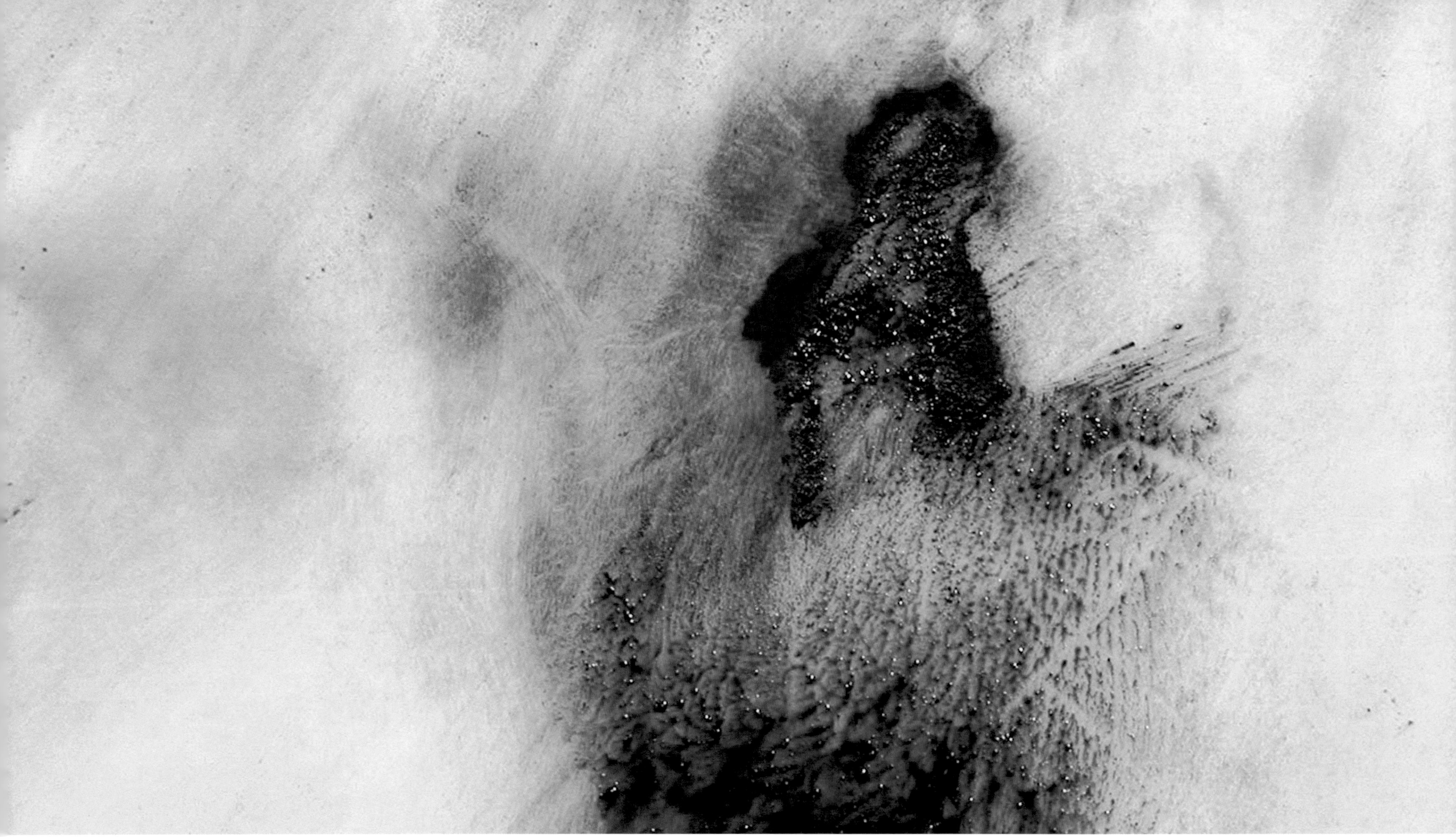

Figures and Ground II (2009) [65], video stills

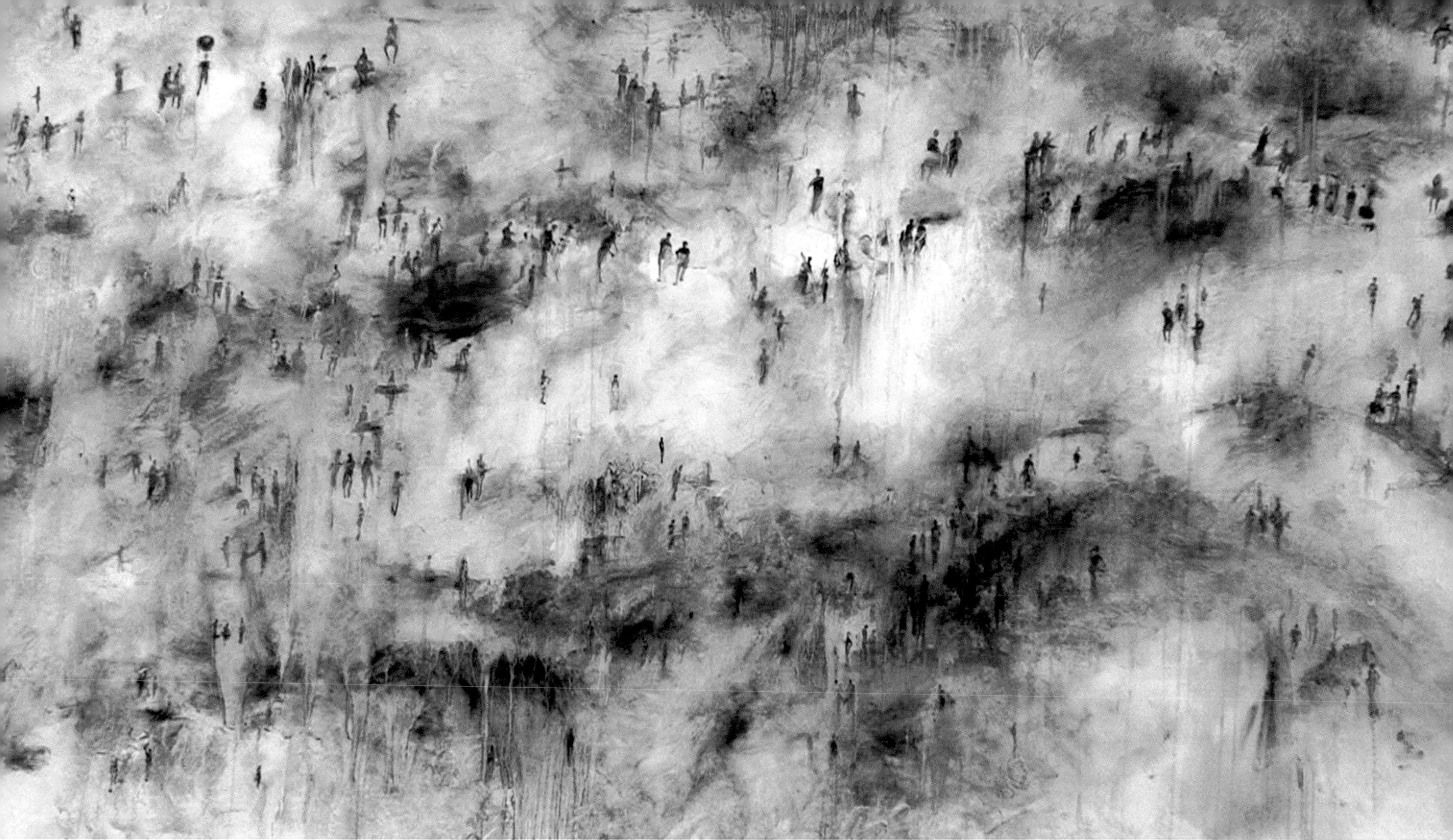

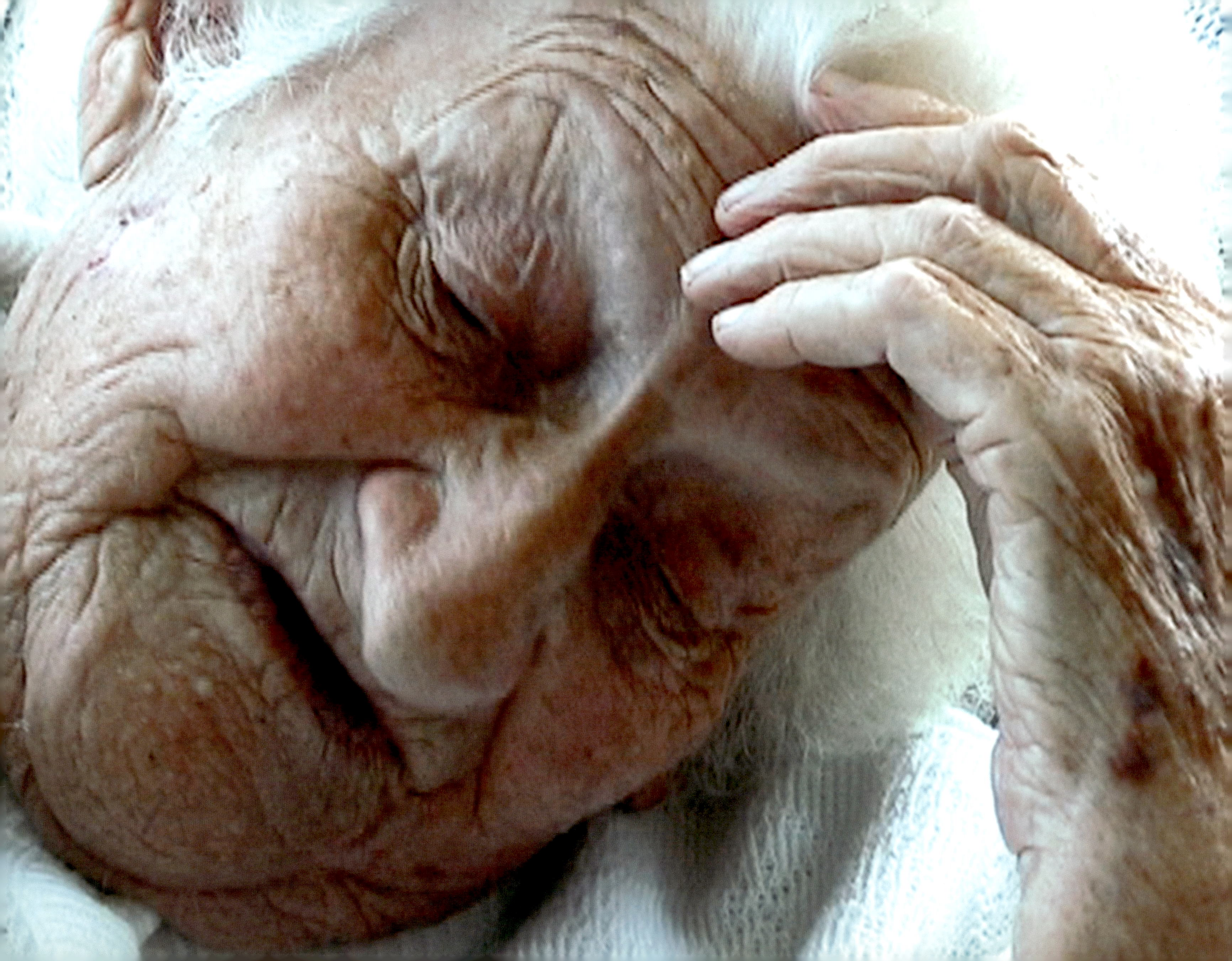

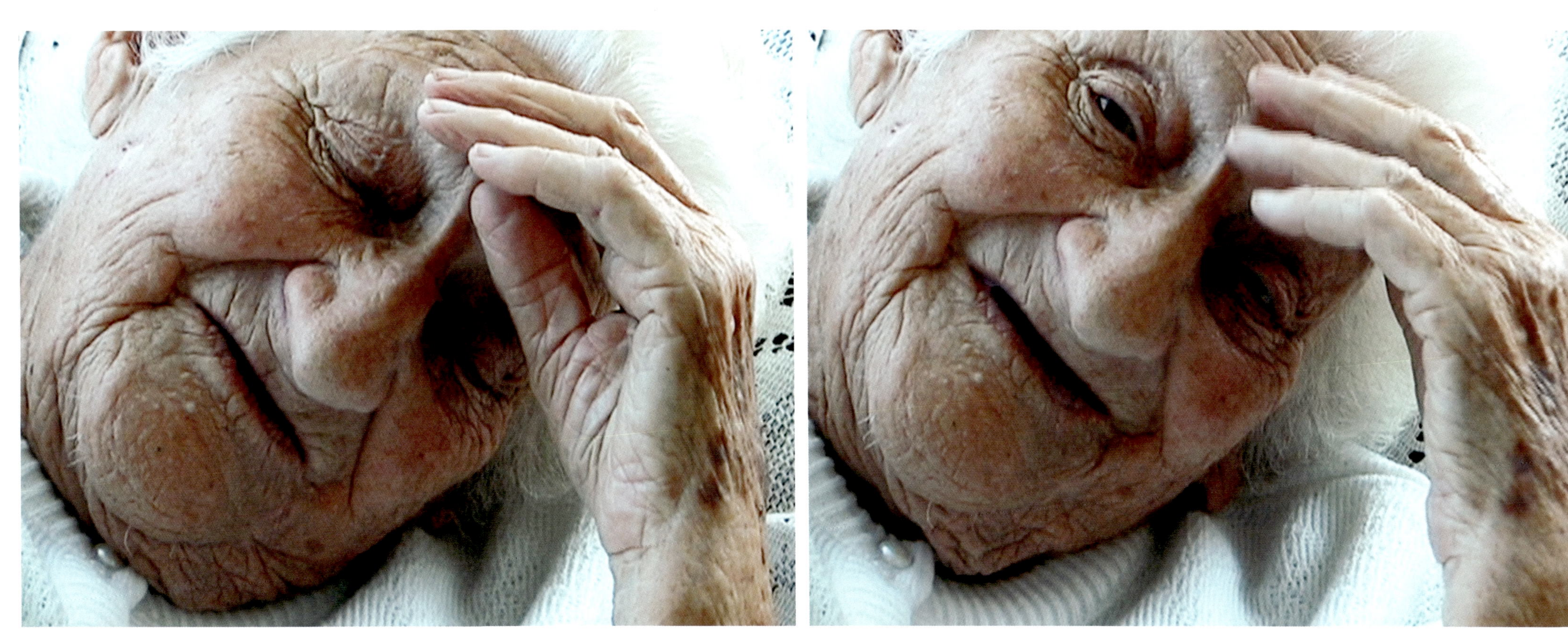

Gladys: A Life (2005) [19], video stills

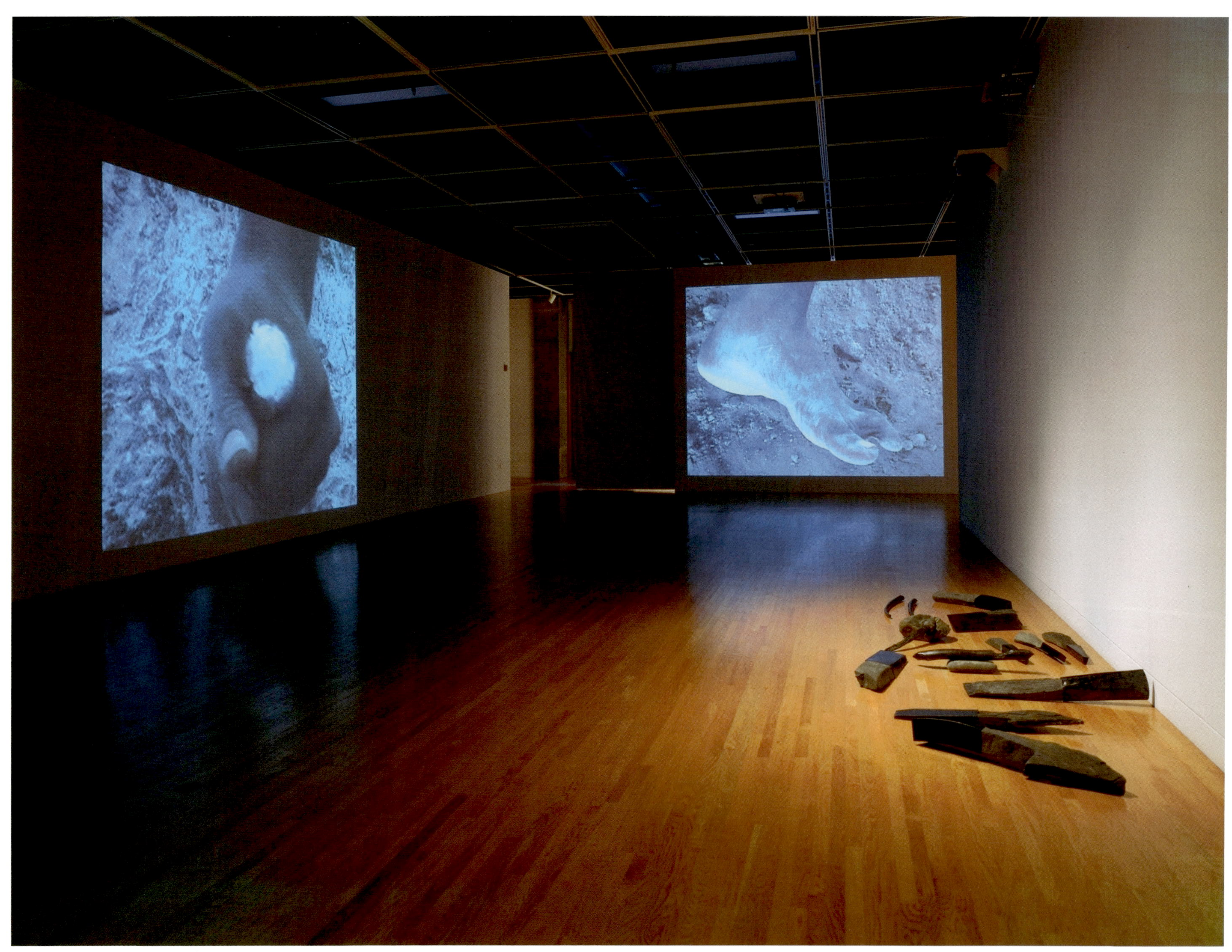

Stone Cutter (2003) and *Foot* (2003), video installation. Leonard and Bina Ellen Art Gallery, 2003. Photograph: Richard Max Tremblay

This emphasis on rhythm endows Safdie's subjects with a mesmerizing sense of fluidity. At times, the fluidity is enhanced by Safdie's lyrical presentation of bodies, many of whom are musicians captured in the act of making music. At other times the fluidity becomes tantalizingly liquid, tactilely wet, as Safdie layers movements of the becoming body with images of moving water. In Safdie's portrait of the trumpet player Joe McPhee (*Joe*, parts I and II, 2005 [26.1 and 26.1]) the technique is a reflection on how the movement of breathing – as the most essential of lifelines and the cradle of all rhythm – resonates and ripples throughout the body to produce what Jean-Luc Nancy describes as the sonorous or resonant body.[5] As a metaphoric representation of sound as waves, it also links Joe's exploration of sound (or, some might argue, music) as the roots of expression to the larger life-renewing cycles of nature such as the movements of the tides and the sound of the wind. With the textured folds of Joe's furrowed brow (at times slipping seamlessly in and out of the water), we are seduced by the ebb and flow of the wave, both visually and aurally, as Joe seeks not only a sense of inner synchronicity but also a deeper and more fundamental attunement with the world around him.

In this sense, there is an alluring tension in all of Safdie's works between movement and stasis. Through looping and/or the play of sound and sight, sight and sound, there is a "continual vanishing away," "a strange weaving and unweaving" of Safdie's subjects to avoid the lulling or sophoric powers that an extended period of

synchronicity or oneness brings.[6] The weaving and unweaving is perhaps never more poignant than in Safdie's portrayal of the improvisational musician Lori Freedman (*Lori*, 2008 [41]). In this work, Safdie visualizes Lori's internal dialogue as a dance between the inner and outer by employing floating images of head and feet, which are themselves in motion. She conveys the tension between movement and stasis as a function of the gravity of Lori's step, where she constantly comes into place despite the forward thrust of the unfolding music-making that pushes her onward. As Lori's head vanishes in and out of the performing space with her feet ever-present at the top of the screen,[7] her dialogue seemingly engages place through a play of light and shadows such that it too seemingly dances. And, as we watch Lori fade in and out only to be spurned on anew by the synergy of the place (now reconstituted as novelty[8]), Safdie repeatedly entrances us with an image that captures the lightness of being that is experienced at the height of a step – when energized by a dance that seems to know no end, we feel ourselves most fully alive.

On a variety of occasions, this dance and its weaving and unweaving leads bodies separated in time and space by the solid border of the picture frame to seemingly recognize something of themselves

5. Jean-Luc Nancy, *Listening* trans. Charlotte Mendal (New York: Fordham University Press, 2007), 39.

6. Walter Pater quoted in Henry Sayre, *The Object of Performance* (Chicago: University of Chicago Press, 1992), 1.

7. This position emphasizes not the groundedness of place, but what Erin Manning describes as the "tensile rhythm of landing." See, Erin Manning, *Relationscapes: Movement, Art, Philosophy* (Cambridge, MA: MIT Press, 2009), 204.

8. Gaston Bachelard, *Air and Dreams: An Essay on the Imagination of Movement*, trans. Edith and Frederick Farrell (Dallas: The Dallas Institute Publications, The Dallas Institute of Humanities and Culture, 1988).

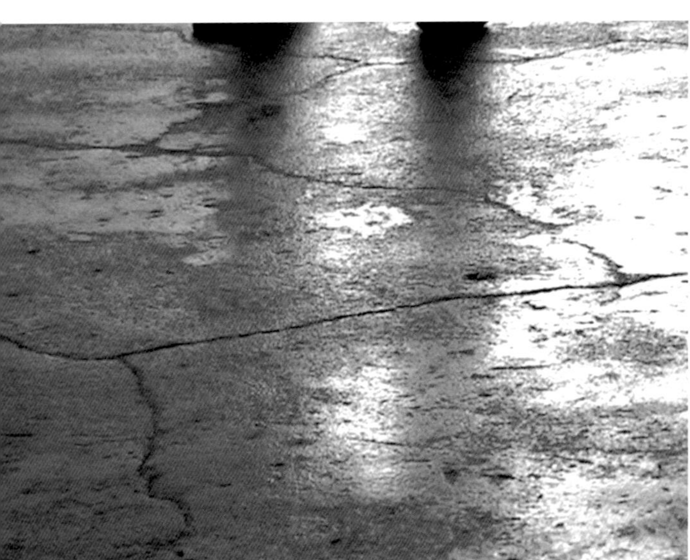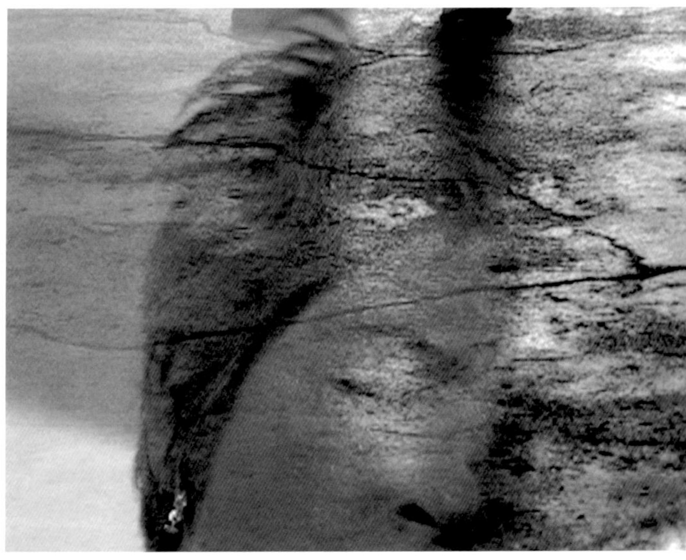

Lori (2008) [41], diptych, video stills

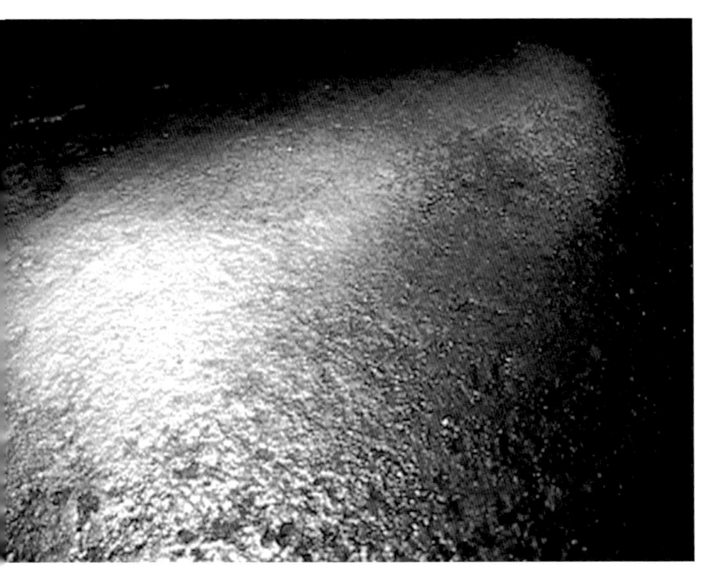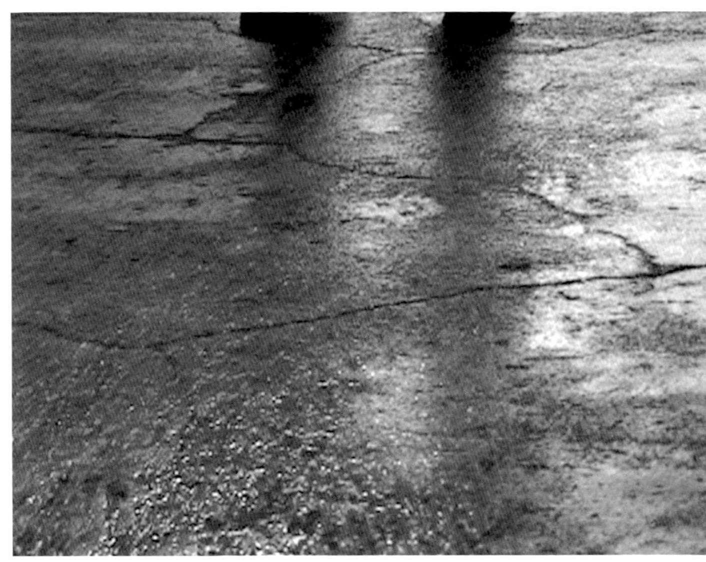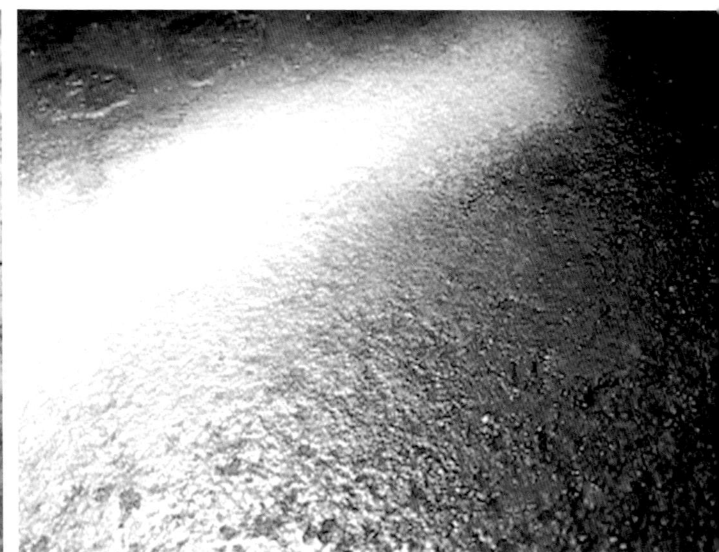

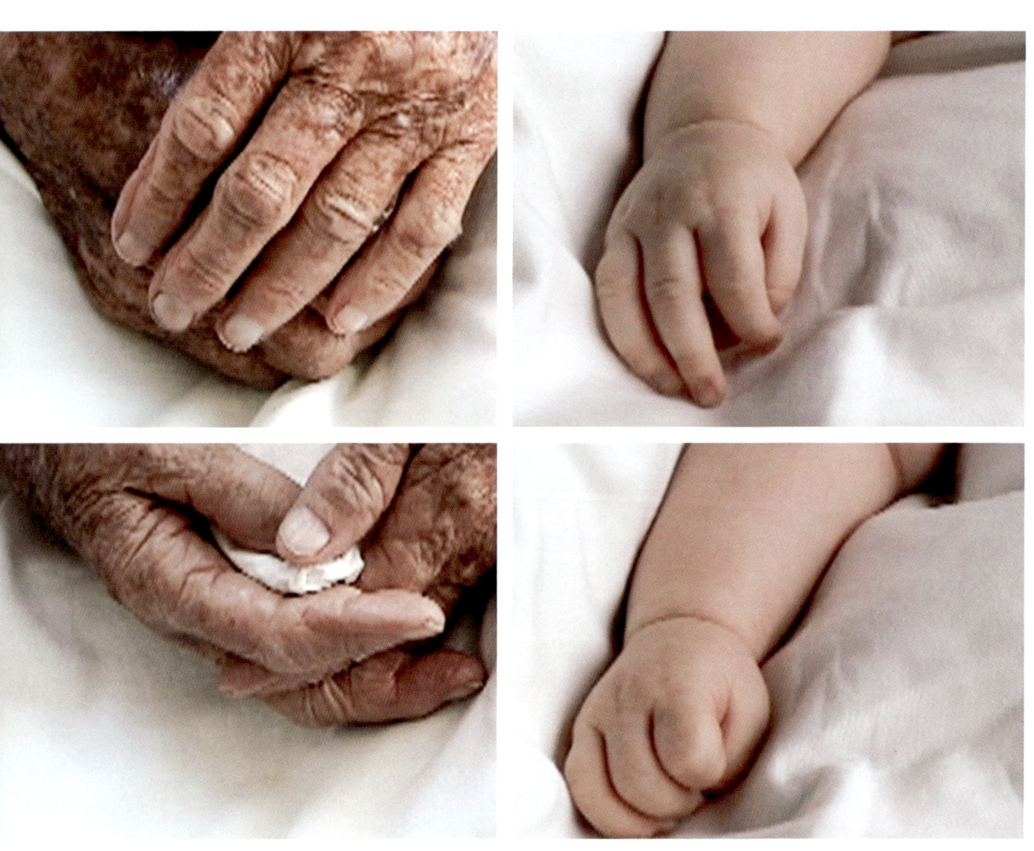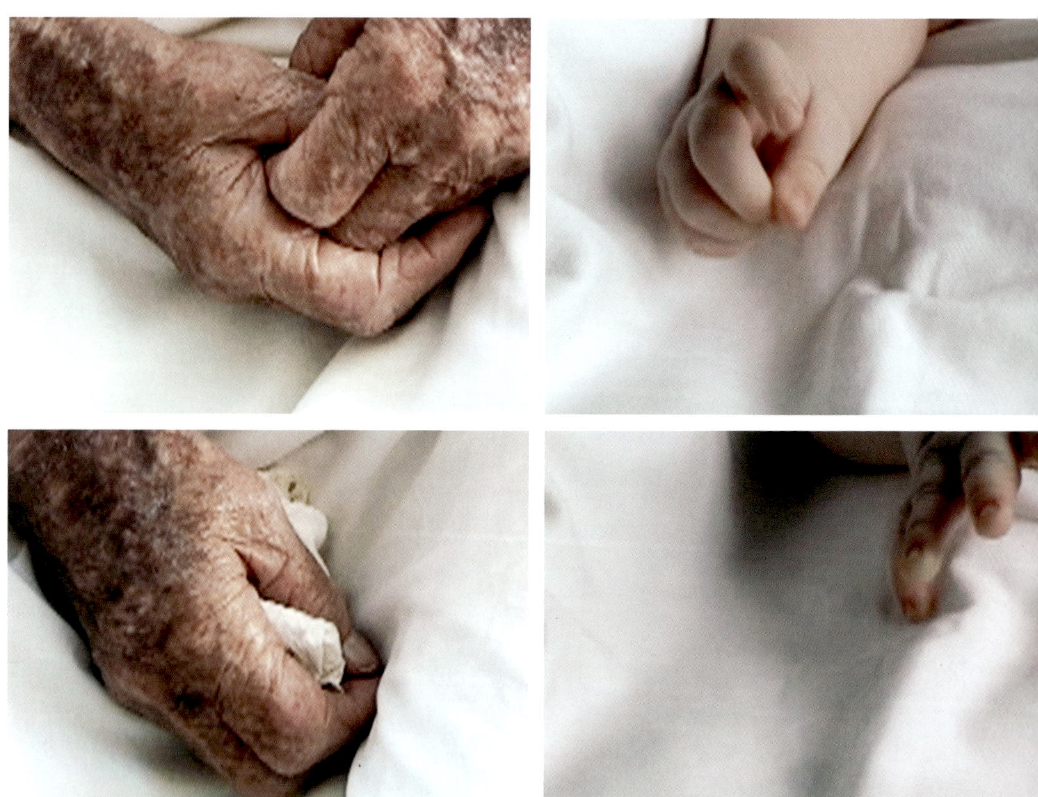

Time Passing (2005) [20], diptych, video stills

in each other. In some cases, we sense this recognition through the accompanying soundtrack and the ways in which the music directs and sustains our attention and gives Safdie's collaborator John Heward a vital bodily presence even in his absence. In other cases, recognition is forged through hand gestures to reveal something of the hand's essential nature and power as an instrument of transformation. For example, in *Time Passing* (2005) [20] Safdie combines images of an old woman's left hand and a baby's right hand – as if they are conversing – in order to articulate the connectedness of the hand as one of a pair. The combination also shows how, as a repository of memory, the hand knows the present through its gestures, evolving movements, and the duration of those gestures as the corporeal lifelines that connect the present to the past and future, or, what the French describe through the homonym for "now" as *main-tenant*, the "hand held." Through the paired hands of a sculptor and drummer, *Solo* (2005) [17] connects the hand to eye and ear, space and time, thought and feeling, and in so doing, presents the essential unity of dichotomies such as hot and cold, dark and light, hard and soft.

The video of pianist Dana Reason and Ben Harkarvy (*Dana/Ben*, 2005 [22]), in turn, foregrounds the transformative power of Safdie's own hand as the hand that gathers and brings bodies together. The gathering hand is visually apparent in the video's close-up approach to the headshots, her interest in the emotional expressions of the face as a window into the mind, and the characteristic way in which she layers Ben's visage with moving water to reflect the interiority of his thought and his connection to his natural surroundings. We experience the tactility of her hand's touch, however, as a function of our own sentient engagement as listeners and viewers while the video unfolds. Luce Irigaray explains that as the gesture through which bodies are connected one to the other, touch is at root a probing beneath the surface.[9] In joining the images of Dana and Ben, seemingly engaged with one another as performer and listener, Safdie creates a play of sound and sight that draws us into the picture as one of her subjects. And, with our perceptions of the world and the possibilities of our bodies changing and evolving around the image of the moving water (now as a dynamic metaphor for the fluidity of the unfathomable), we too feel her touch as if we ourselves have been set in motion.

There is consequently an essential continuity between Safdie's videos and video installations and her earlier paintings and sculptures in that film has become an extension of her own identity as a collector. In the *Body/Stone/Water* series (2010) [73] we feel something of Safdie's own weaving and unweaving as subject (or artist). In this work, she layers images of her own moving body with previously collected images of water and stone to explore the ways in which they meet, affect, and are affected by each other as a measure of the inventiveness of her own hand. She describes her approach as painterly, but it is more musical in conception as it is seemingly driven by a body that Jean-Luc Nancy would describe as "all ears."[10] Not only does Safdie combine the layers as one would lines in a

---

9. Luce Irigaray, *I Love to You*, trans. Alison Martin (New York: Routledge, 1996), 79ff.
10. This is a frequent posture that Safdie documents in many of her videos, such as the *Late Afternoon Raga* series (2007) [40], *Padmaran* (2008) [37], and the *Head* series (2009) [67–69]. See Nancy, *Listening*, 40–1.

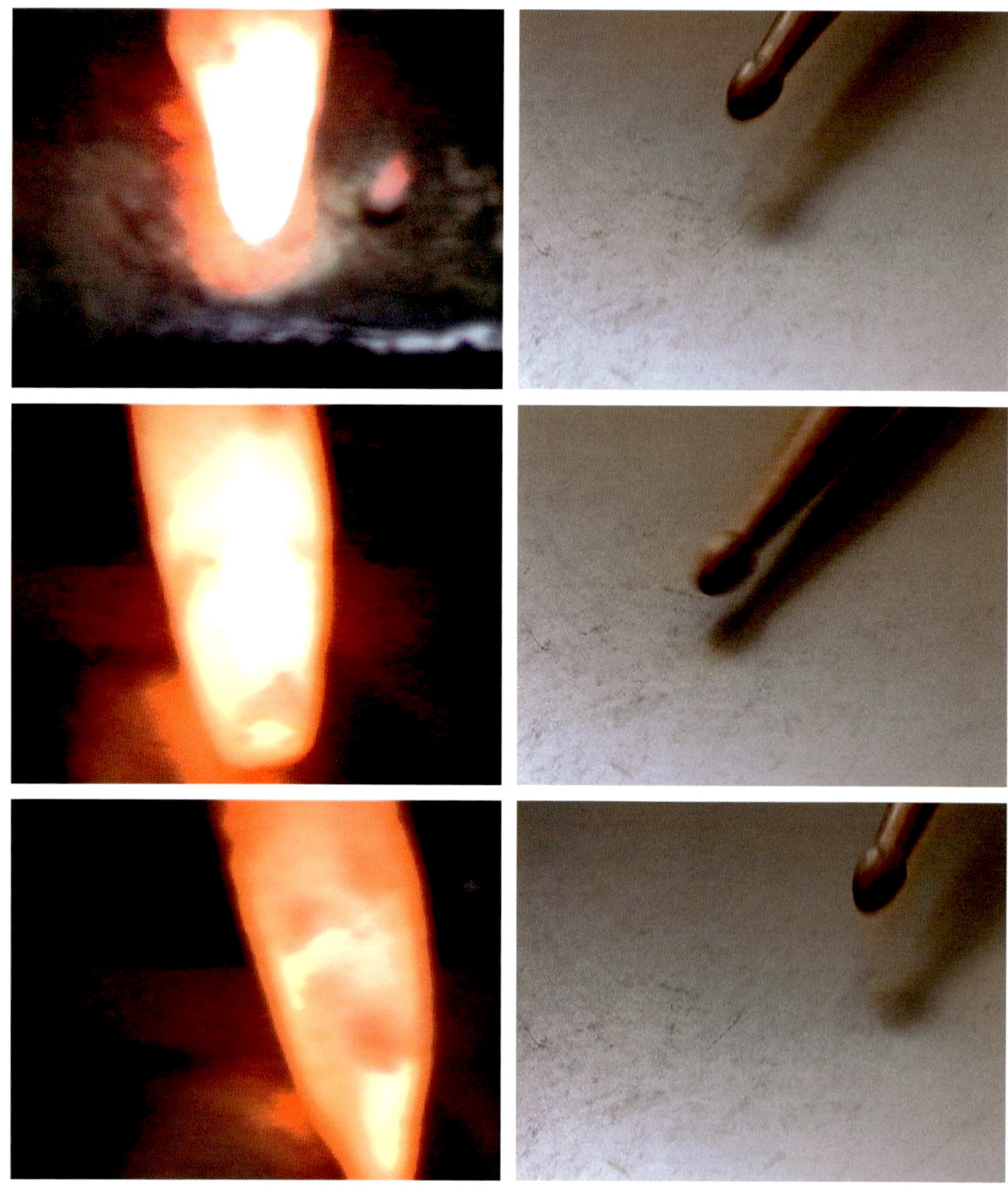

Solo (2005) [17] diptych, video stills

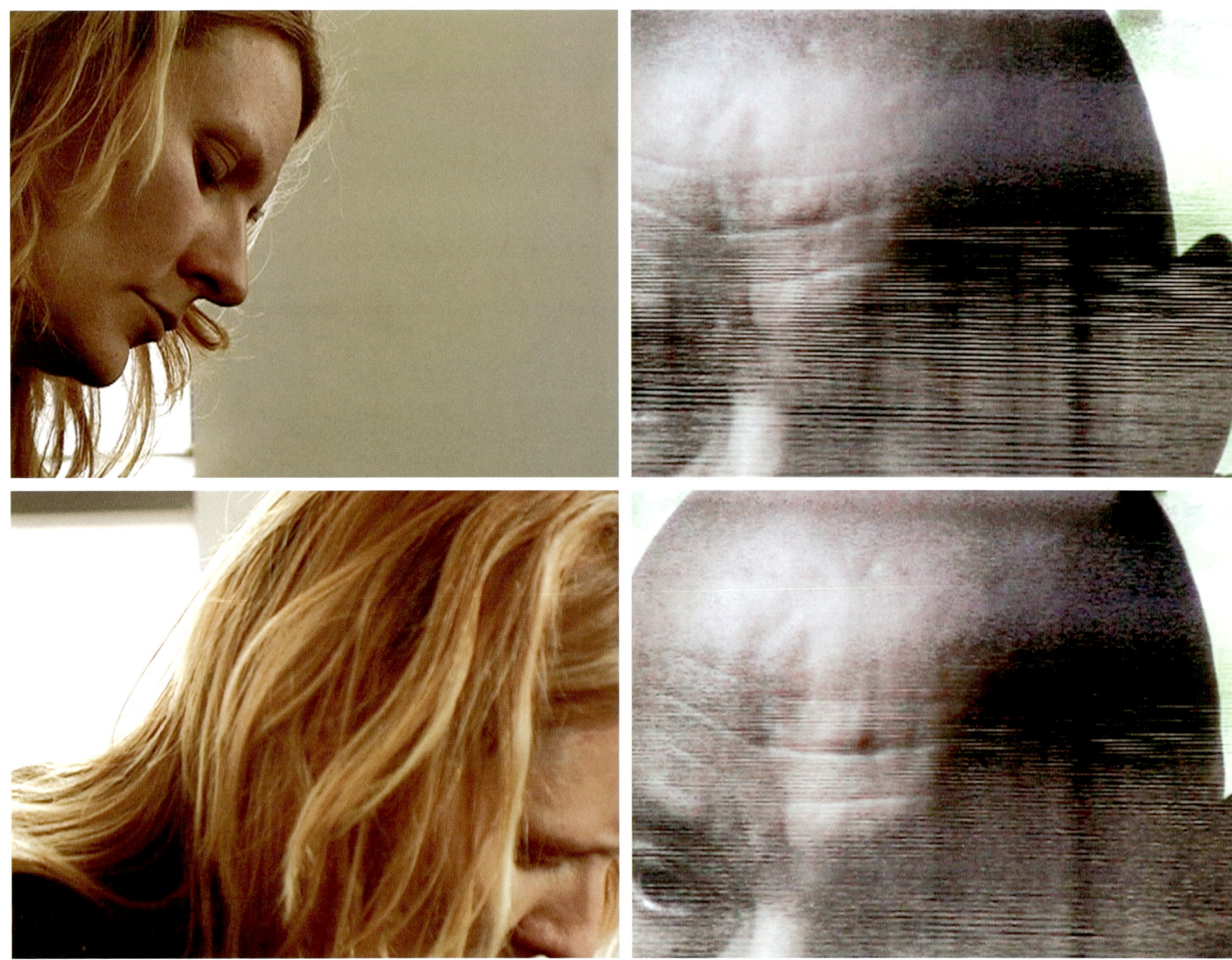

Dana/Ben (2005) [22], diptych, video stills

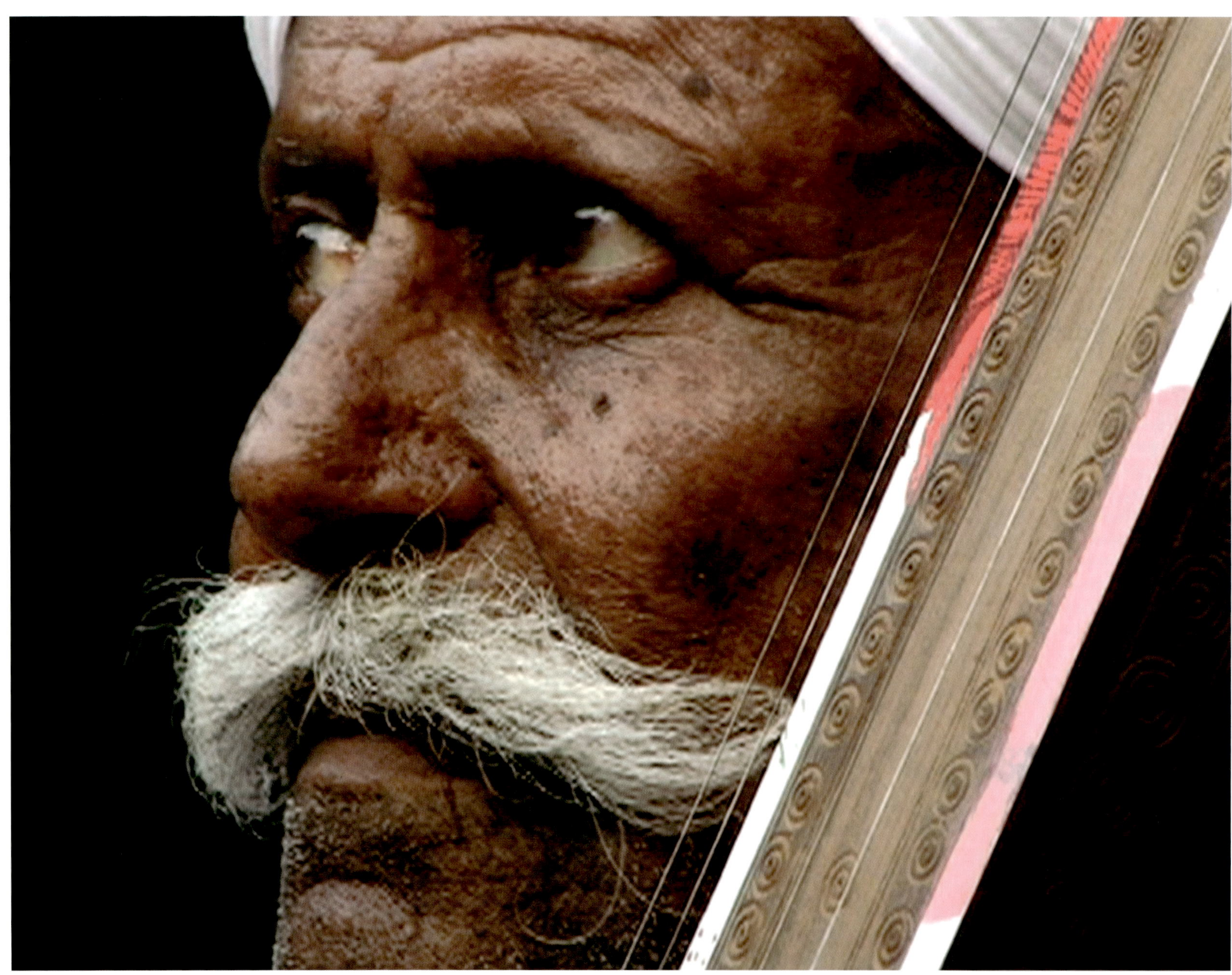

Song (2008) [38], video stills

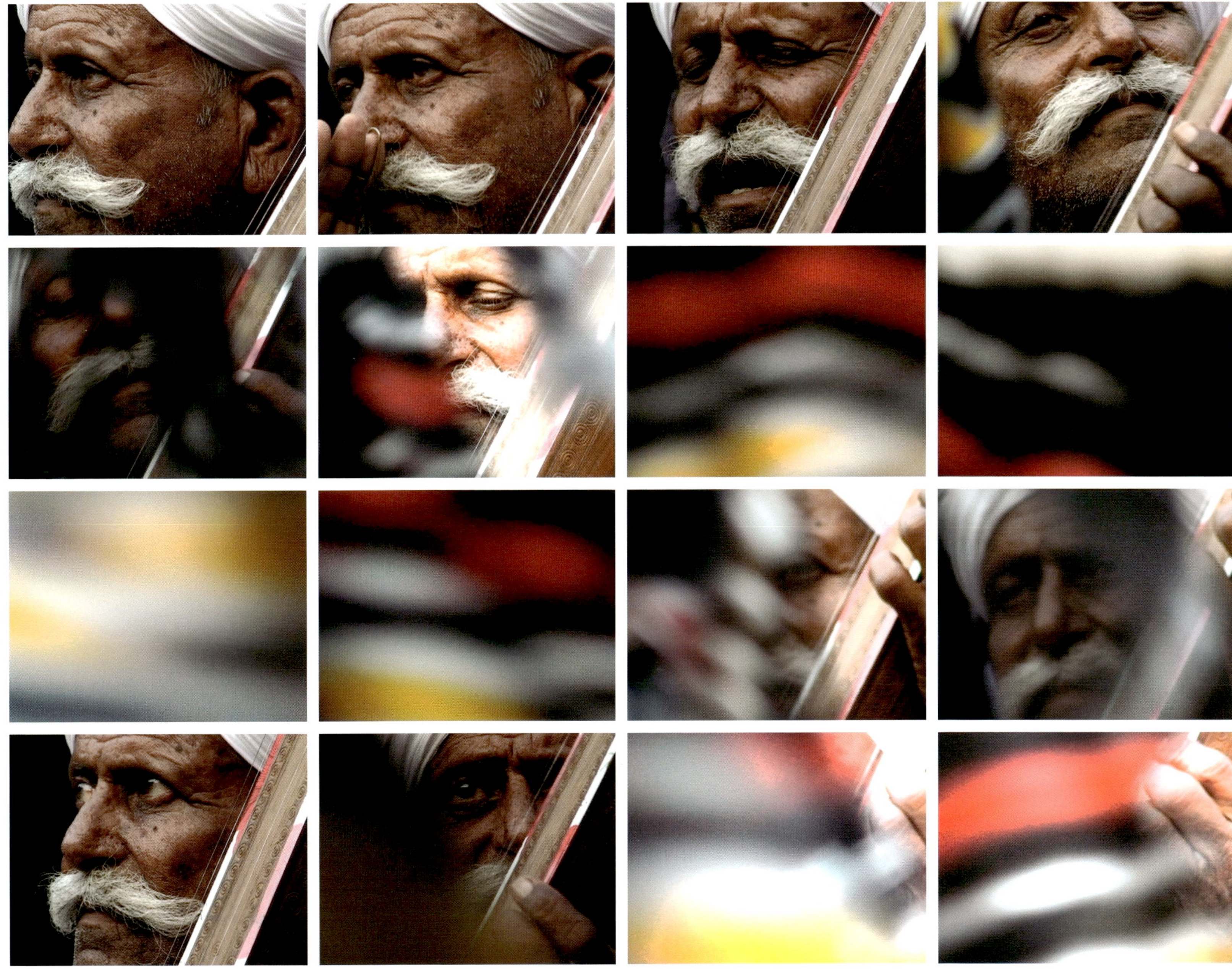

musical composition, she manipulates them as movement-images for their temporal qualities, listening for the ways in which they echo, resonate, and reverberate with each other as a reflection of the body's transformational potential. Where we typically see water for its fluidity and stone for the way in which it endures, Safdie shows us the flux and solidity in both and in so doing reveals the plasticity of the body becoming. Through the play of bodies between screens her body becomes multiple, such that the ground of our perception is constantly shifting and to paraphrase the words of Henry David Thoreau in *Walden*, "We are all sculptors and painters: our material our own flesh and blood and bones."

Body/Stone/Water VI (2010) [73.6], video stills

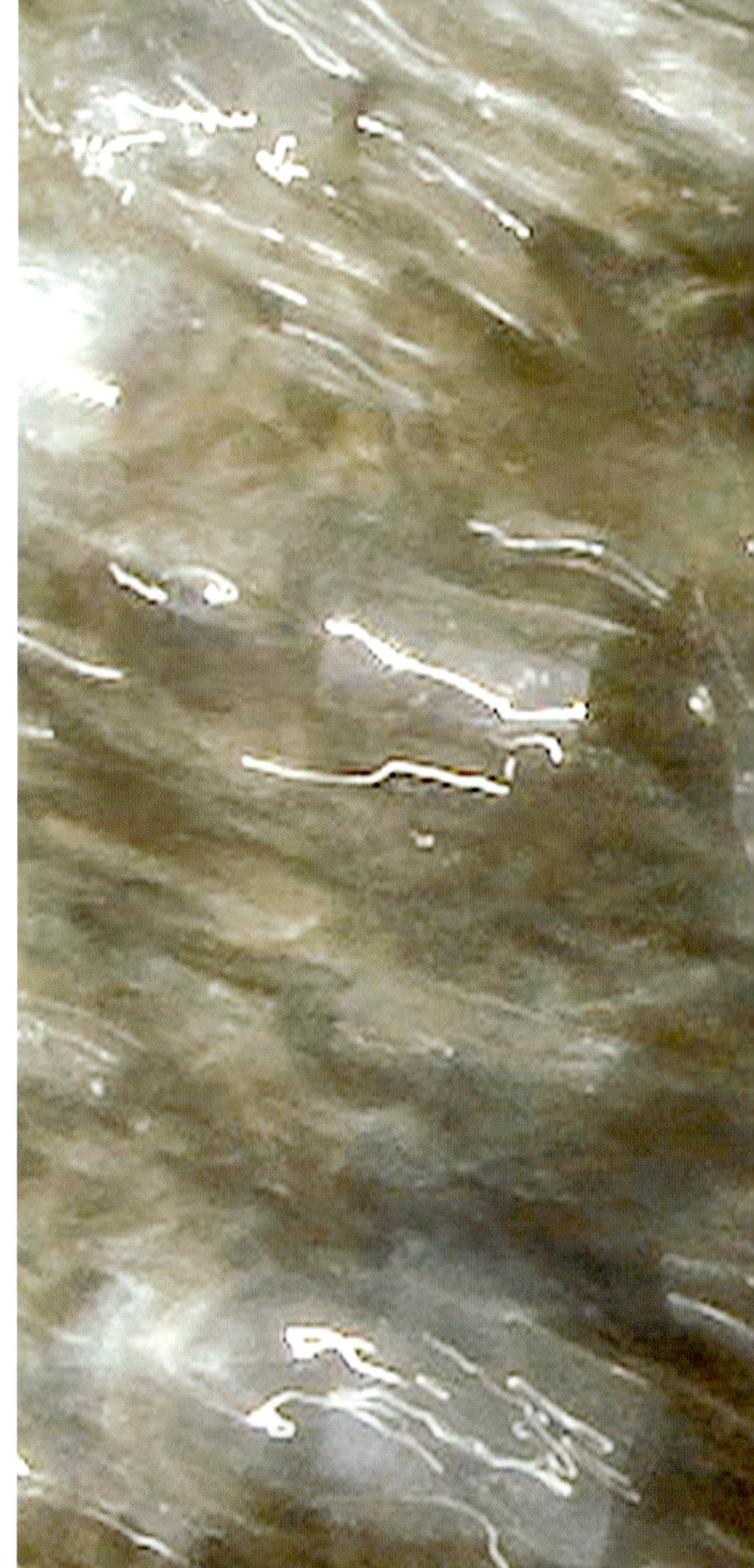

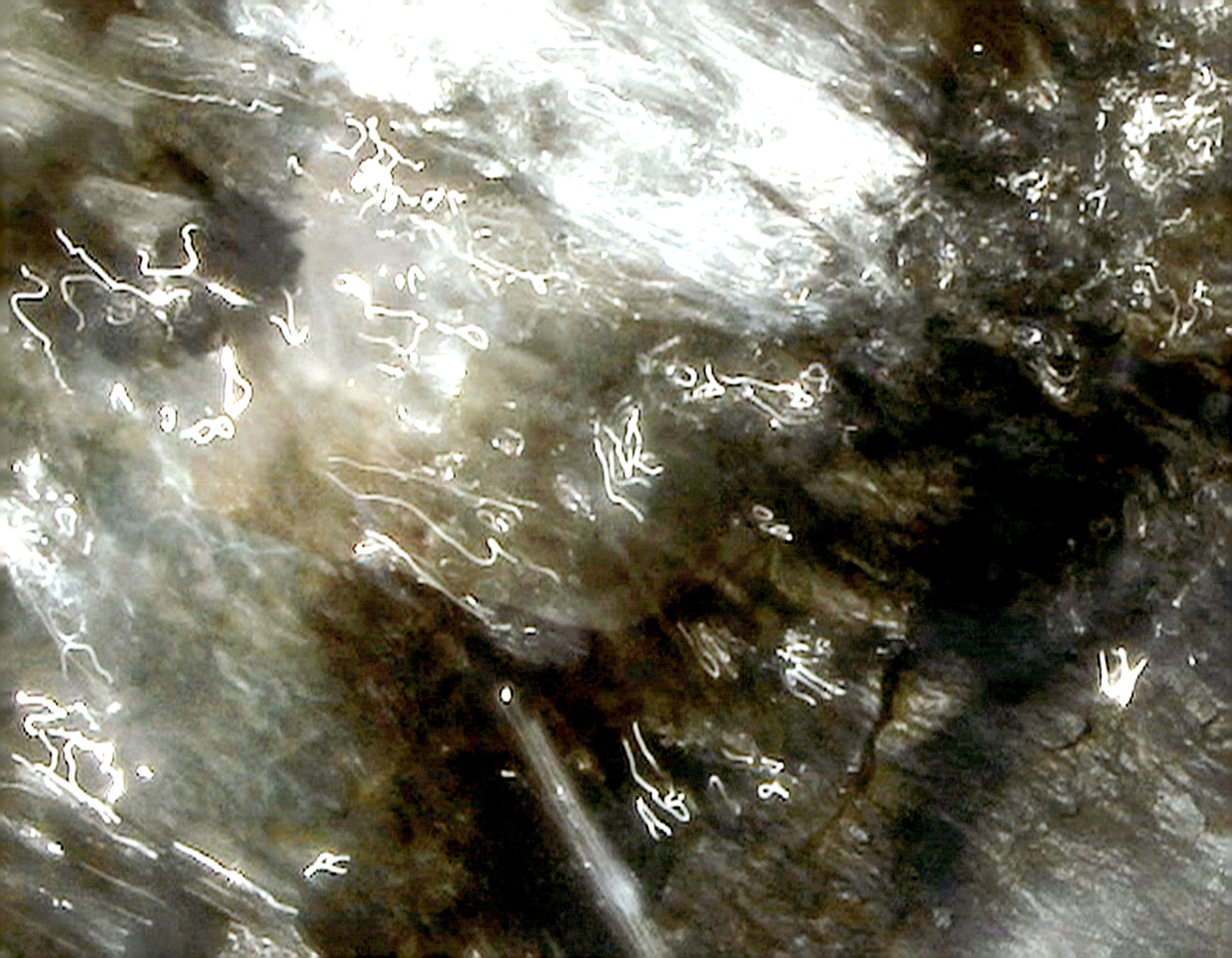

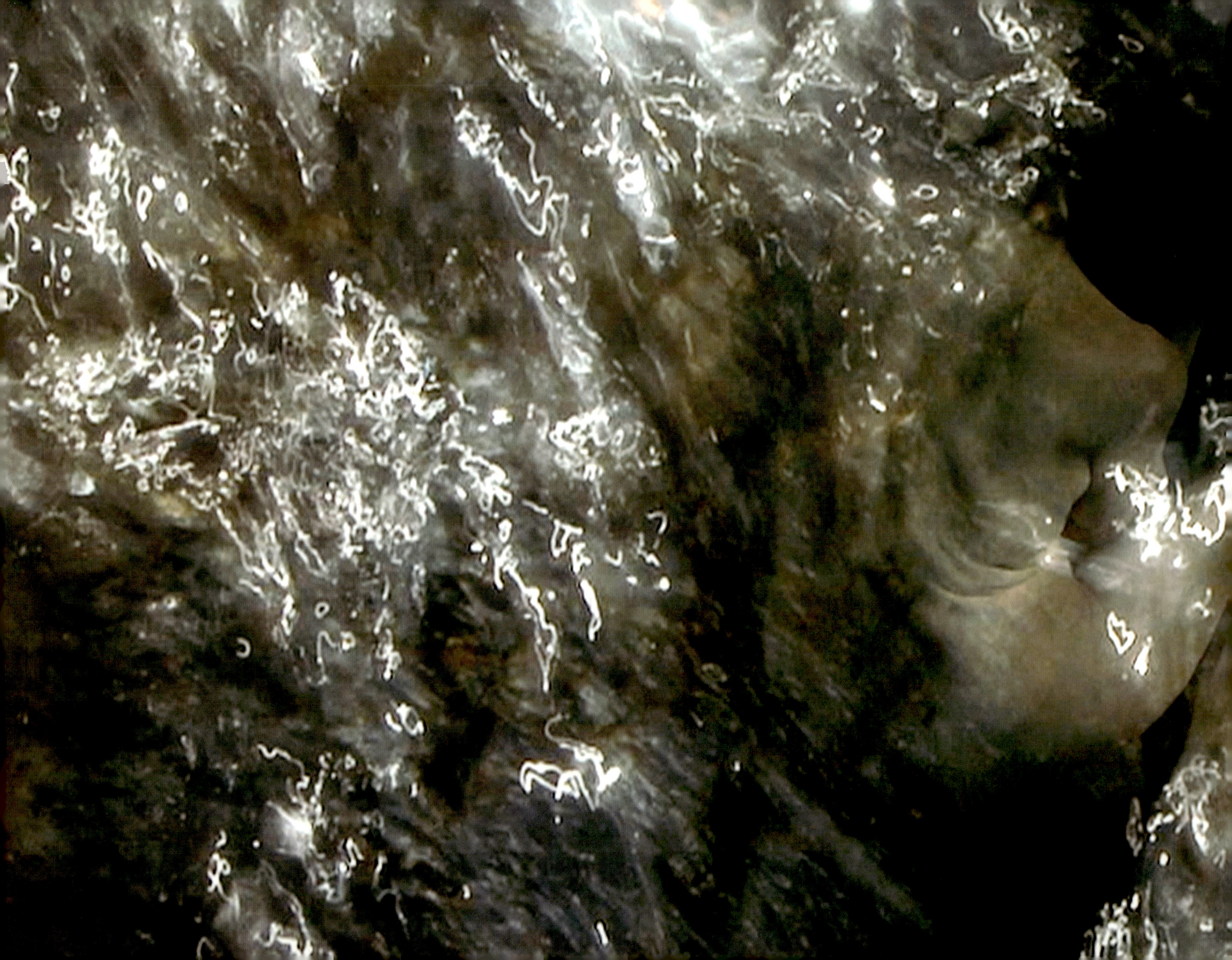

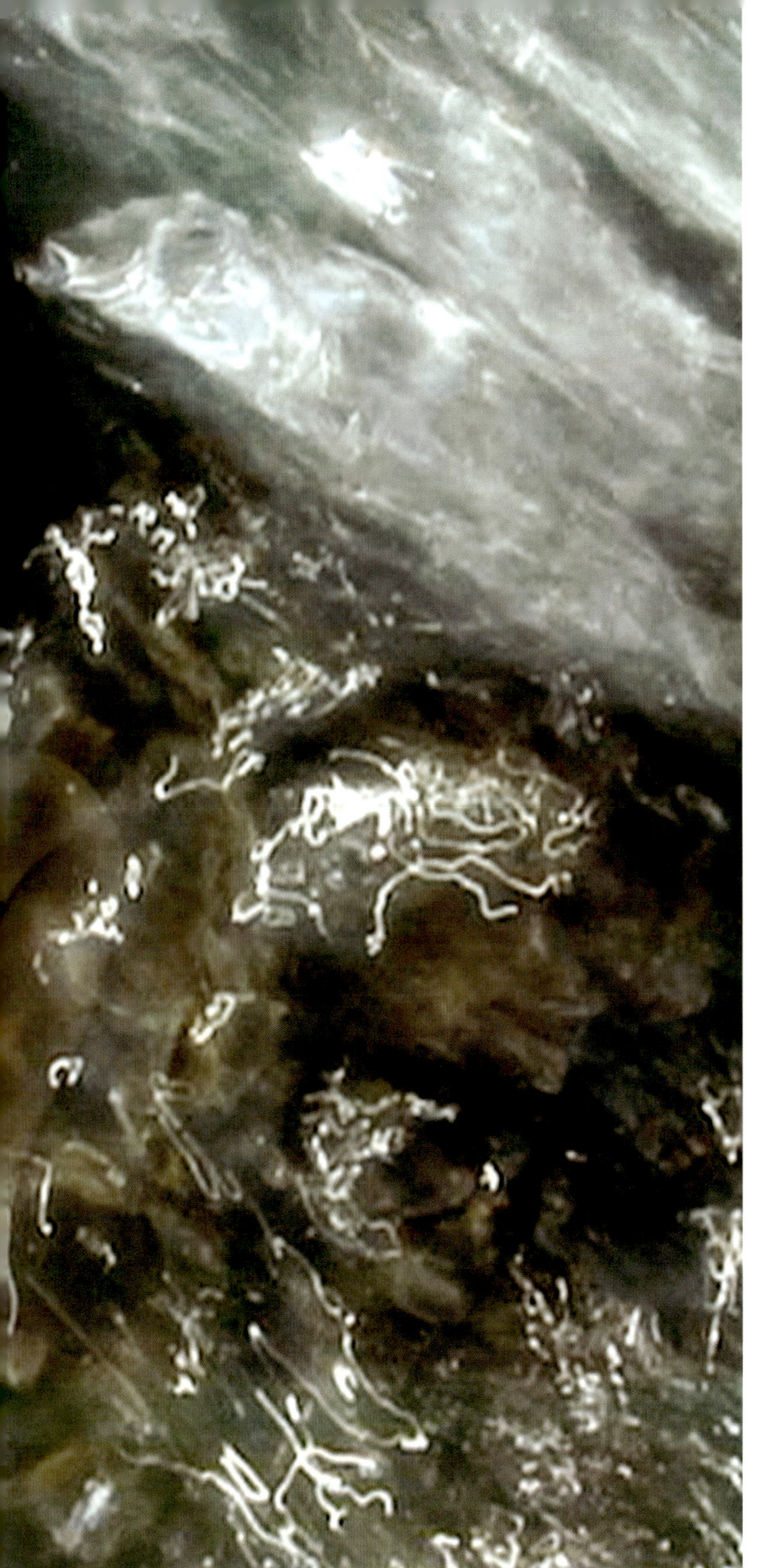

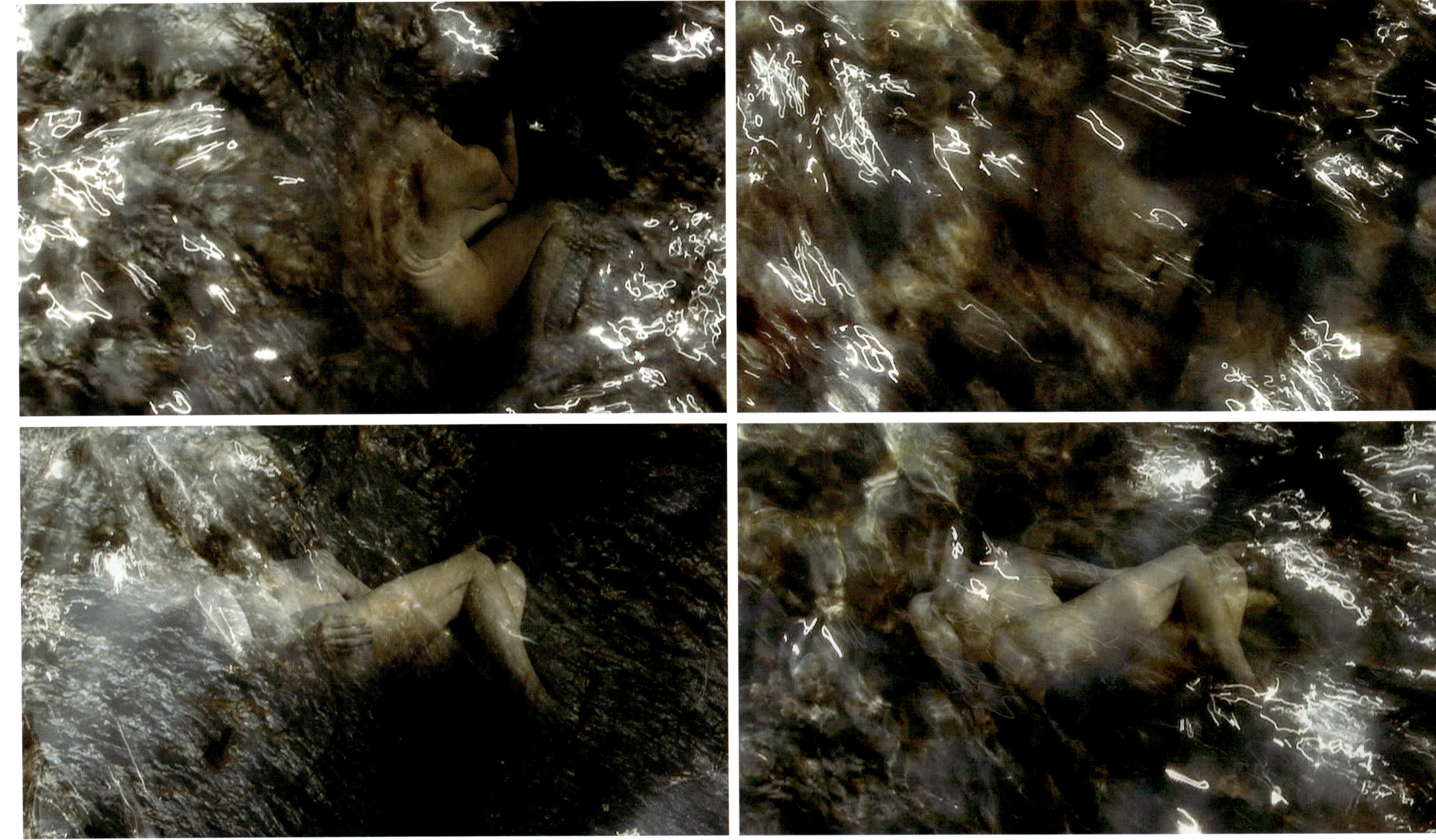

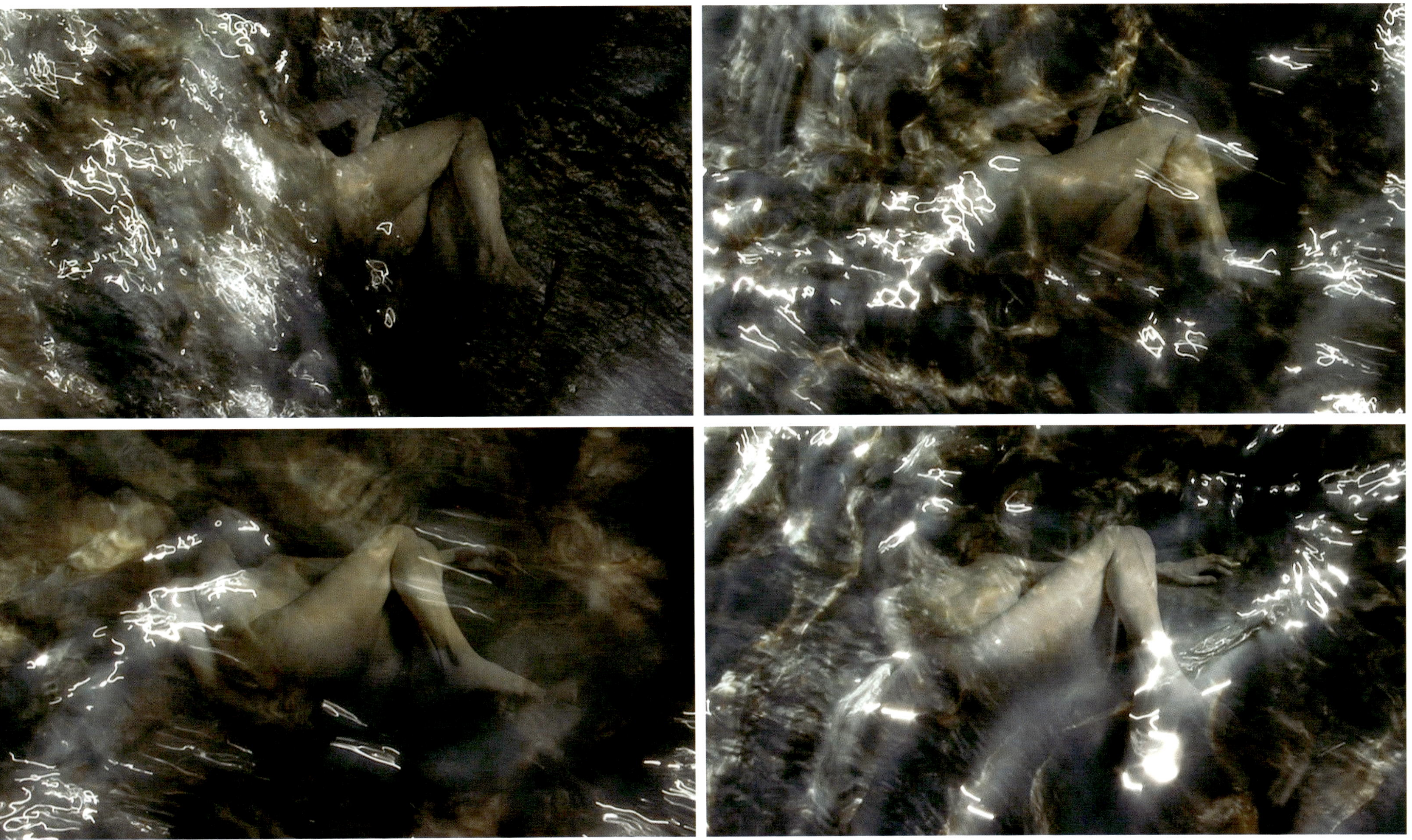

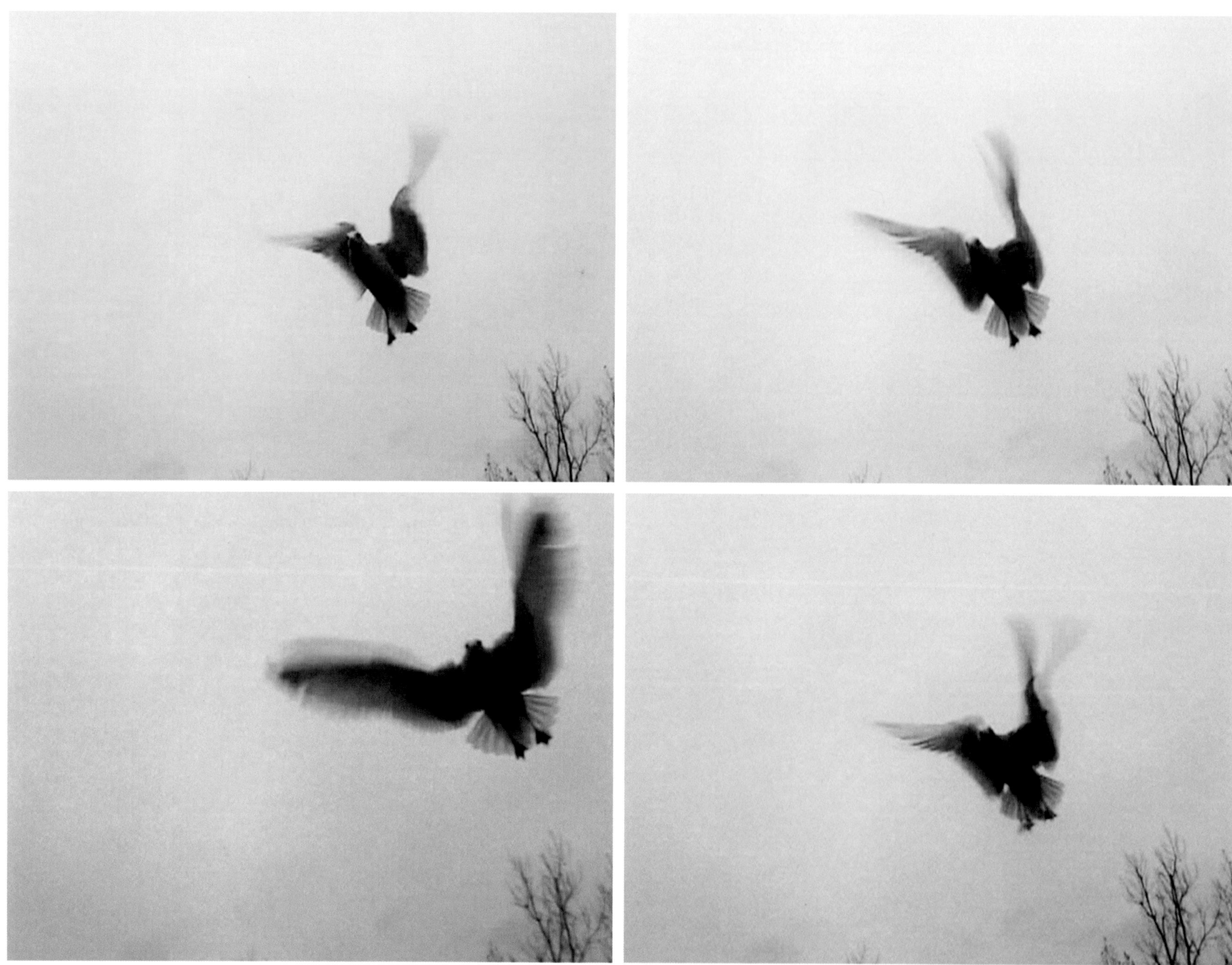

Gulls (2002) [2], video stills

Sounding Breath–Breathing Sound
The Video Art of Sylvia Safdie

Eric Lewis

A bird hovers obliquely overhead, its wings beating as it remains suspended in space. The image is arresting, yet also somehow familiar. While the video (*Gulls* [2]) is unaccompanied by sound it is very loud. The thrust of the bird's wings seem to corporealize the air and roar like a sudden wind. You can almost see the sounds created. The looping of the image creates a momentary caesura in your perception. The bird, jerking slightly, seems to suddenly recede back in time, only again to hover, as if forced to relive this moment. Your attention is fixed, while you ponder notions of time, space, silence, and sound. Suddenly the familiarity of the image comes into focus – you have seen such images, however static, thousands of times in western paintings. In Christian iconography it represents the Holy Spirit, hovering, perhaps over you, waiting to descend.[1] The precise location of this bird and the subject of its gaze, are off-camera, obscured, and a subject for one's imagination, suggesting a way in which the viewer needs to complete the scene.

This early video by Sylvia Safdie (her second, in fact) shot in 2002 suggests many of the themes she goes on to explore in subsequent video works. That a simple and silent continuous-loop, fixed-camera video can contain the seeds of years of subsequent video art, grounding and sustaining its development, is a testament both to the clarity of Safdie's artistic vision and to her determination to resolve the aesthetic and philosophical tasks she has set for herself.

---

1. The representation of the Holy Spirit as a bird, usually a dove, is perhaps the most ubiquitous symbol in the canon of Christian symbolism. A classic study is *Iconographie chrétienne*, by Adolphe Napoleon Didron, first published in French in 1843. The biblical texts this symbol is drawn from include Matthew 3:16, "As soon as Jesus was baptised, he went up out of the water. At that moment heaven was opened, and he saw the spirit of God descending like a dove and lightening on him." See also John 1:32 and Genesis 8:10–11.

Safdie has repeatedly said that one goal of her video art is "to capture breath," a universal hallmark of life. The Holy Spirit is, of course, breath; the original Greek for "Holy Spirit" is *pneuma*, and the most common meaning of pneuma is breath. In the western art tradition the iconography of the Holy Spirit centres on the dove, water, fire, and clouds – all elements central to Safdie's video imagery. Breath's symbolic presence is found in her use of these images, while, as we shall see, its literal presence is also deeply felt in many of her works. The literal and symbolic presence of breath interacts to create a metaphysical middle ground. This is one of the major accomplishments of Safdie's videos – to make the invisible visible by merging the symbolic and the actual.

The symbolic influences on Safdie's video art extend far beyond Christian iconography and her themes are universal. The Holy Spirit is not only the best-known iconic element in western Christian painting; it is also evoked in the Hebrew Old Testament, and in related Jewish religious texts, where we find the expression "holy spirit" in both Psalm 51 and the Book of Isaiah. Ancient Stoicism conceived of the soul as a breath with wave-like motions and viewed the whole cosmos as animated by such a breath.[2] This idea of breath as motion, and its role in animating the cosmos, is also found in a number of Safdie's videos. Her explorations of breath, and the

various ways she represents its presence in the world, draw upon a range of philosophical and theological traditions from antiquity onwards. Her focus on the animating power of breath allows her work to present in new ways aspects of the history of Judaism in the twentieth and twenty-first centuries, particularly the challenges raised by the Holocaust and the Jewish diaspora when they are the subject of visual depiction and commentary. Through her artistic use of breath Safdie both presents and resolves her relationship to these signal events of modern Jewish history.

Crucial to understanding Safdie's video art is recognizing her painterly treatment of the medium and the continuity between her video, sculptural, and painting practices. Her video work is a natural extension and transformation of her earlier work in other media. First, almost all of her videos employ a fixed, unmoving camera, and each scene is carefully framed. The subjects in these videos are in motion and changing – motion is not produced by the camera. This creates the effect of a painting-in-motion. Although a painting can depict its subject in the act of being transformed, video can present the transformations themselves. Given that so much of Safdie's earlier artistic output is preoccupied with transformation, particularly bodies transforming, the move to video was a natural step.

Safdie's interest in both absent and transforming bodies is longstanding. In 1983 she began painting and drawing the human body, focusing on the female figure. In 1996 she began mixing earth, collected in the course of her travels, with oil to form the material for her drawings and paintings. In these works human forms are often highly abstracted, and figure and ground have imprecise

---

2. For a judiciously chosen selection of primary texts, with commentary, on these themes in Stoicism see: A.A. Long and D.N. Sedley, *The Hellenistic Philosophers*, vol. 1, (Cambridge: Cambridge University Press, 1987), especially chapter 46, "God, Fire, Cosmic Cycle," and chapter 47 "Elements, Breath, Tenor, Tension." The Stoic account of the relations between breath, soul, and God influenced early Christian theorizing on these same topics.

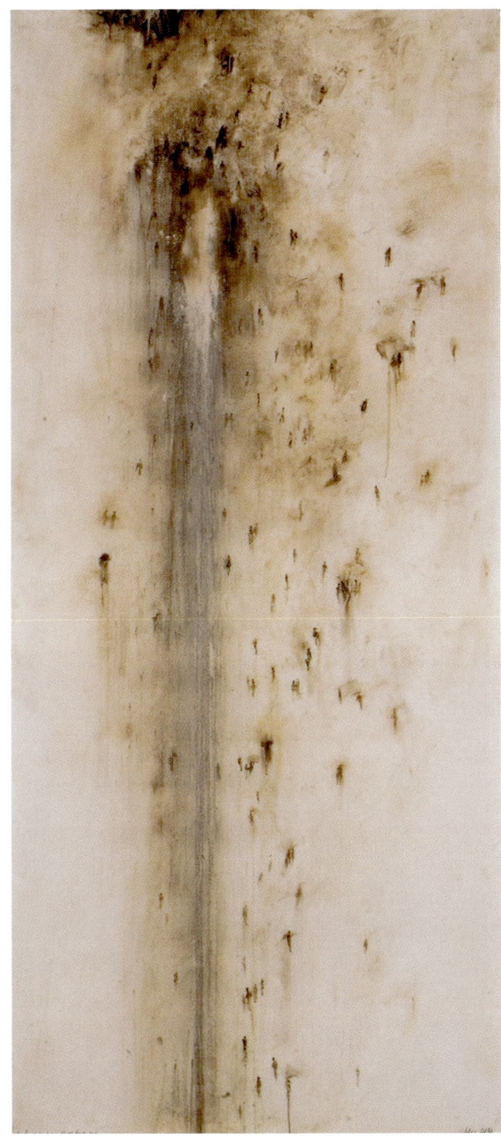

Earth Marks Series XVI no. 3 (2010)
Earth and oil on mylar, 239 x 107 cm

Earth Marks Series XVI no. 4 (2010)
Earth and oil on mylar, 239 x 107 cm

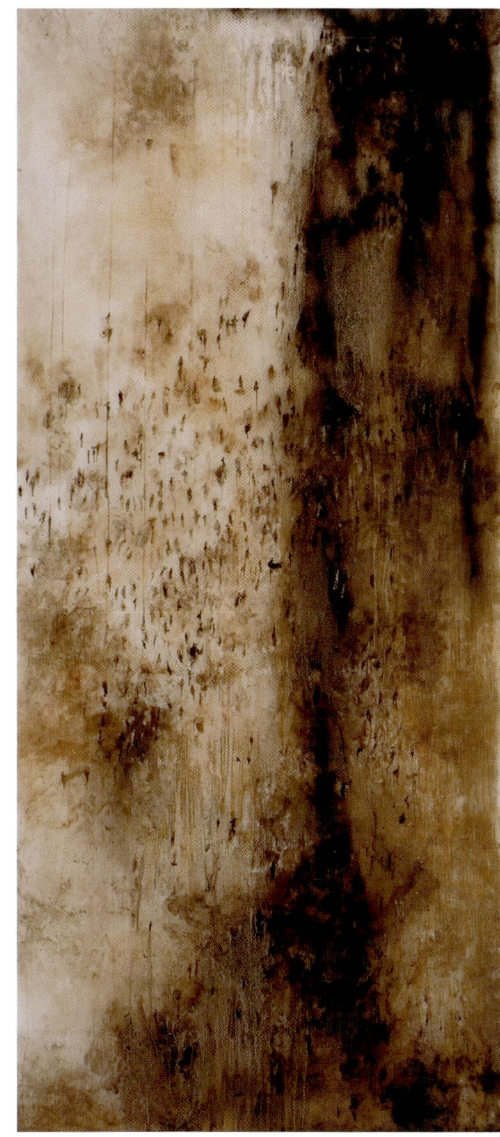

Earth Marks Series IV no. 3 (1998)
Earth and oil on mylar, 239 x 107 cm

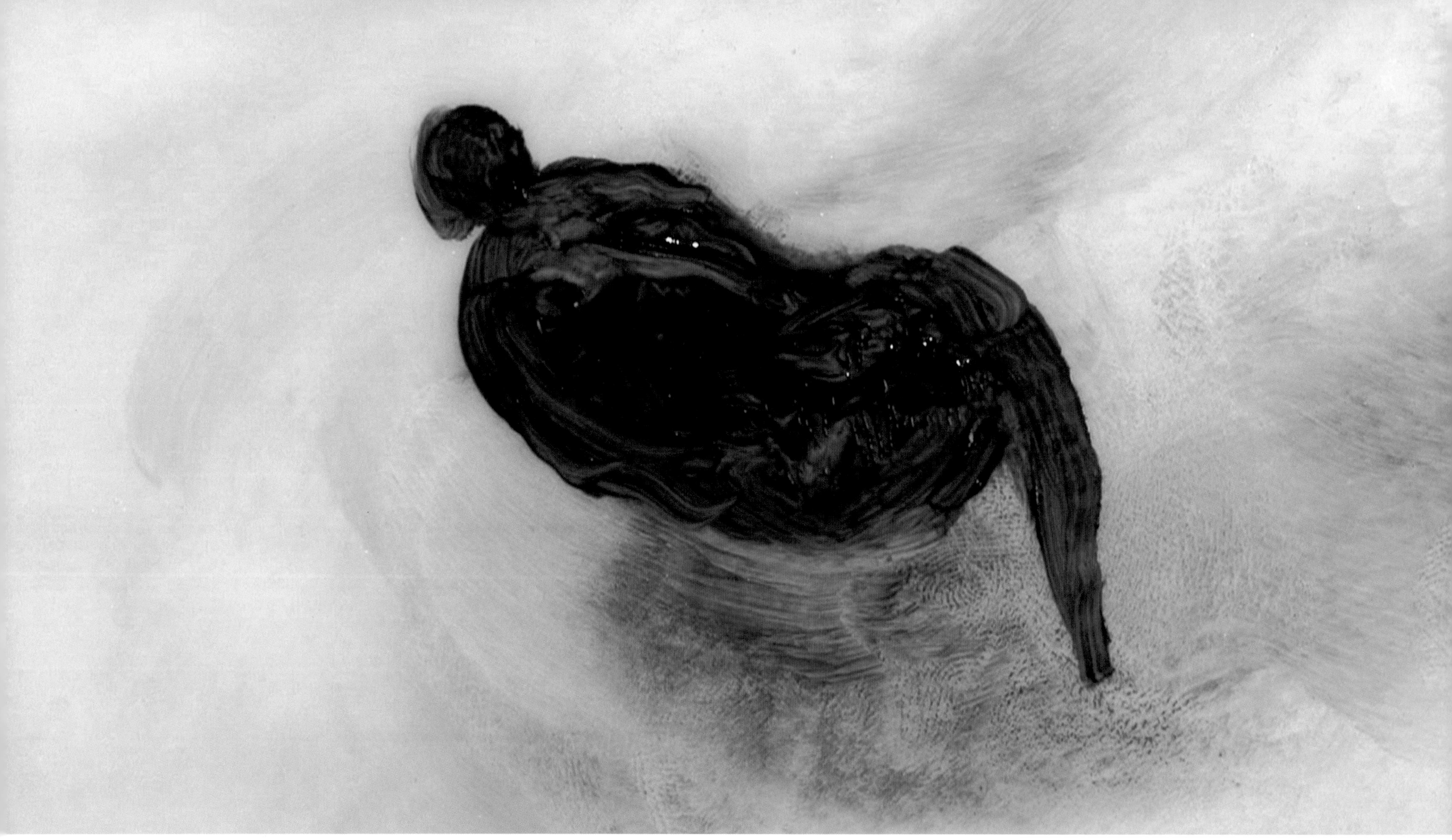

Figures and Ground III (2009) [66], video stills

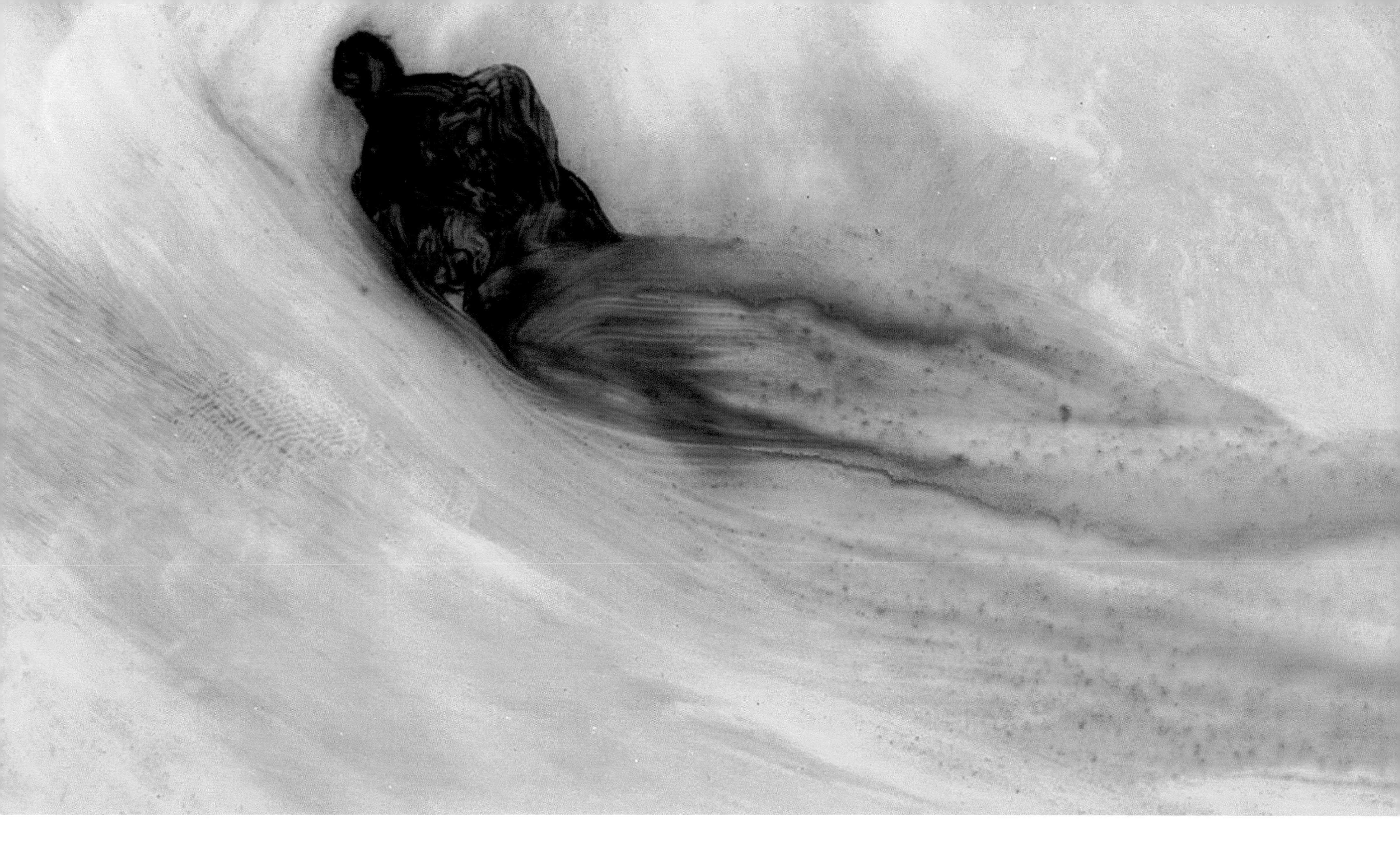

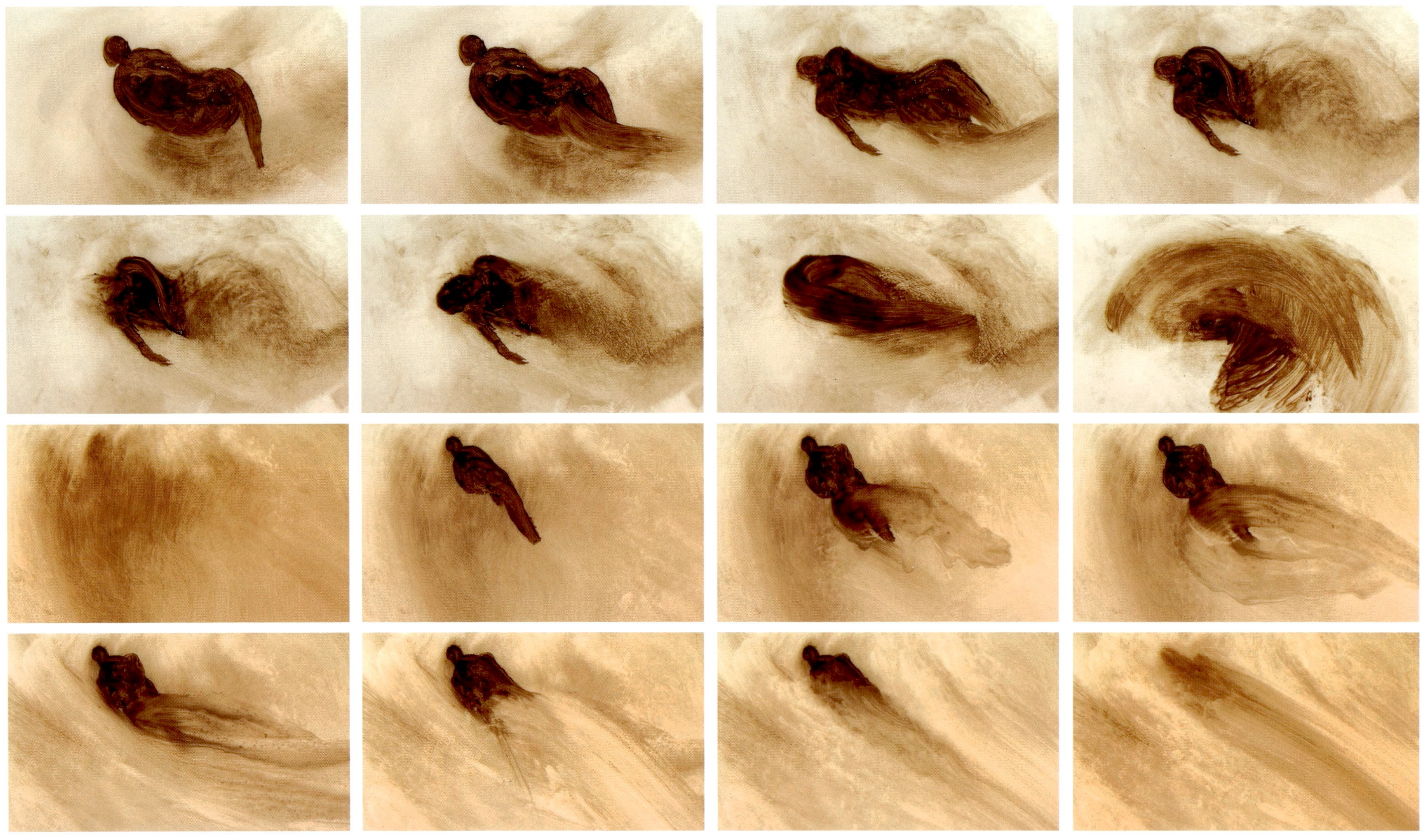

boundaries. The bodies in many of these paintings emerge out of their backgrounds, which often resemble the walls and stones that play such a prominent role in her videos. The bodies are depicted mid-transformation, with occluded faces, engaged in mysterious movements. Small bodies seem to ascend as if in a wind, like dust blown about. Barely discernible faces bleed into their surroundings. The series of sculptures *Heads* (1977 and onwards) presents found stones as heads, further blurring the boundary between the animate and inanimate. These transformations of bodies into and out of their surroundings are a theme of many of Safdie's videos. Bodies emerge out of rocks, and rocks symbolically stand in for absent bodies, which follows a thread of her sculptural work. Where once Safdie transformed nature and place by physically taking rock and earth and producing pigment from them to depict the human form, she now, through video, directly effects this transformation.

Safdie's videos are akin to living dynamic versions of the static images seen in some of her large canvases that depict painted bodies against a backdrop resembling a mottled wall, or the surface of a cave, with each body caught in the act of becoming something else. "Our gestures in the present connect us to the past and to the future. They are our lifelines," Safdie has said. Similarly, the gestures in Safdie's works, whether in paintings, drawings, sculptures, or videos, connect the mediums to each other, unify her corpus, and put these works into dialogue. Just as an improvisation takes place in the moment while reaching back to the past, these works improvise with each other. They are simultaneously about transformations and examples of transformations. In effect Safdie's videos animate

her paintings and sculptures, introducing breath or spirit to them, in sympathy with the ancient understanding of the soul as a capacity for self-motion.[3] It is as if the hovering bird resides in all the videos.

A good example of how breath enters into her videos is Safdie's recent series of videos filmed at Auschwitz [74–80]. In *Gulls* the spirit – the life-giving breath – is out of reach; it is a mysterious, unresolved subject. In the Auschwitz series this spirit, a breath both divine and human, enters into the subjects and animates all it touches. Safdie's videos, when considered diachronically and developmentally, can be seen as exploring a variety of themes, which, upon their resolution, allow her to bring the breath (and importantly her own breath), back into the world. The videos allow spider webs to pulsate with pneumatic power, allow Safdie to face down the metaphysical impossibilities that Auschwitz embodies with a cosmic breath, allow her to reanimate her own body in her videos, as well as be able, after a deep engagement with sound and music, to allow silence to speak loudly again, and to have one hear the life-giving breath with the eye and see it with the ear. The journey these videos reenact is simultaneously personal and metaphorical. After viewing them we emerge with an invigorated understanding of certain themes: the place of breath in the world, the cycle of life and death, the nature of sound and image, the unity of nature, and also of Safdie the individual, who is seen as an integral part of nature in

---

3. Viewing the hallmark of soul as a capacity for self-motion is the most ancient, and most persistent, definition of the soul. It is found in the earliest philosophical account of the soul, as developed by Thales (see Aristotle, *On the Soul*, 405 A11f.), and forms the backbone of Aristotelian psychology.

the recent video series *Body/Stone/Water* [73]. The hovering bird is finally brought to earth, and enters, as spirit, into the content of the video images.

Safdie's videos enact a subtle interplay between the personal and the universal which is coordinated through her literal and symbolic treatment of breath. Considered collectively these videos are autobiographical and at the same time speak to universal themes. This synthesis fulfils a desire shared by many artists to create works that do more than narrowly represent their own experiences and do not lecture the viewer from on high. The force and aesthetic interest of Safdie's videos (and ultimately their importance) are products of the interplay between background and detail, the mundane and the cosmic. They are compelling to the eye, ear, mind, and spirit, because even at their most abstract and universal, the personal remains present. They ring true. They breathe, and invite onlookers to breathe with them, drawn to the videos' universality without a sense of suffocation or alienation.

In some senses Safdie's video art may be seen as part of the Romantic tradition – a tradition that values beauty as an aesthetic ideal, fuses both the personal and the universal, and elevates painting to the highest level of artistic expression. Shunning many of the common tropes of contemporary video art, which often foreground the complex technologies behind their creation, Safdie's videos hide their craft. Although the raw footage she shoots documents her real-time encounters with her environment, she subjects this footage to careful scrutiny and manipulation. The final product nonetheless always appears natural, almost inevitable. Even when the action

depicted in one of her videos is literally impossible – as when a rock becomes a human body – it is treated in such a natural way that the mind does not resist but instead acquiesces to the transformation. Much like earlier painterly traditions that aimed to hide the presence of the painter (for example, producing paintings devoid of brush marks and other artifacts of creation), Safdie's videos use their technological sophistication to reveal their subject, not themselves. The sense in which many of these videos can be seen as paintings-in-motion (and Safdie often describes them in these terms), is that we see the transformation of what is being represented in progress, we witness *its* development, but not the development of their making. These videos are not self-referential.

Of course the most obvious suggestion of a Romantic aesthetic is the sheer beauty of the images. They are immediately captivating, entertaining the eye and ear as they engage the mind. Yet this is not to suggest that Safdie's work is backward-looking, old fashioned, or anachronistic. Rather she engages with art's history literally (by using symbolism drawn from the history of art) and literately.[4] By relating her work to certain classical themes and texts, I hope to reveal the sense in which these works represent a new stage in art's long engagement with questions concerning temporality, life, death, transformation, body, and soul.

■

4. That is to say, although Safdie's art uses new technologies it does not align itself with postmodern art movements that assume a radical break with previous artistic movements (usually modernism and it precursors) at the level of aesthetics, techniques, themes, content, and function.

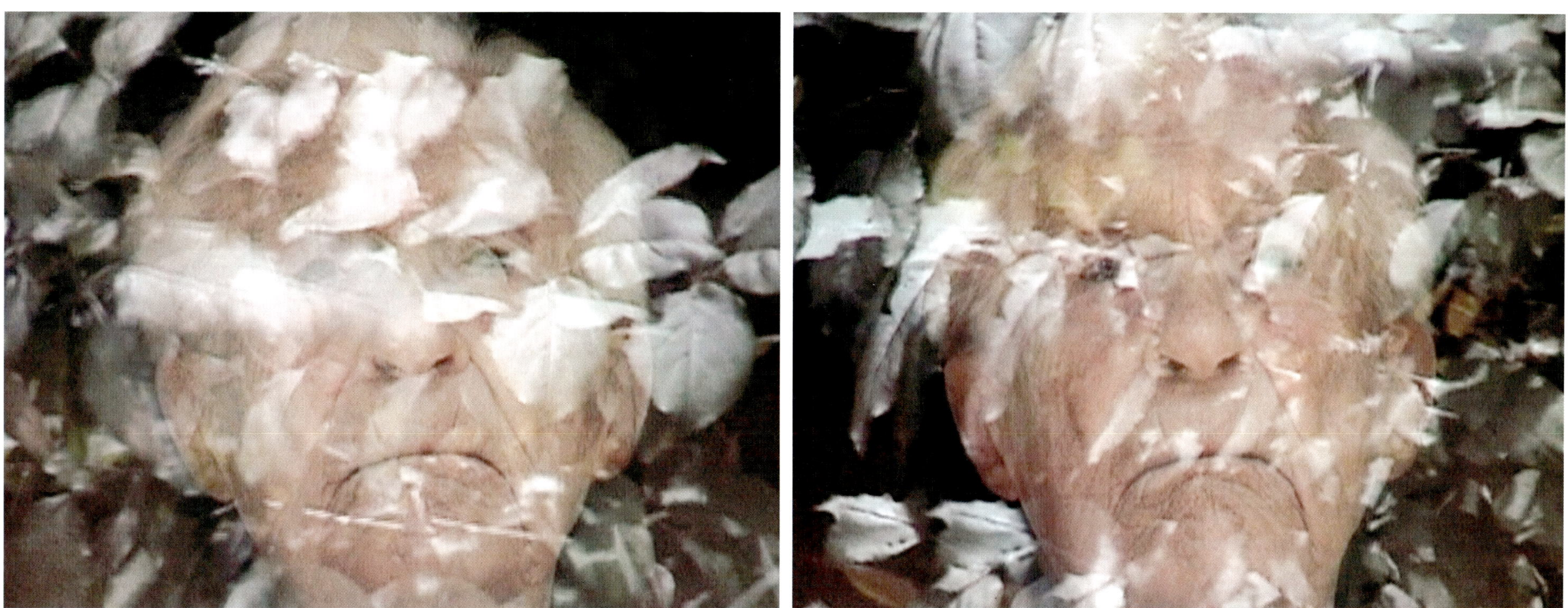

Walter/Leaves (2002) [1], video stills

Safdie's videos are either silent or are accompanied by music. However, the music is not merely a soundtrack for the images, but interacts with them, and the interaction between sound and image is often the subject of the videos. Safdie sets up a dialogical relationship between sound and image, the kind of dialogue that is central to improvisation. Often the images themselves are of improvising musicians, although they are never presented in anything resembling a documentary style. The subject is often obscured or presented to the gaze obliquely.

Safdie's early and sustained interest in breath may have triggered her interest in (and use of) improvised music to help realize her artistic vision. Music propelled by voice or by wind instruments is literally breath in motion. Her use of improvisers was prompted by her many collaborations with the visual artist and improvisational drummer John Heward, who helped integrate Safdie into the diverse community of improvisers based in and passing through Montreal.

Certain features of improvisation render it highly complementary to Safdie's art. First, improvisation foregrounds the body. Far from attempting to ignore or hide the body, improvisation is about "sounding" bodies. While performing an improvisation one is literally performing one's body. Improvisation does not hide the fact that bodies work to produce sound, but displays this work and production, and breath, whether the proximate source of the sound or a necessary adjunct to its production, is always central in improvised music. Improvised music is both able to speak (a form of breath with meaning) and to breathe. Its speech is a dialogue between the improvisers that involves, among other things, the negotiation of

intentions, desires, and identities in real time. When this dialogue proceeds harmoniously improvisations seem "to breathe" – to be imbued with a single life-force, the product of collective action. Improvised music concerns process far more than product, and one of Safdie's goals in moving from painting to video is to make assorted natural processes apparent – to bring back time, change, development, and duration into her artworks while retaining an essentially painterly vision.

In these senses Safdie is herself an improviser and time and again she refers to her videos as collaborations between herself and her surroundings, where her own agency is only partially in control. This may not be obvious since these videos lack many of the hallmarks postmodernism tends to identify with the improvisational – rapid edits, bricolage, a lack of apparent structure and subject, and the use of random processes. Safdie's work is not improvisational in these superficial respects. Her work is highly dialogical, intentional, created with form and structure, transformative, and imbued with meaning – all features of improvisation as theorized by its practitioners.

It is worth thinking about the importance of breath for Safdie while considering her first video, *Walter/Leaves* (2002) [1] and the later videos *Joe Part I* and *II* (*Breath* and *Sound*) (2007) [26], which feature close-ups of the multi-instrumentalist Joe McPhee, an improviser with an international reputation. *Walter/Leaves* reveals the face of the then ninety-seven-year-old Walter, in a state that Safdie calls "sleep/awakening," a state of mixed consciousness which she says is her favourite. Superimposed over the semi-somnolent face of Walter are gently swaying leaves, seemingly both animated by Walter and animating him. "I have captured breath here," Safdie says about her first video work, and the regular movement of the leaves does seem to stand in for Walter's breath. As long as the leaves continue to move, Walter continues to be. "A lot of my work is about life and death, about being and not being." Again breath, and what results from its presence or absence, is foregrounded. Walter, who passed away on the day this video was first exhibited, symbolically lives on in the image of the bird in *Gulls*, as a breathing spirit and in the rustling leaves, his breath made visible and natural.

The relations among breath, sound, life, and death permeate many of these works. In *Joe Part I* and *II* (*Breath* and *Sound*) [26] Joe McPhee is filmed close up playing a poignant solo on his trumpet. McPhee conceived of his participation in this video as a way to honour his father in what was the tenth year since his death, and would have been the hundredth year since his birth. As McPhee comments immediately prior to the filming of these videos, he wished to pay homage to the gifts of breath and music his father gave him, by summoning his absent father with his own breath and sound. McPhee's playing style here is somewhat uncharacteristic of his recorded work, but expressive and moving as always. Safdie comments: "When I worked with Joe, he told me he made sounds that he had never made before ... it was an elemental sound." The camera captures his rapture, his "sleep/awakening" state, and also suggests his own finitude.

McPhee's playing is all about his breath, breath made both corporeal and musical. He does not hide the fact that it is his life-force passing through his horn. Far from it, he forces us to hear his very

essence in his playing, complete with wheezes, puckers, throat sounds, and whistles. The superimposed images of water become a corporealization of his breath, and, like the role of pneuma in Stoic theories of God, soul and body animate what they touch through their vibrating movement.[5]

As in many of Safdie's videos, the real subject – here, Joe's father – is not seen. Here too we find her characteristic fusion of the particular and universal in Safdie's works, for while the video is deeply personal, it also raises questions about the birth of sound. McPhee's elemental playing, coupled with images of water (themselves seemingly propelled by the music), suggests a sort of primitivist creation of sound. By personalizing the evocation of sound and spirit Safdie avoids the vexing issues surrounding the reception of so-called primitive art and imagery that high modernism faced. The videos are not a primitivizing generalization of a people or culture because Safdie captures Joe McPhee in an act with sacred overtones that is of his own choosing and a product of his own history and experiences.[6]

The trust that McPhee has in Safdie's ability to treat such a personal moment with artistry and honesty allows him to reveal so much of himself. It may be worth recalling that in the early history

5. For the Stoics, soul is a form of breath, called pneuma, which moves in waves, both inwardly and outwardly, thus both unifying a body, and granting it psychic capacities. This kinetic wave-like pneuma is also identified as God – the God in us – by the Stoics.
6. See William Rubin (ed.), *"Primitivism" in 20th Century Art*, vols 1–2, (The Museum of Modern Art, 1984), for the classic, and controversial, discussion of the relationship of modernism to the so-called primitive. See also Alfred Appel Jr., *Jazz Modernism* (Yale University Press, 2002) for a (problematic) discussion of the relationship of jazz to modernism.

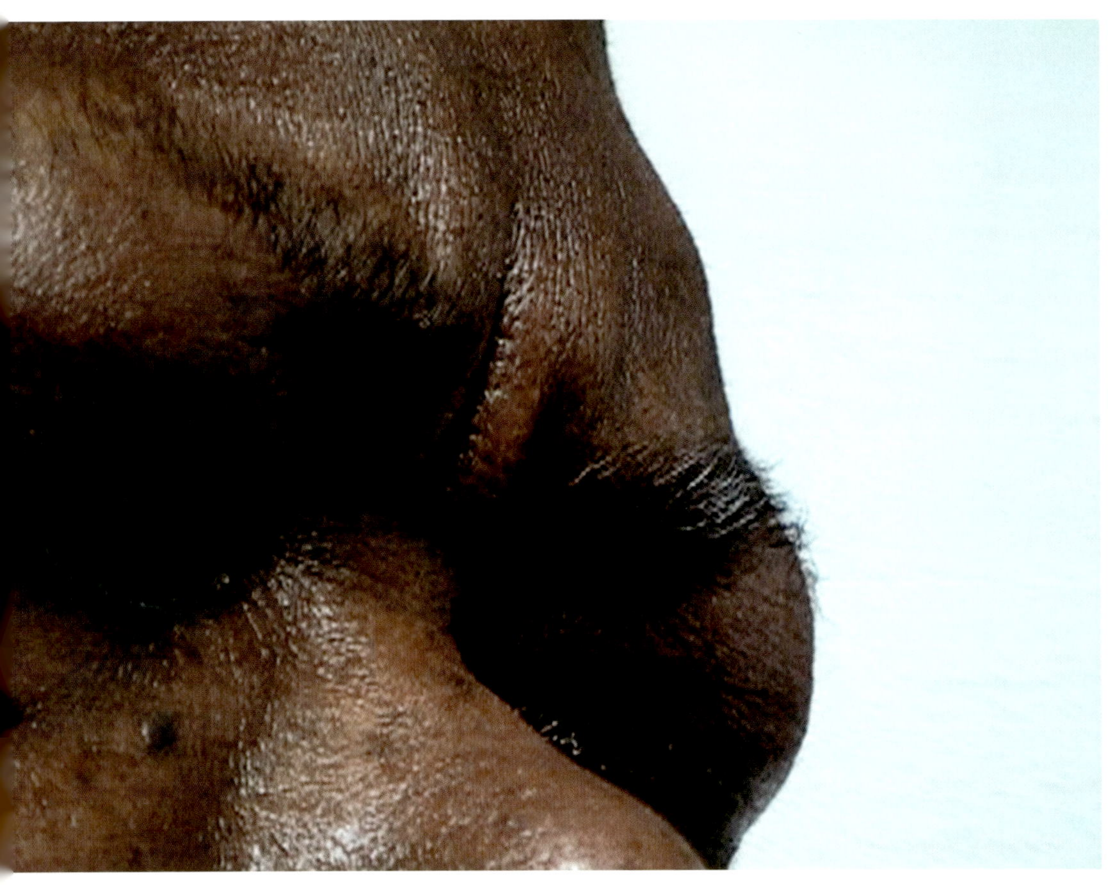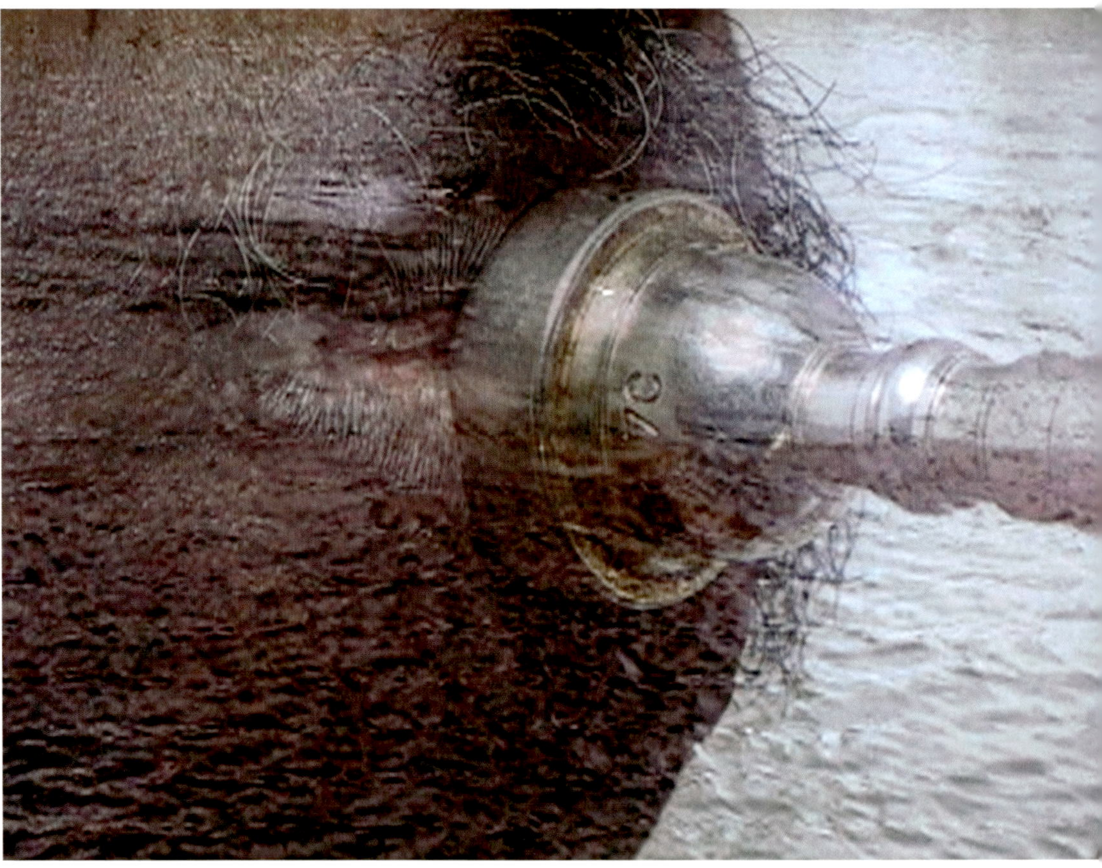

Joe, Part I: Breath (2007) [26.1], video stills

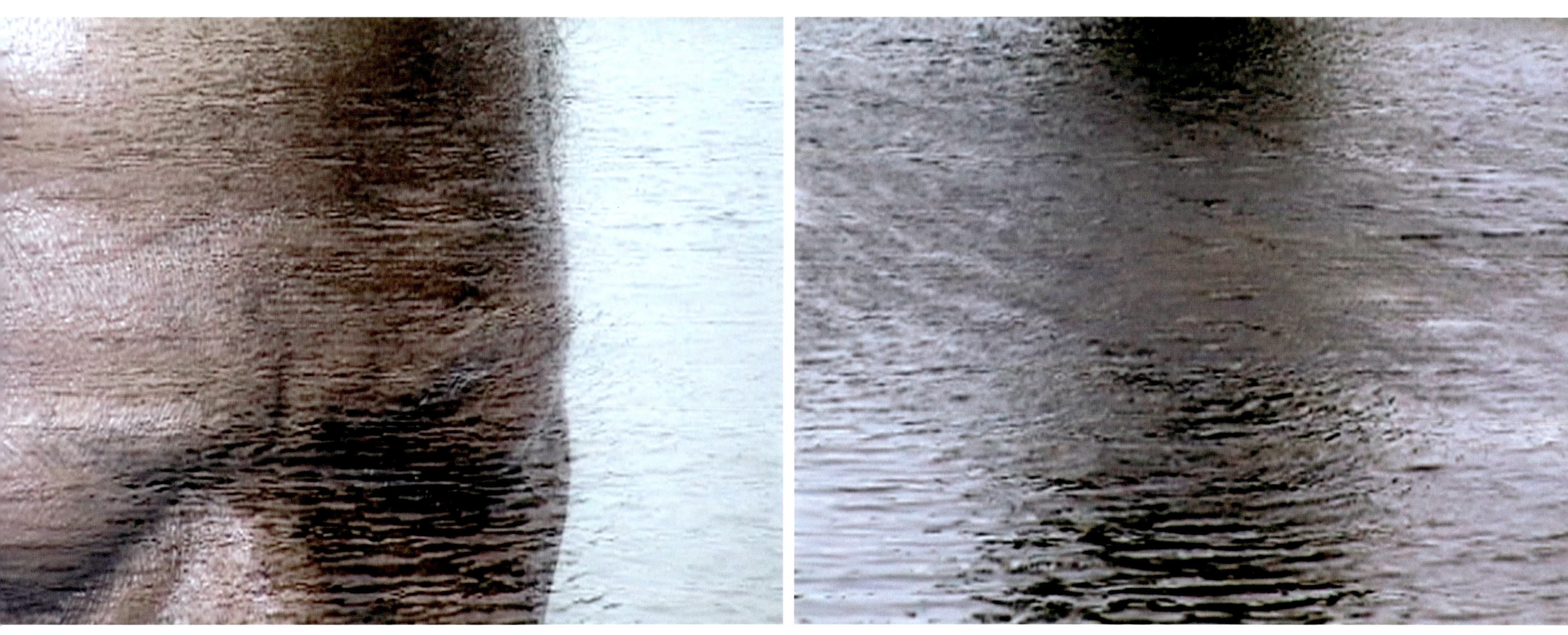

Joe, Part II: Sound (2007) [26.2], video stills

of jazz, when mechanical means of recording were introduced, many jazz musicians were unwilling to be recorded out of fear that their sound (and so their very essence) would be both captured and stolen. Their breath/essence as music was at risk. Given the intimacy of the sounds captured in *Joe Part I* and *II* one can see why this was a real fear.

Already we can discern not only a number of unifying themes in Safdie's work, but also a consistent motivation behind them. Many videos concern the liminal space between the animate and the inanimate, the living and the dead, and the conscious and the unconscious. Bodies merge into and emerge out of rocks and water (*Untitled I* [70]; *Body/Stone/Water* [73]), subjects occupy middle grounds between distinct states of consciousness, and assumed inanimate objects are imbued with breath, with a life force. Such videos occupy ambivalent spaces between the symbolic and literal – they are both of this world and a world of abstractions. Sound and image also have their boundaries blurred and the opposition between them questioned as images take on rhythms and sounds materialize as rock, water, dust, or shadow. These features of Safdie's art can perhaps be partially explained by her interest in the "sleep/awakening" state. It is in this state where perceptions report features of the external world but also seem deeply symbolic and where the categories we normally use to carve up the world at its joints (animate, inanimate, etc.) are often discarded for lacking relevance. In such a state we can hear images and see sounds – so what is left to distinguish them?

Safdie's focus on breath as a vital force, her use of occluded or absent subjects, the distinctions between the animate and inanimate, and the cycles of change, all affect her treatment of bodies in general and her own body in particular, although her own body does not enter into her video art until 2009–10. Previously, her body appeared symbolically in her videos. This can be seen in *Water over Stone* (2002) [4], which despite being silent is also a very musical video. "You are not hearing the sound, but you are feeling it physically," Safdie says. The video, which is a loop of water moving over and around a stationary rock, has rhythm, tempo, and dynamics. It is a corporeal, kinetic, silent music. The movement of the water and the inner and outer vibrations that it suffers are akin to the Stoics' idea of the movement of the pneumatic soul, where outward motion gives rise to an en-souled being's qualities, while inner motion unifies and holds the being together. At the core of this pneumatic motion is the body, which is represented by the rock in the video.

Safdie says that the resemblance of this stone to a body was immediately apparent to her, and that the resemblance started her to think again about her own body with respect to her art. "The memory of that image was deeply implanted in my mind." This image returns in *Untitled III* (2010) [71] where Safdie's own body takes on the shape and position of this rock and is also the inspiration for the series *Body/Stone/Water*. In the eight years between *Water over Stone* and *Untitled III* bodies go from being symbolically present to being actually present (if still obscure and indistinct), but always in the process of becoming. While actual bodies have always informed Safdie's work, by 2010 she saw a way to integrate the natural rhythms of the body with those of nature, merging the transformations that

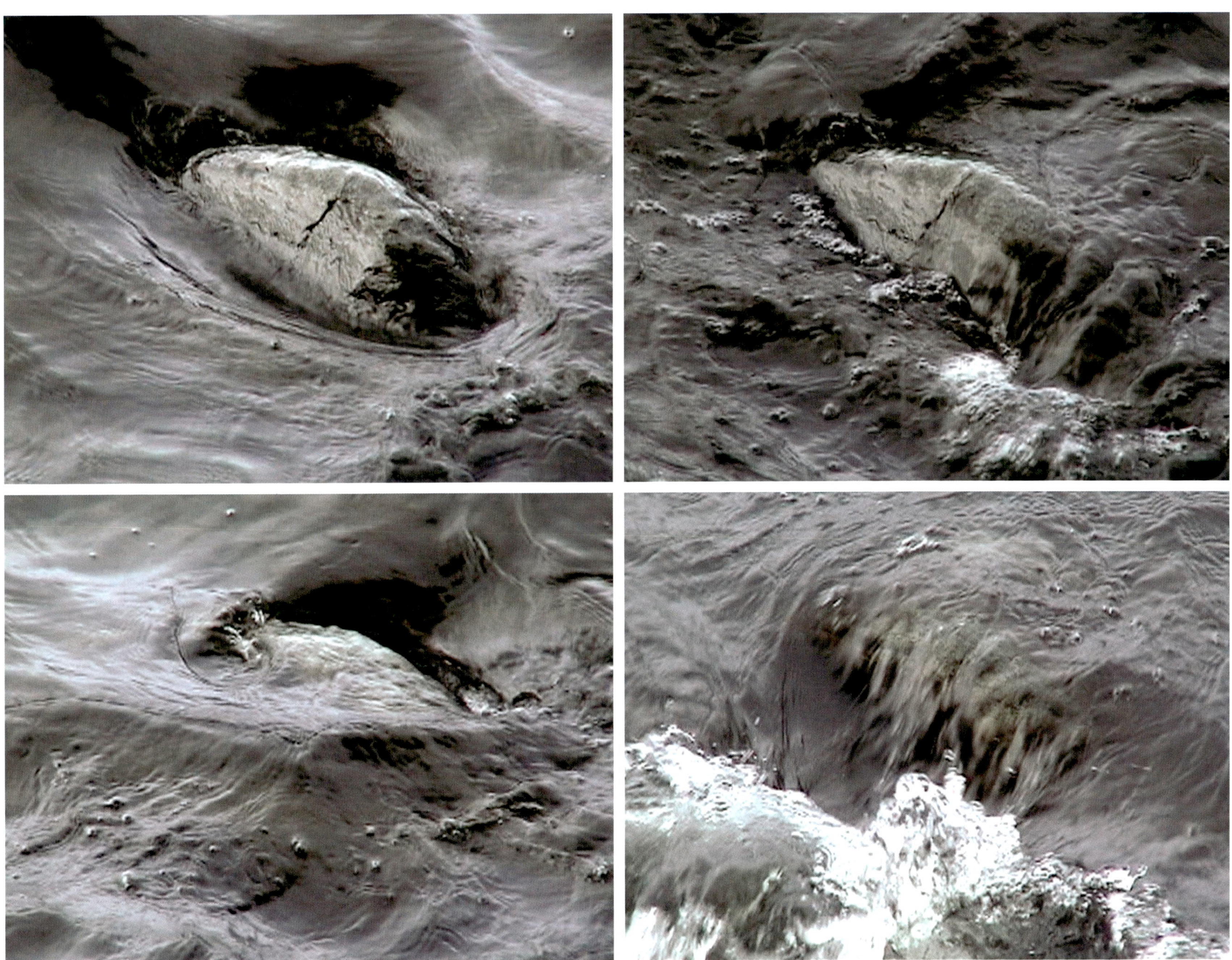

Water over Stone (2002) [4], video stills

both bodies and nature undergo. She no longer "merely suggested" the unity of the human body with nature, but turned to the direct depiction of this unity. The seamless merging of the movements of nature and bodies found in the series *Body/Stone/Water* was inspired by *Confluence* (2010), a dance choreographed by Canadian dancer and choreographer Peggy Baker. The movements were in turn based on Safdie's video *Dance* (2005) [16], featuring the "death dance" of a dying insect to the music of Heward's hand-drumming. While filming a performance of *Confluence* Safdie was inspired to introduce her own body into her videos, while remaining committed to presenting bodies (often with unclear identities) in process.

Implied and occluded bodies feature in a number of Safdie's works. *Solo* (2005) [17] focuses on a metal worker's chisel and the drum sticks of John Heward. In this video the bodies of both the worker and Heward are implied, while remaining just off camera. In *Movements* (2005) [15] the camera focuses on the hair and barely revealed shoulder of the improvising pipa player Liu Fang. The fluid sensuousness of this image suggests the otherwise absent whole body without any of the implications of fracture and violence that much contemporary art criticism focuses on when faced with body parts. While the image is not of a whole body, the allusion invites the mind to make the absent body whole, not to further deconstruct it.

Similar treatments of absent bodies are found in *Dance* (2005) [16], where Heward's hands are implied but absent, and with *Hands* (2005) [21] and *Touching* (2007) [30], which depict only hands, or implied hands, respectively. Sometimes bodies are implied by the tools they use, as with *Act/Shadow* (2006) [25] which follows the bow of Malcolm Goldstein as he performs his piece "Gentle Rain Preceding Mushrooms." In *Lori* (2008) [41], the clarinetist Lori Freedman, playing her instrument, is shown at first at the base of her feet. Soon her face fleetingly appears, dim and indistinct, only to fade again into the background. In *Late Afternoon Raga* (2008) [40] the bodies of musicians and singers are only suggested, and in *Sumitra Maina* (2008) [36] (both shot at the Rajasthan International Folk Festival) a female singer is shown singing from behind a decorative veil. A similar treatment of heads appears in the 2009 series *Head I, II, III* [67–69], where, as the video progresses, one is never sure if it is a real or sculpted head that slowly comes into focus. In fact this series uses the heads of both Safdie and Heward, but they remain so indistinct that it is difficult to argue that this series is "about" Safdie's body in any definite sense. The use of darkened heads in this video series is very much like her use of large heads in a series of paintings (*Heads*) shown in 2005, where the painted heads, depicted in varied states of transformation, are anonymous and generic at the same time that they are curiously personal. Like dream images or thoughts in a state of sleep/awakening, these heads are familiar, yet just as the mind affixes an identity to them, they change or fade away.

These videos with implied bodies are conspicuous for the absence of Safdie's own body. In *Body/Stone/Water* (2010) [73], the first video in which she uses her own body, we see a stone slowly morph into her limbless back, then briefly become her whole body before fading again into the surrounding rock and water. Having worked for years on the artistic evocation of breath, soul, and

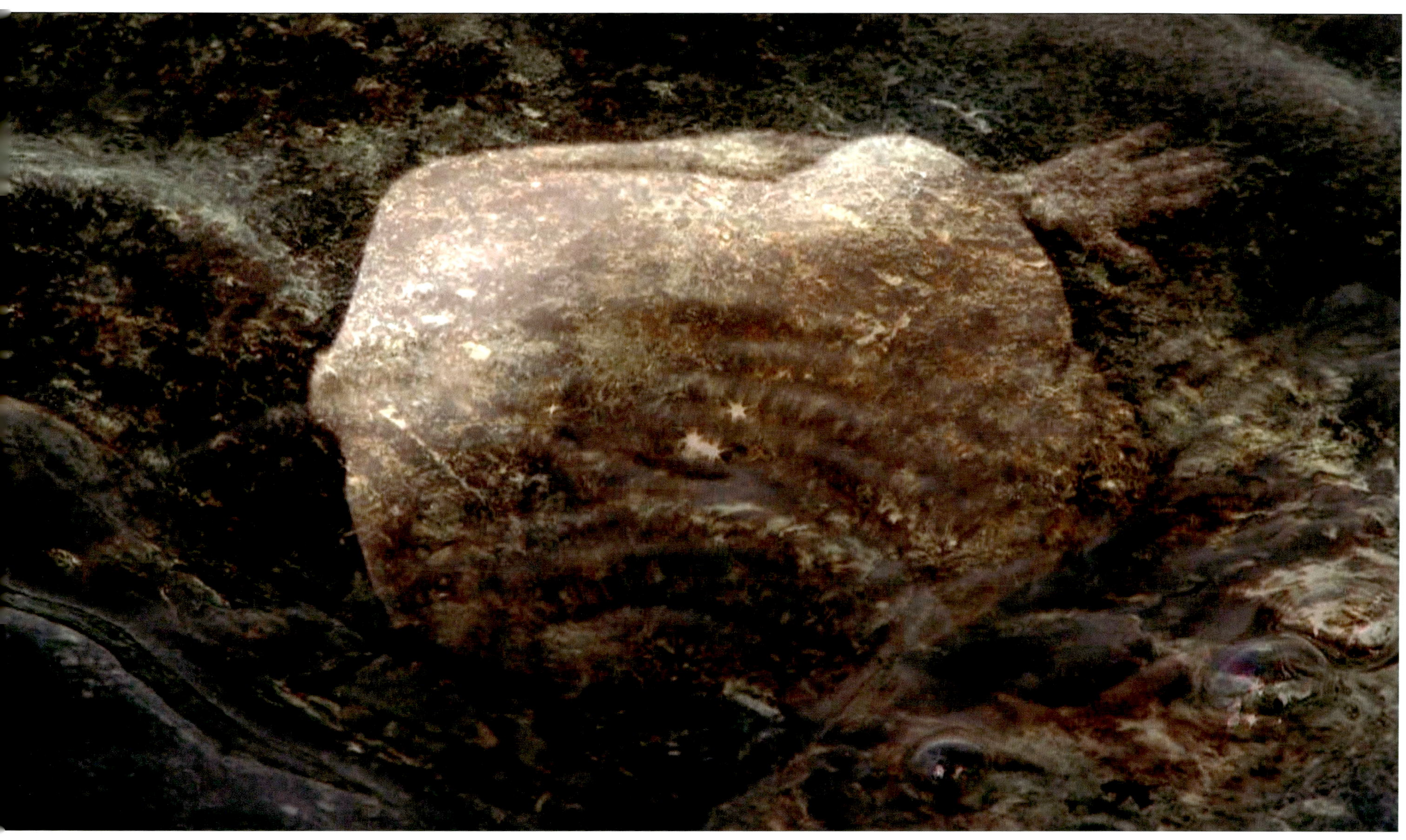

Untitled III (2010) [71], diptych, video stills

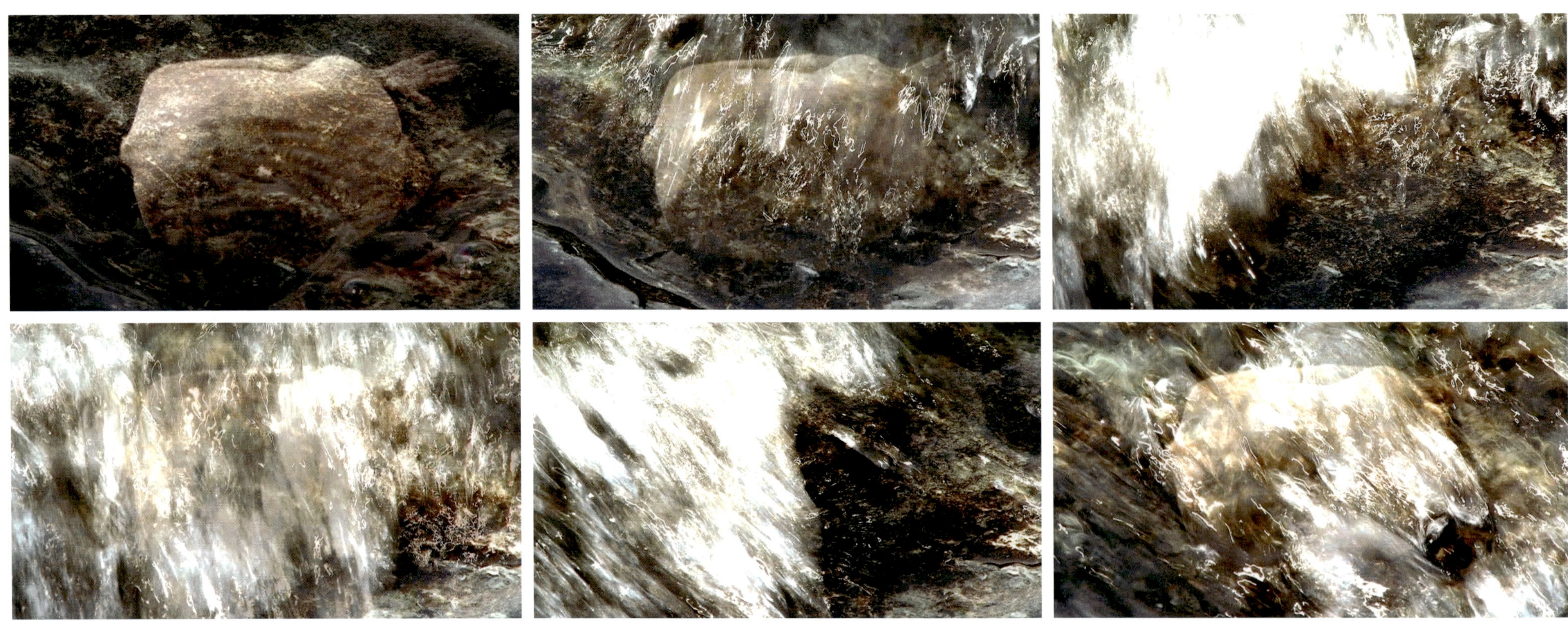

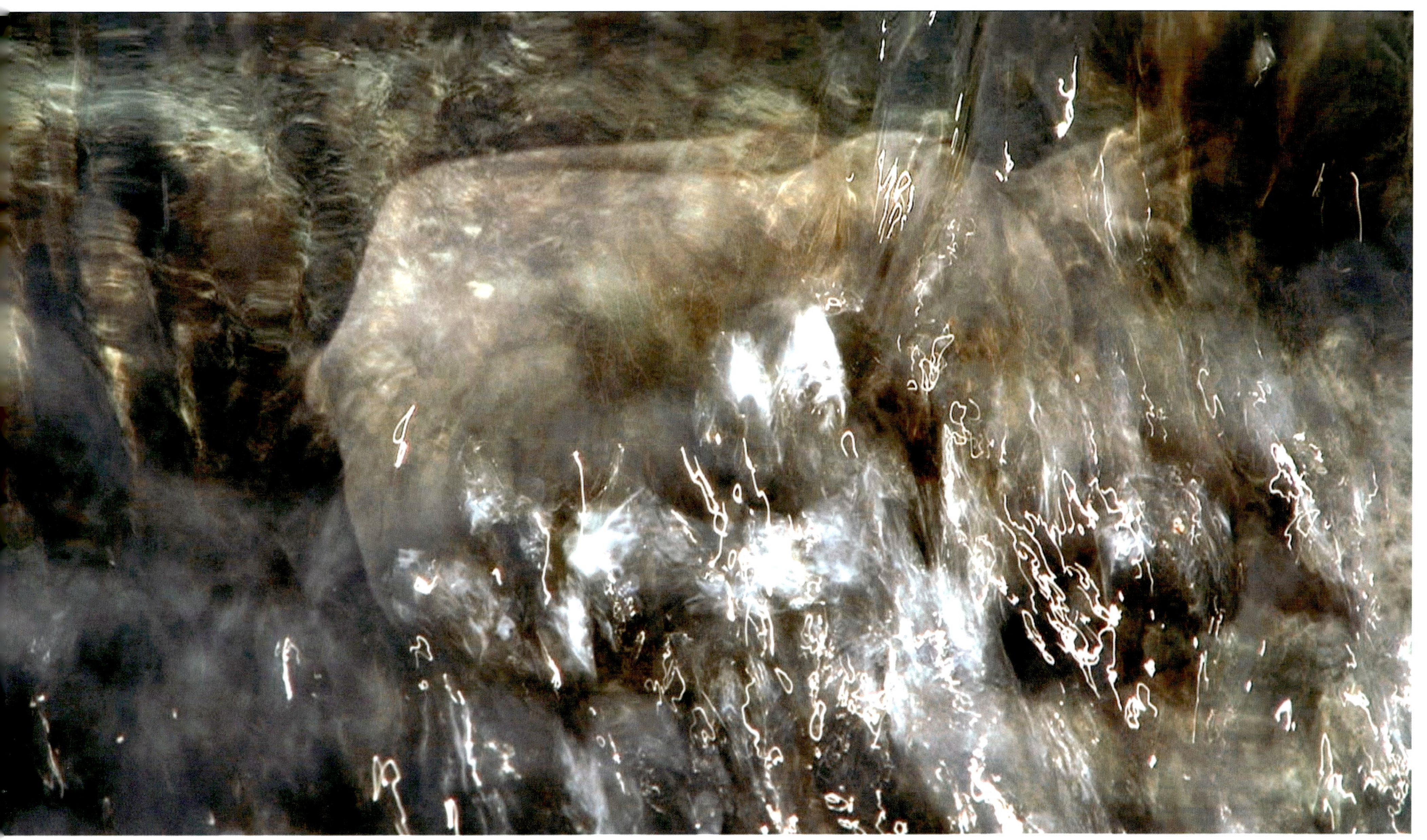

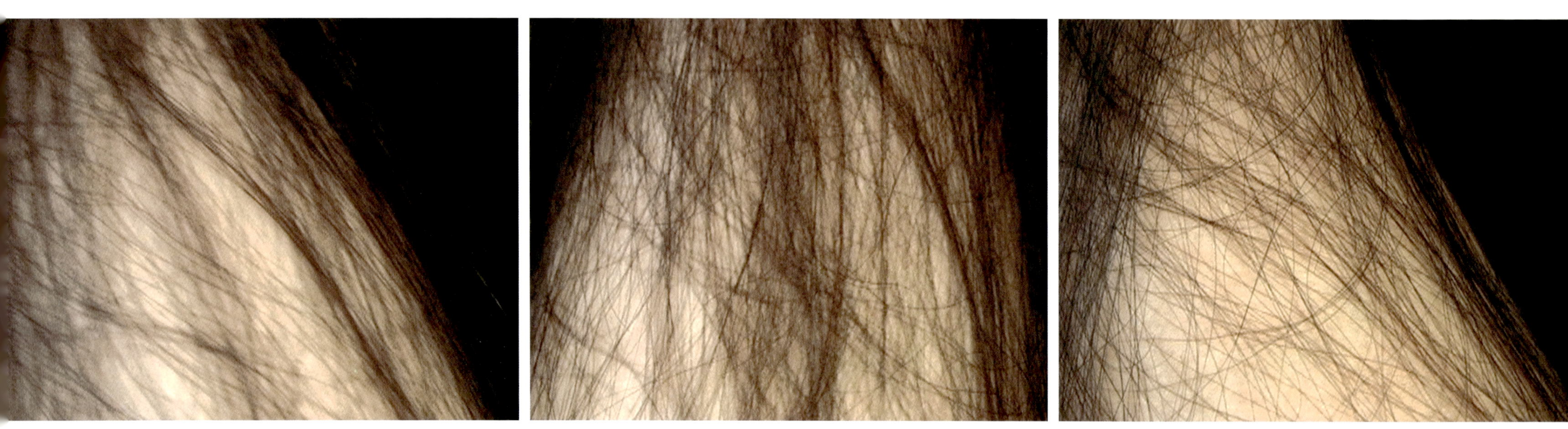

Movements (2005) [15], video stills

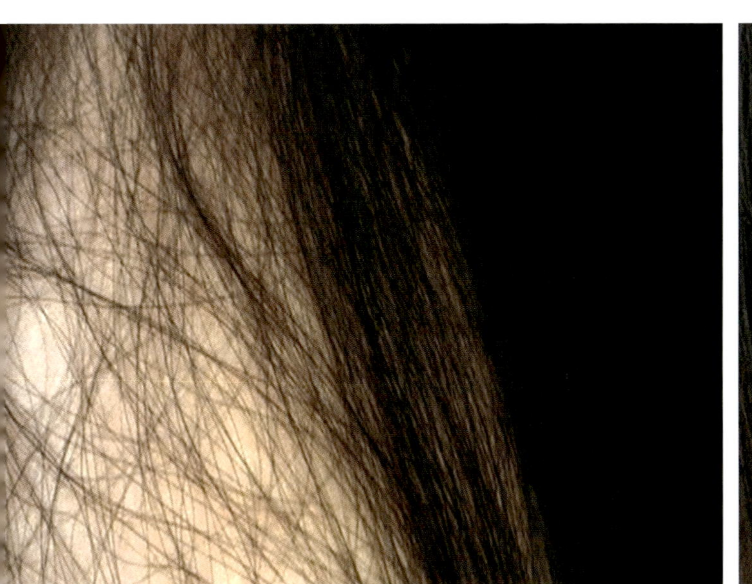
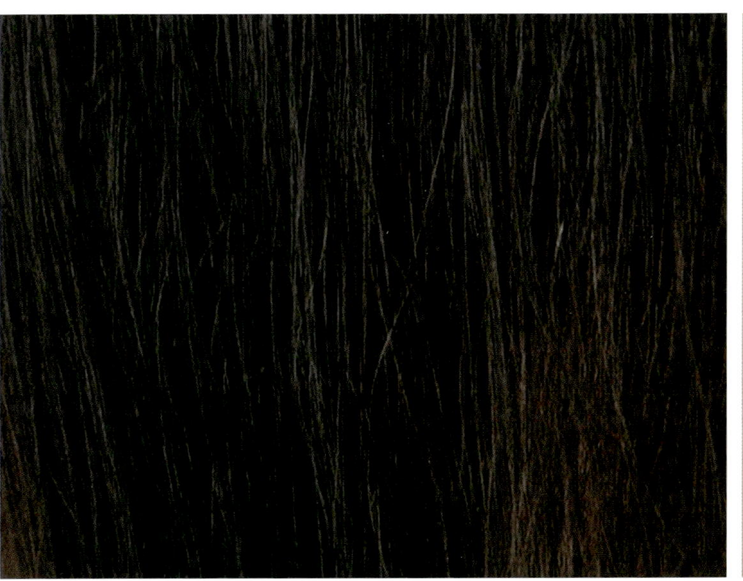
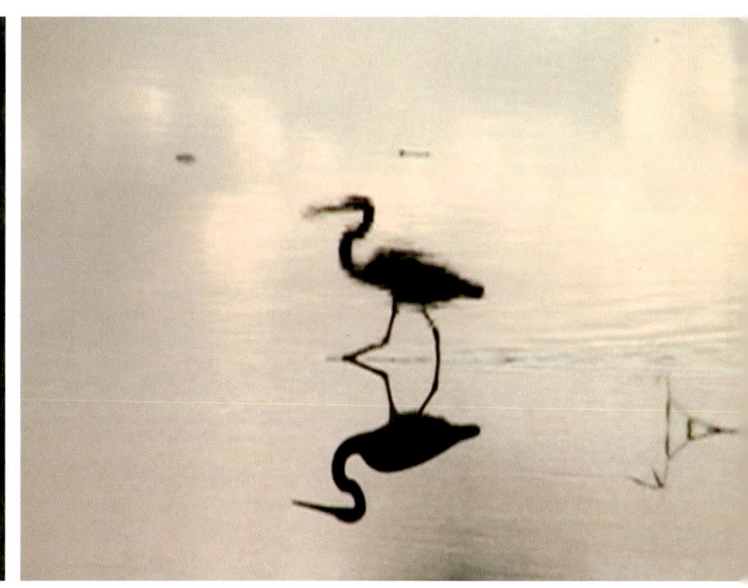

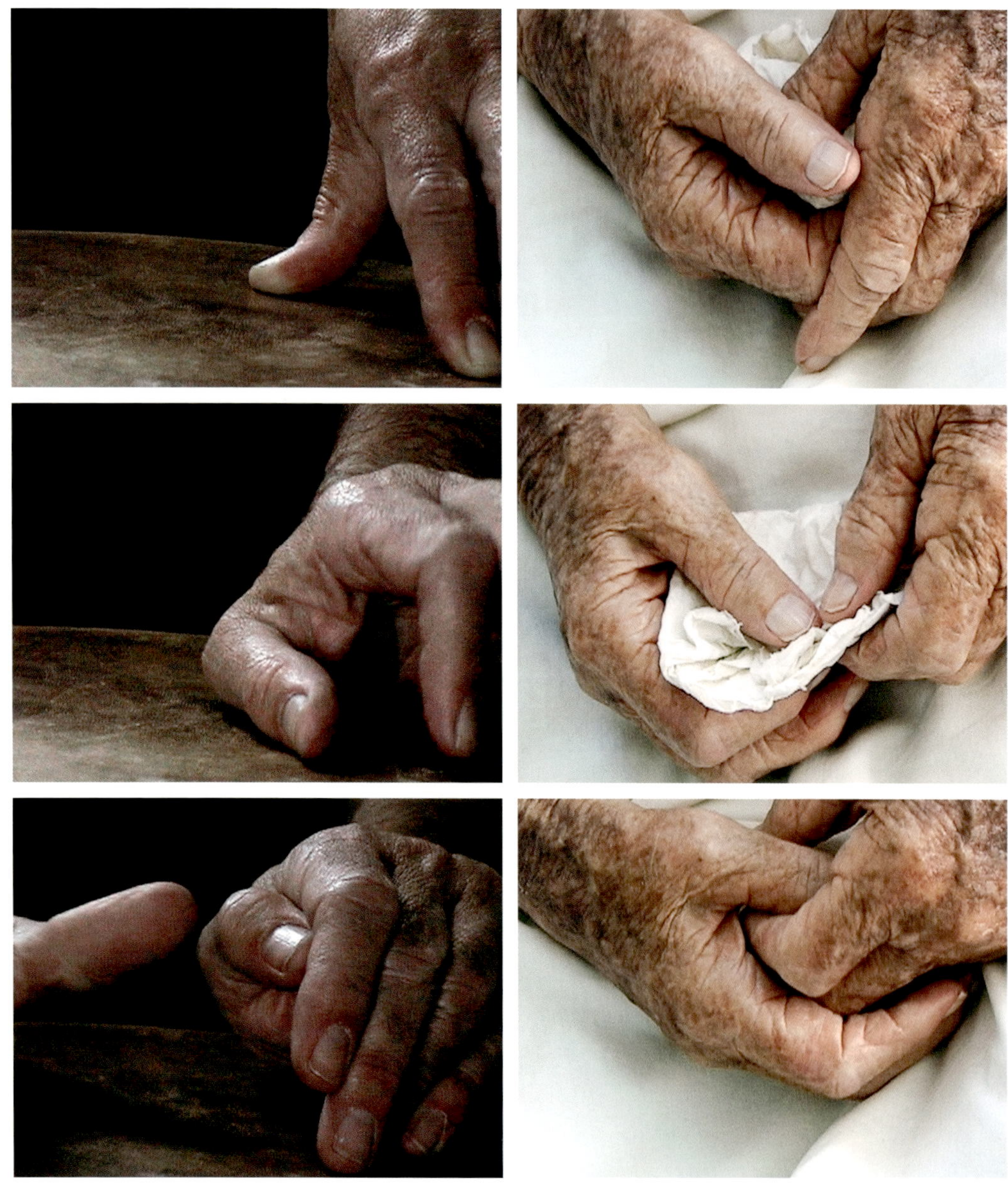

Hands (2005) [21], diptych, video stills

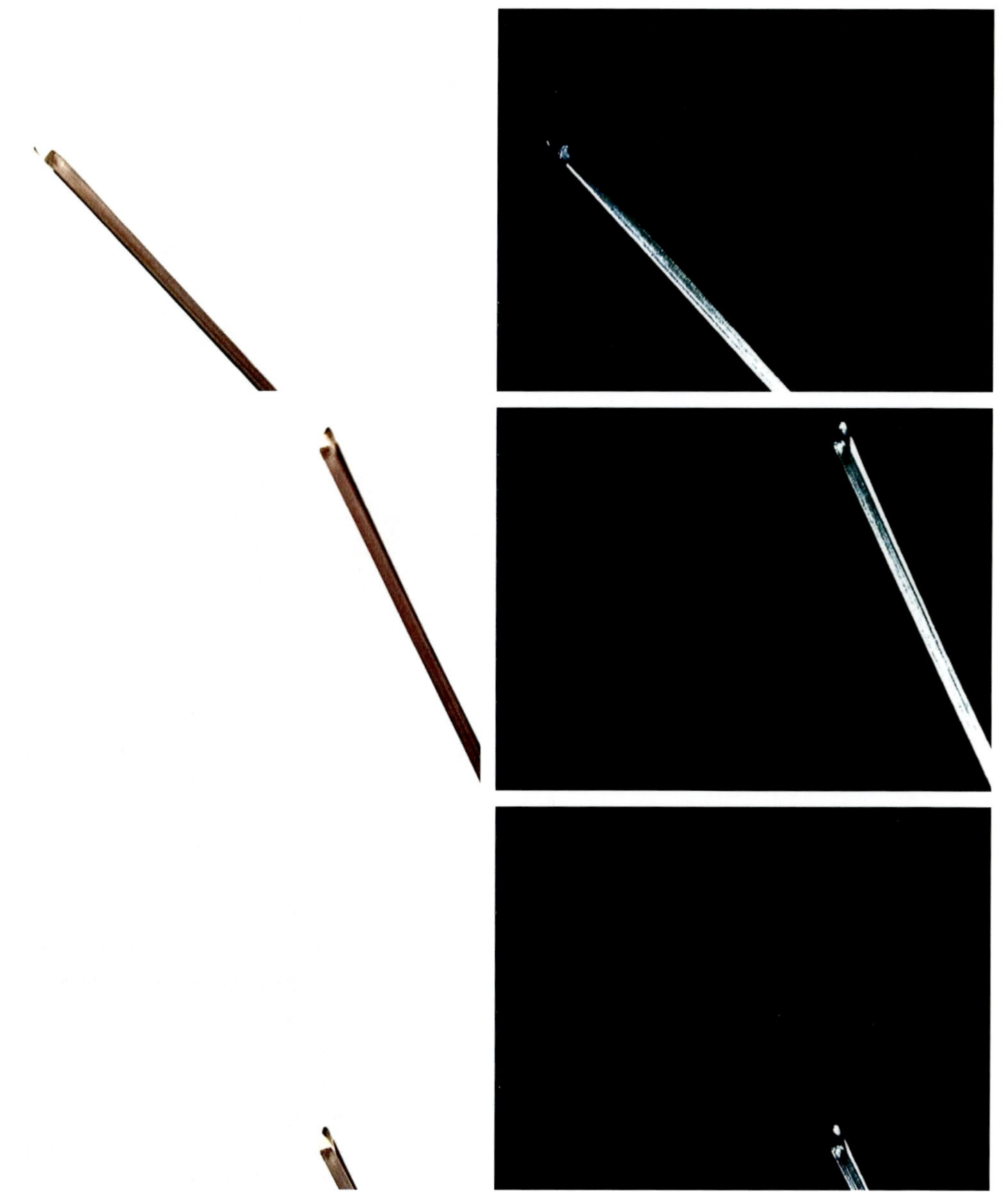

Act/Shadow (2006) [25], diptych, video stills

Late Afternoon Raga (2008) [40], diptych, video stills

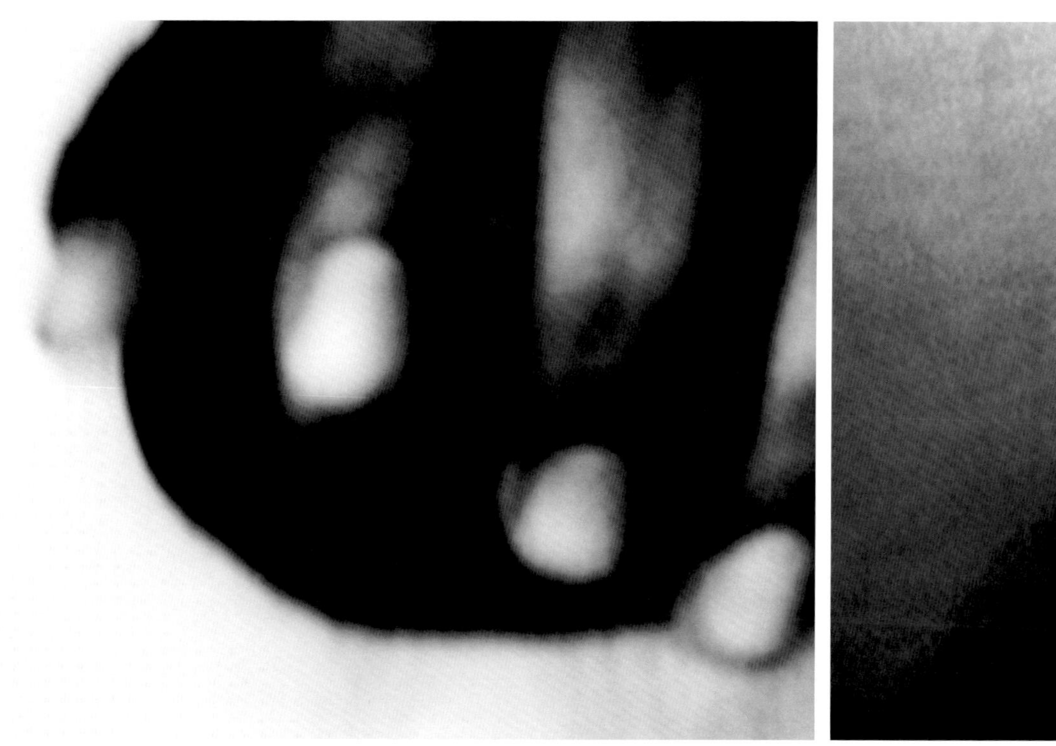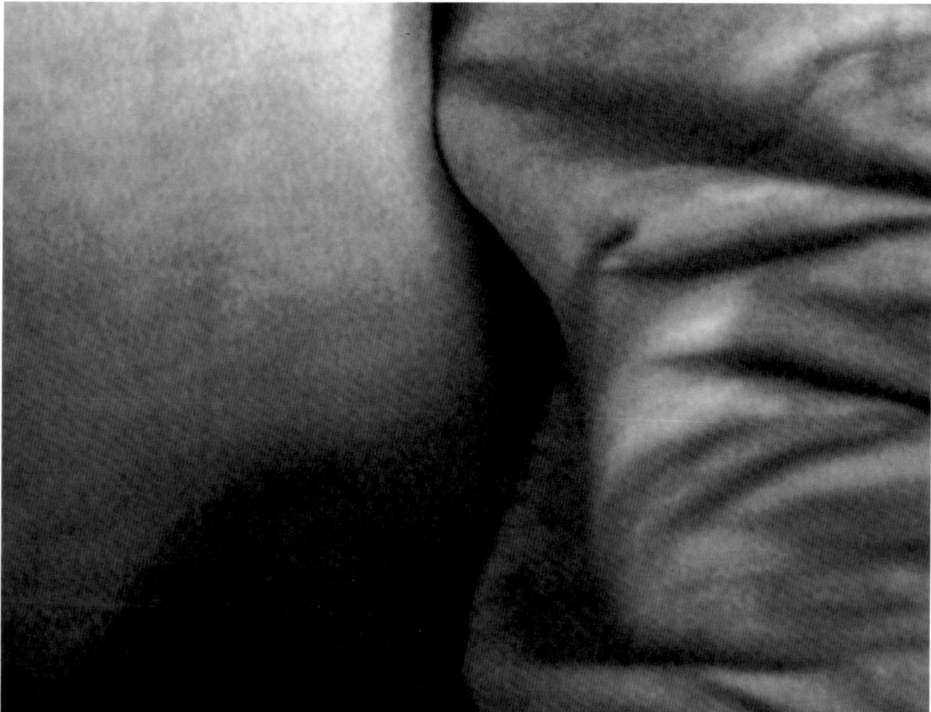

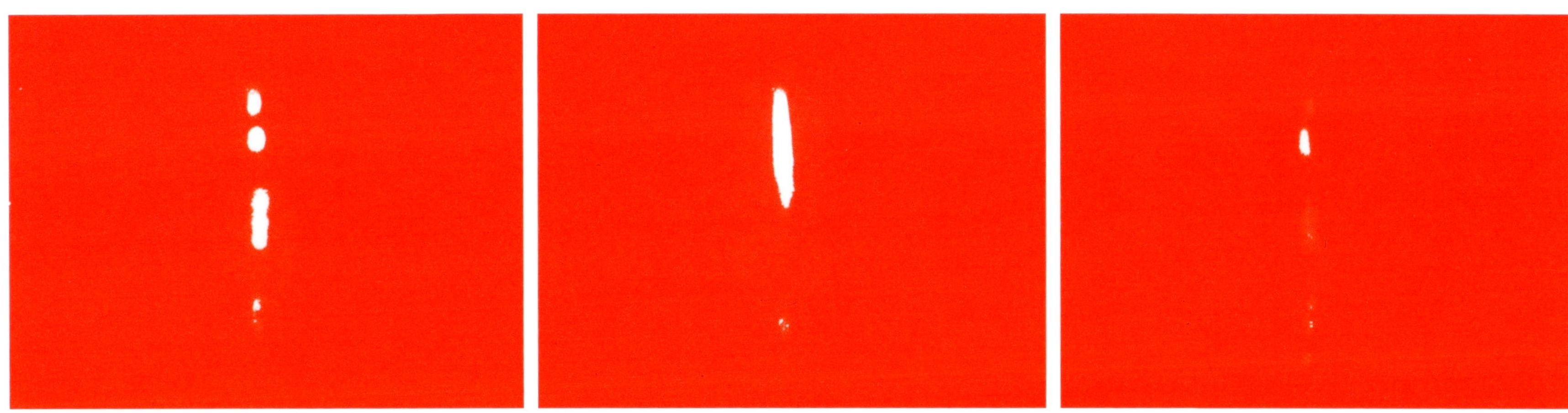

Rajasthan (Red) (2008) [39], video stills

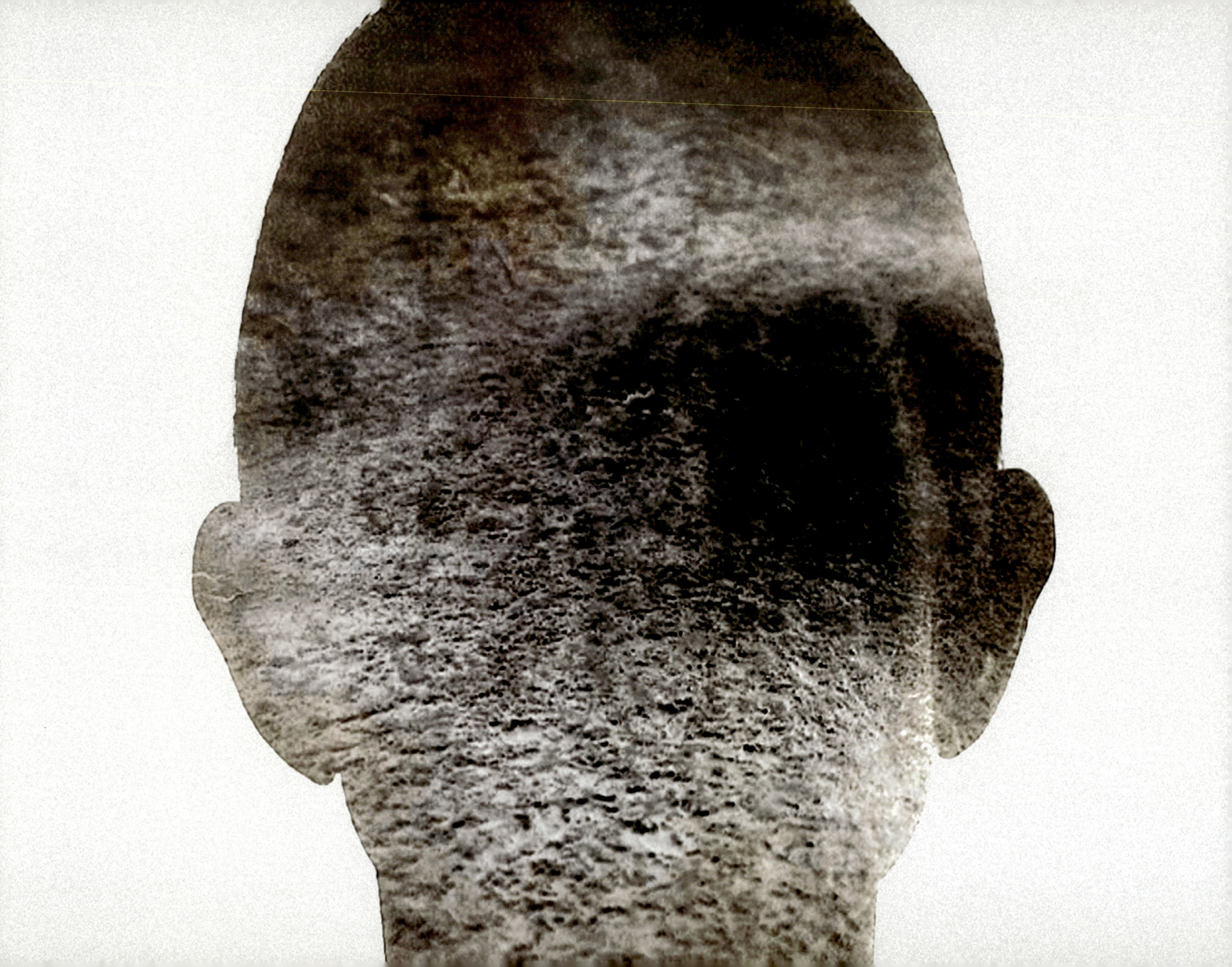

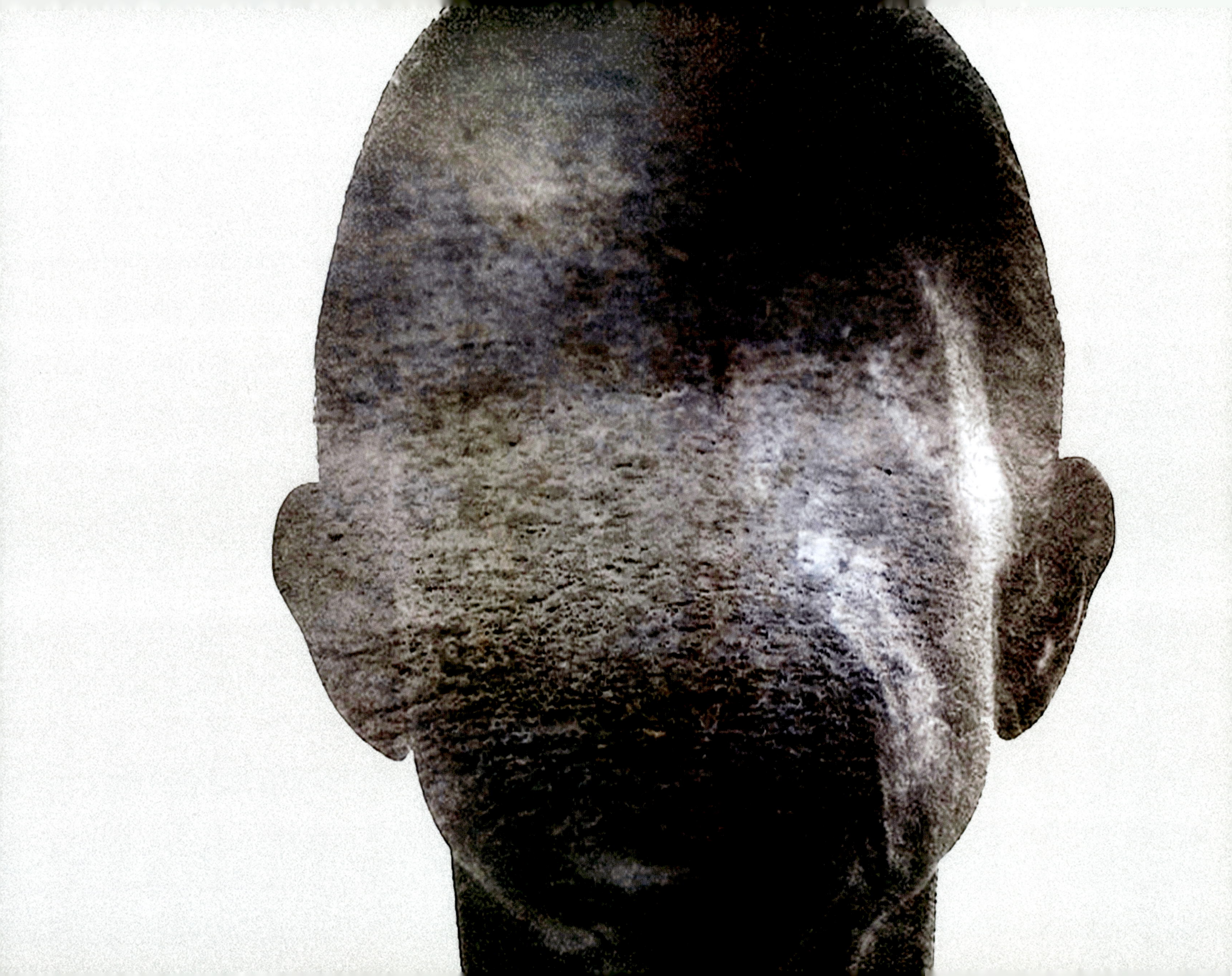

spirit, and making them corporeal and visible, now Safdie brings her own body into our gaze, a body wholly integrated into nature. As Safdie has said: "Where do we go? Into the earth. Where do we come from? Water. It is a cycle." At ease with her now older body and the transformations it has undergone, accepting of her place in her environment, and at peace with her own mortality, we see in these videos an artful statement of the principle that we are all part of nature – depicted by Safdie as a living, breathing organism. Referring to this series in general, Safdie states, "I could not have done these pieces when I was younger. My meditation practice has intensified my awareness of breath, mind, body, and nature." *Body/ Stone/Water* is temporally book-ended by two series of powerful and important videos, the first shot in Morocco [43–64], the second at Auschwitz [74–80]. Both concern missing bodies, lost spirits, absence, and the transformation of spaces, but in different ways and for different reasons.

With the Morocco series Safdie set out to investigate what happens when a community long identified with a particular location is displaced. How are both the community and the place transformed? Her interest and sensitivity to the issue of displacement as transformation is due in no small part to her own heritage as a Lebanese Jew of Syrian descent, communities which now exist almost entirely in the diaspora. Her long concern with the depiction of both absent bodies and bodies in transformation made the diaspora a natural subject of interest.

Safdie traveled to Amzrou, a kasbah in the Draa valley, on the edge of the Sahara desert in southern Morocco. For 2,500 years it was home to a relatively large Jewish community, who lived in peace with their Berber neighbours. In 1958 the eighteen remaining Jewish families living in the mellah (the Jewish quarter) of Amzrou immigrated to Israel, leaving behind their homes, trades, crafts, tools, and traditions, many of which were taken up by the local Draouis families who soon moved into the mellah. Memories of this community are preserved only by the elderly, especially by the Jewish elders who no longer live there, and by the spaces they once occupied, where they cooked, worked, prayed, lived, and died. The first video Safdie shot here, *Morning* (2009) [43], focuses on brightly illuminated, rhythmically moving subjects, while also capturing the sense of absent presence in keeping with this series. In this video, the camera fixates on a distant figure brightly back-lit at the end of a long passageway. Details of the figure are obscure, as are its precise movements and gestures. The video manages to be about this particular subject, with its strong presence as the focal point, and to suggest through the surrounding darkness an absence presence. The figure is a residue, so to speak, standing as a token for the passing of something much greater.

This sense of absence pervades the videos Safdie shot in the long abandoned synagogue of Amzrou, which she sees as "a poetic evocation of a place which marks the dispersion of a society from its home." In a series of videos [44–47] that focus on particles of dust illuminated by a bright column of natural light (set against the mottled backdrop of the synagogue wall), the spirits of these absent persons are almost shamanistically made visible. The dust particles move and dance as if summoned by the violin playing

Previous spread: Head II (2009) [68], video stills

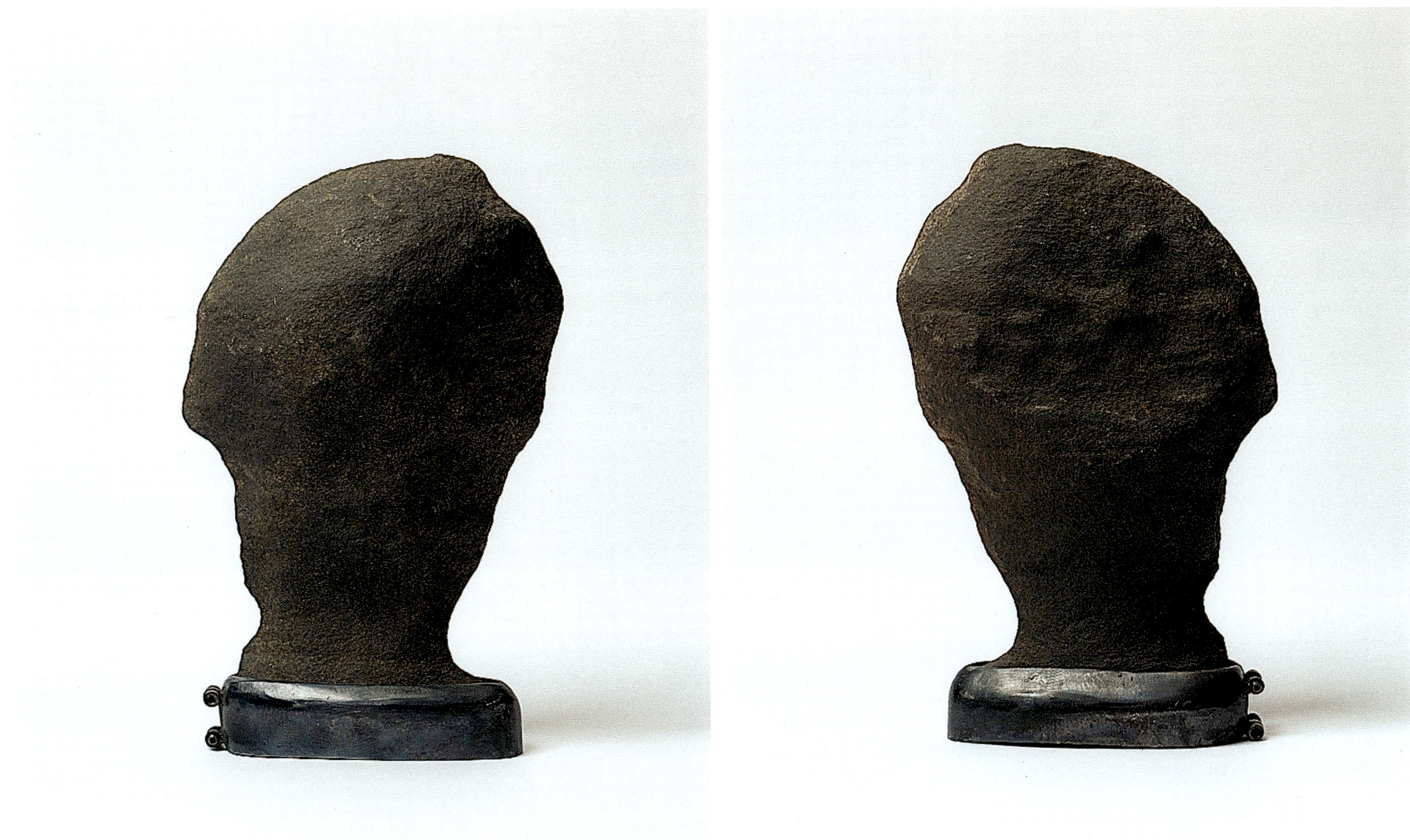

Headstone no. 1, 1993, stone, steel, 29 cm x 16.5 cm x 78.2 cm

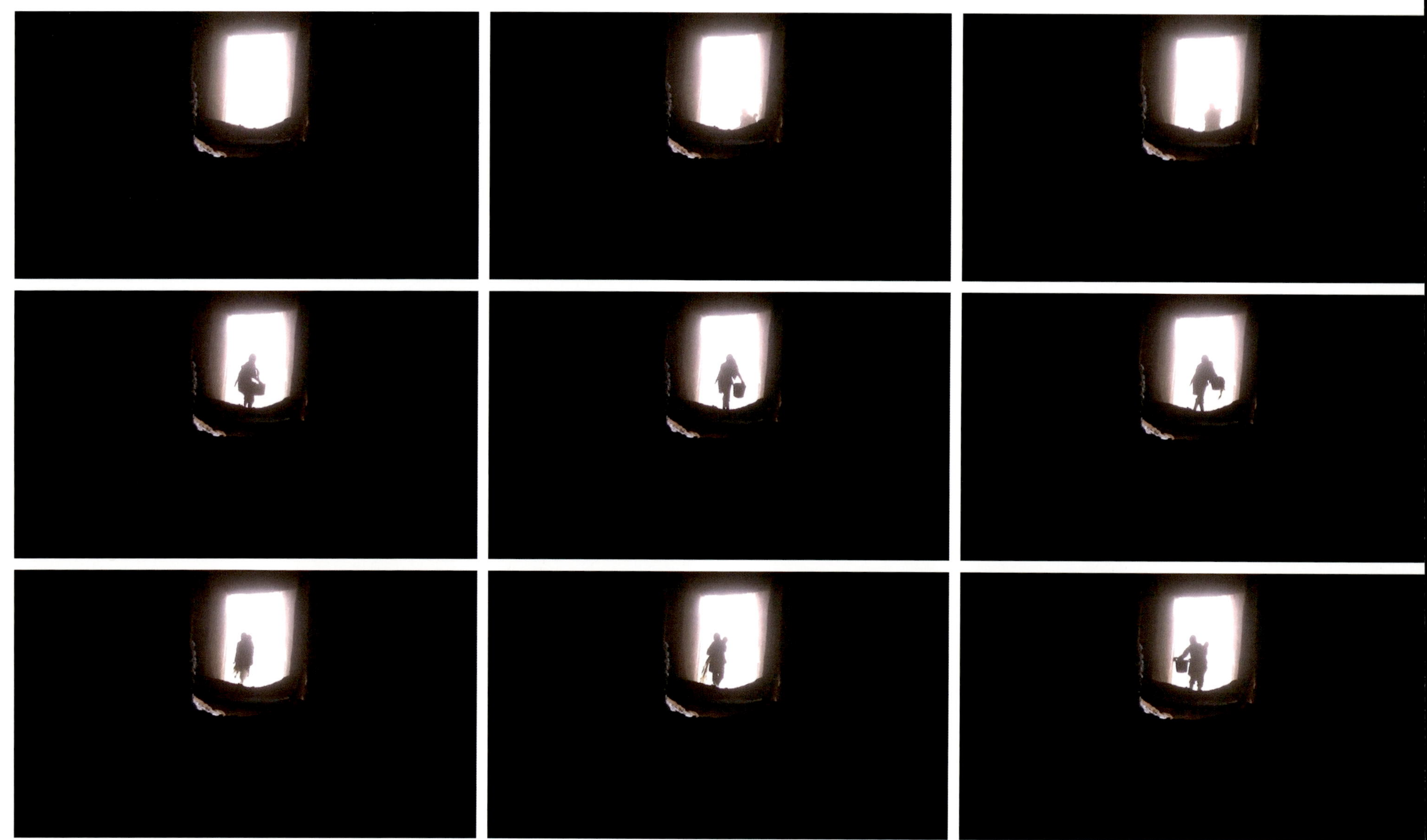

Morning (2009) [53], video stills

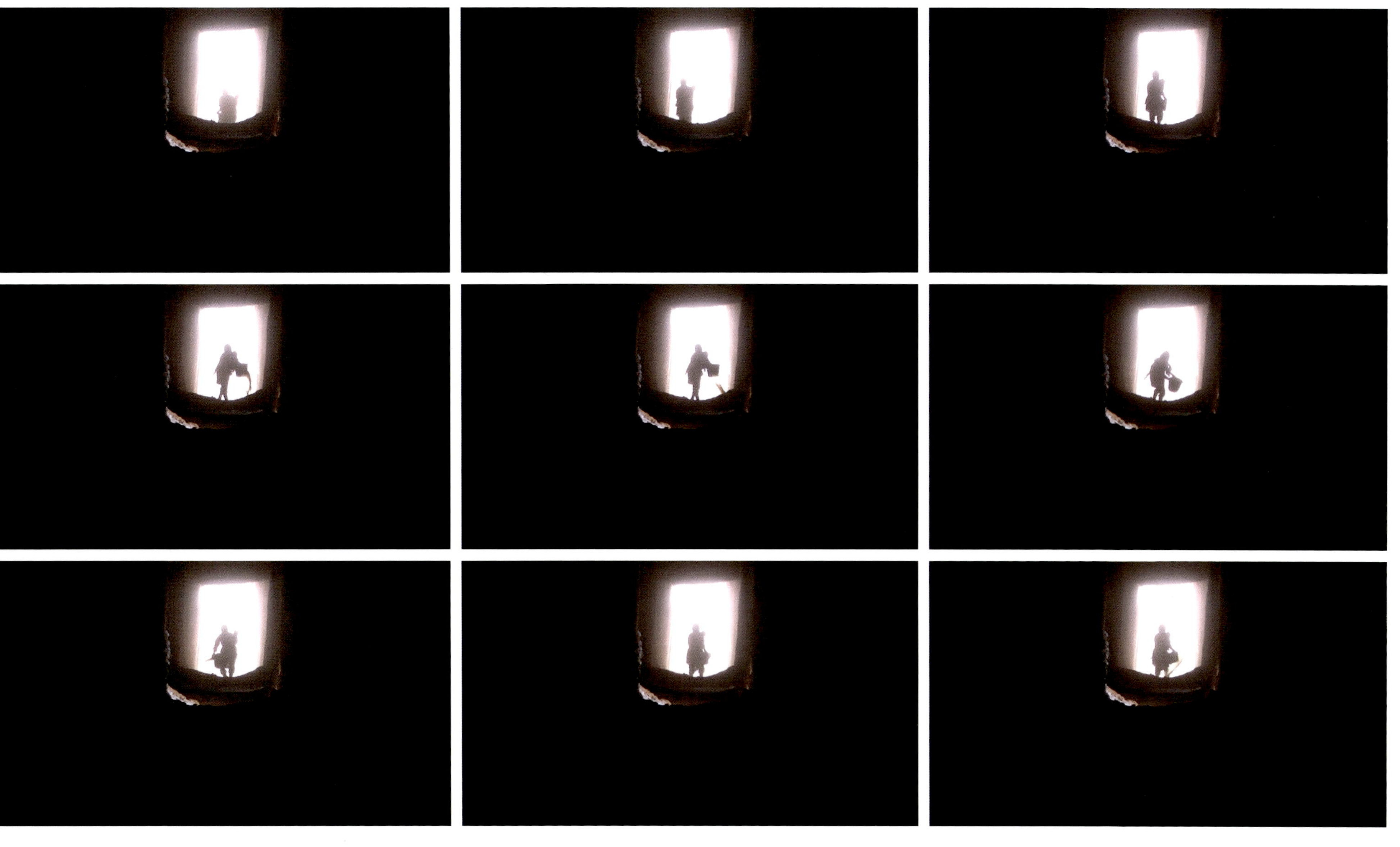

of either Malcolm Goldstein (*Dust*, 2009 [45]) or David Prentice (*Particles*, 2009 [44]). These pieces concern memory and absent presences, the dust as the remains of long gone bodies, and their spirits as breaths. Reflecting on this series, Safdie said, "These pieces have so much lament, so much memory."

Regarding the dust that these videos focus on, Safdie says "the dust found me, and I found the dust." In the piece *Dust* [45] smoke rises through the dust and light like a breath. Here the light (supplied by the sun through a broken window) suggests the spirits that still inhabit this sacred space, while Goldstein's breath and body, his singing and violin playing, help animate the whole scene. A similar effect takes place when David Prentice, in an utterly different musical style, seems to control the motion of the dust through his playing, almost commanding it into reanimation (*Particles* [44]).

Each video in this series is a document of pure process, like watching an action painting unfolding before your eyes. Both the music and the motion of the particles seem to exhibit moment-by-moment randomness, though a distinct structure is apparent overall. By seeing the movement of the dust, one hears the formal structure; by hearing the formal structure, one comes to view the movements of the dust as orderly. In this sense the eye helps one to hear, while the ear helps one to see.

This series manages to pay homage to an absent community without romanticizing it. On one hand the videos are direct about what remains of this community – almost nothing, just dust in a once vibrant place, with scraps of sacred texts scattered over broken floors. However, by presenting the dust as spirit and by giving it breath,

Safdie makes clear that both individuals and communities have a felt presence that often can outlive their corporeal presence. Craftwork once conducted by Jews, such as jewelry-making, is now carried out by Berbers who had been taught by Jews and who now use the very tools they left behind. A place cannot escape its past since its present form is determined by the past. The clouds of dust make it clear that this community has moved on, has been radically and irrevocably transformed, and yet continues to be present in this place.

While Morocco is the site of absent Jewish communities, these communities transformed, leaving behind marks of their long existence in places such as Amzrou. Transformation implies not only change, but continuity; whatever transforms exists both before and after, just altered. This sense of continuity implicit in all transformation is captured by *The Guardian* (2009 [51]), where we view Mbark, the Berber caretaker of the synagogue, reciting the names of the now absent Jewish families of the village while dust swirls around him. The soundtrack blends his voice with village sounds, the sound of the muezzin (the Muslim call to prayer), and the sound of Jewish prayers recorded elsewhere in Morocco. There is a sense of loss in this video, as with the whole Morocco series, but this sense is tempered by the knowledge that this community is still remembered, and in this sense still remains.

Auschwitz, where Safdie next explored these themes, presents different and more alarming issues. Here people were not transformed but annihilated. The Jews sent to Auschwitz had no control over their destinies, no autonomy. Auschwitz was designed to leave no trace of the people imprisoned there, to permit no continuity,

Amzrou Synagogue, photograph (detail): Patrick Andrew Boivin

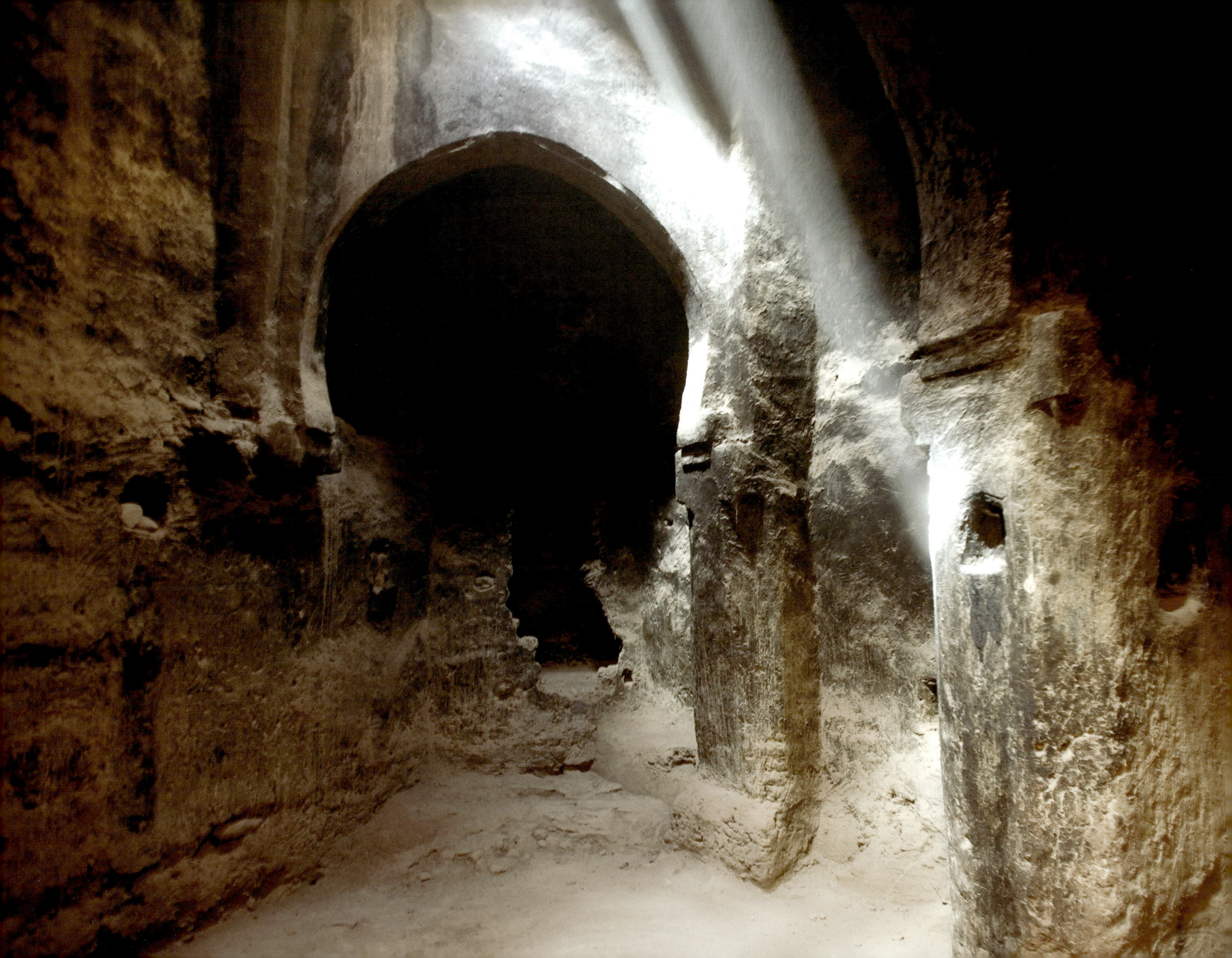

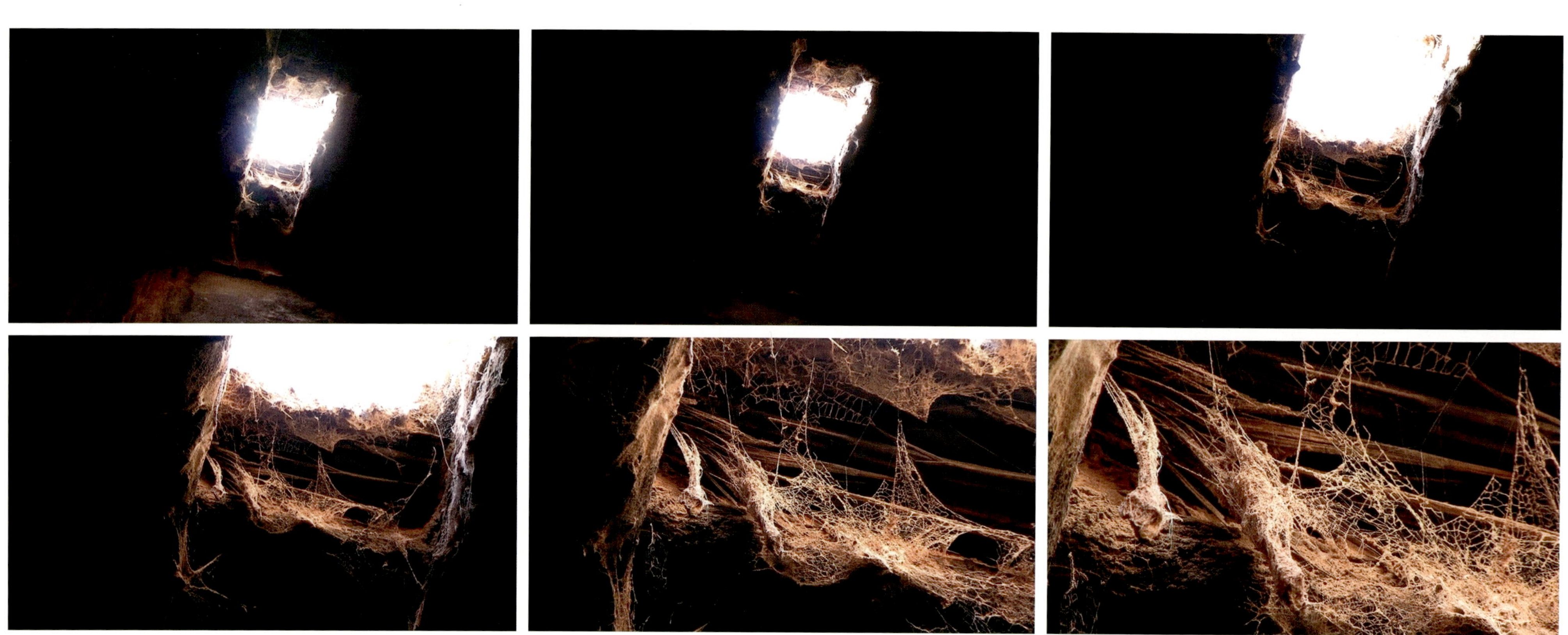

Amzrou Synagogue Interiors, Series I, Interior 3 (2009) [48.3], video stills

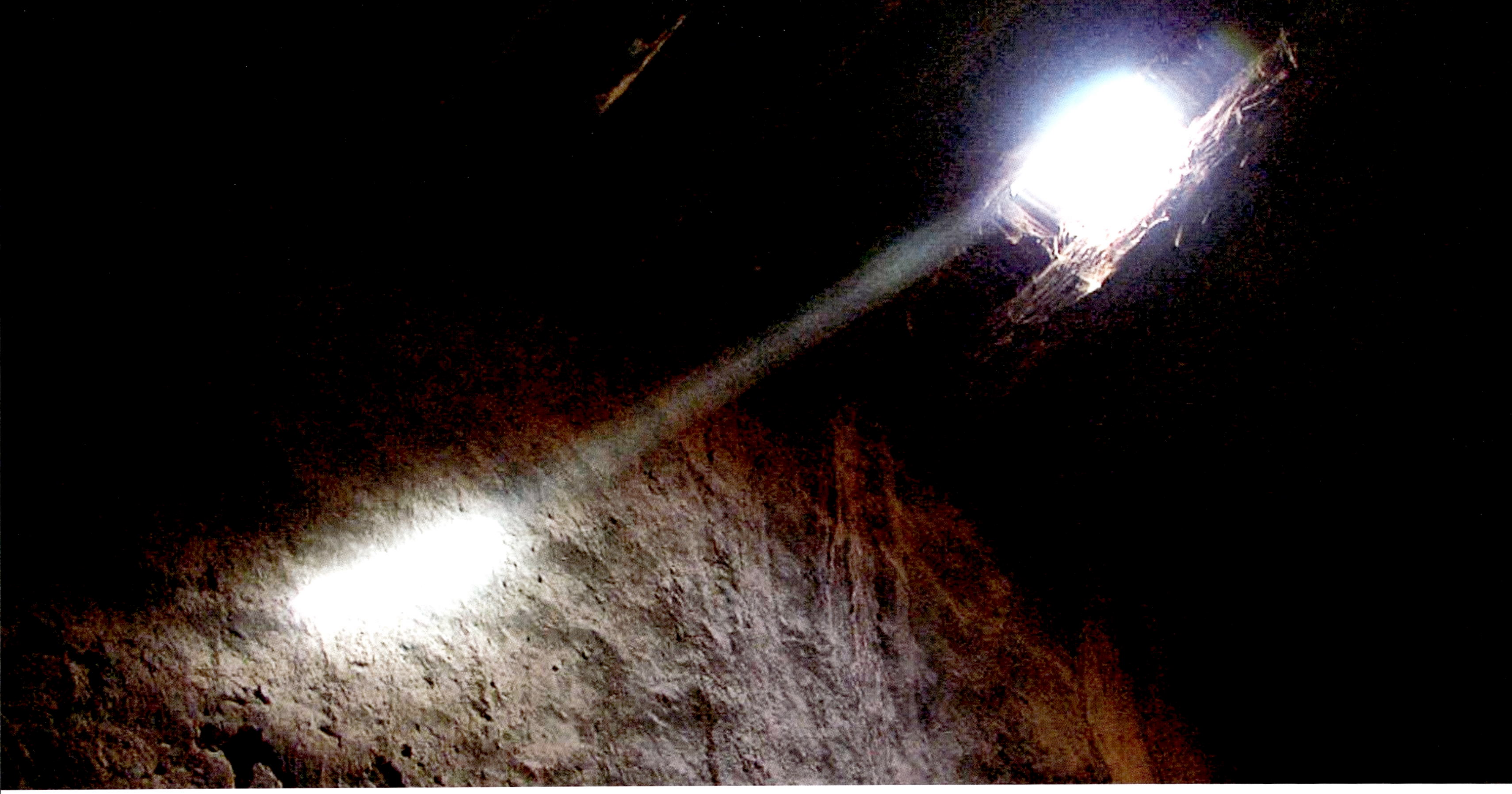

Amzrou Synagogue Interiors, Series I, Interior 1 (2009) [48.1], video still

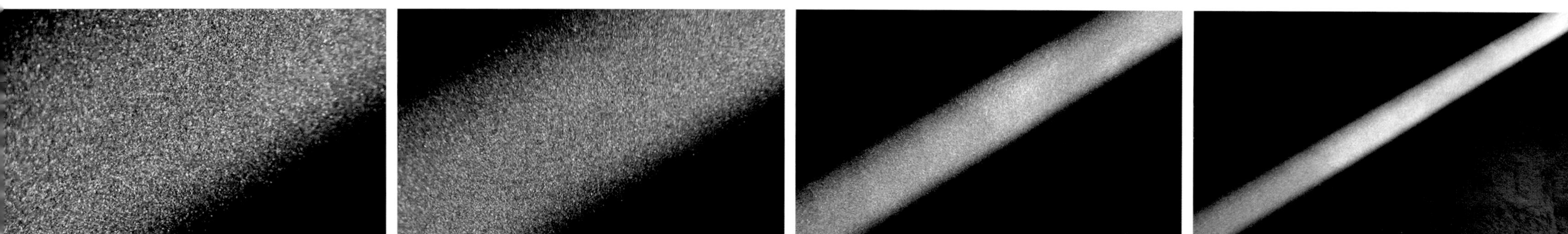

Amzrou Synagogue Interiors, Series II, No. 1 (2009) [49.1], video stills

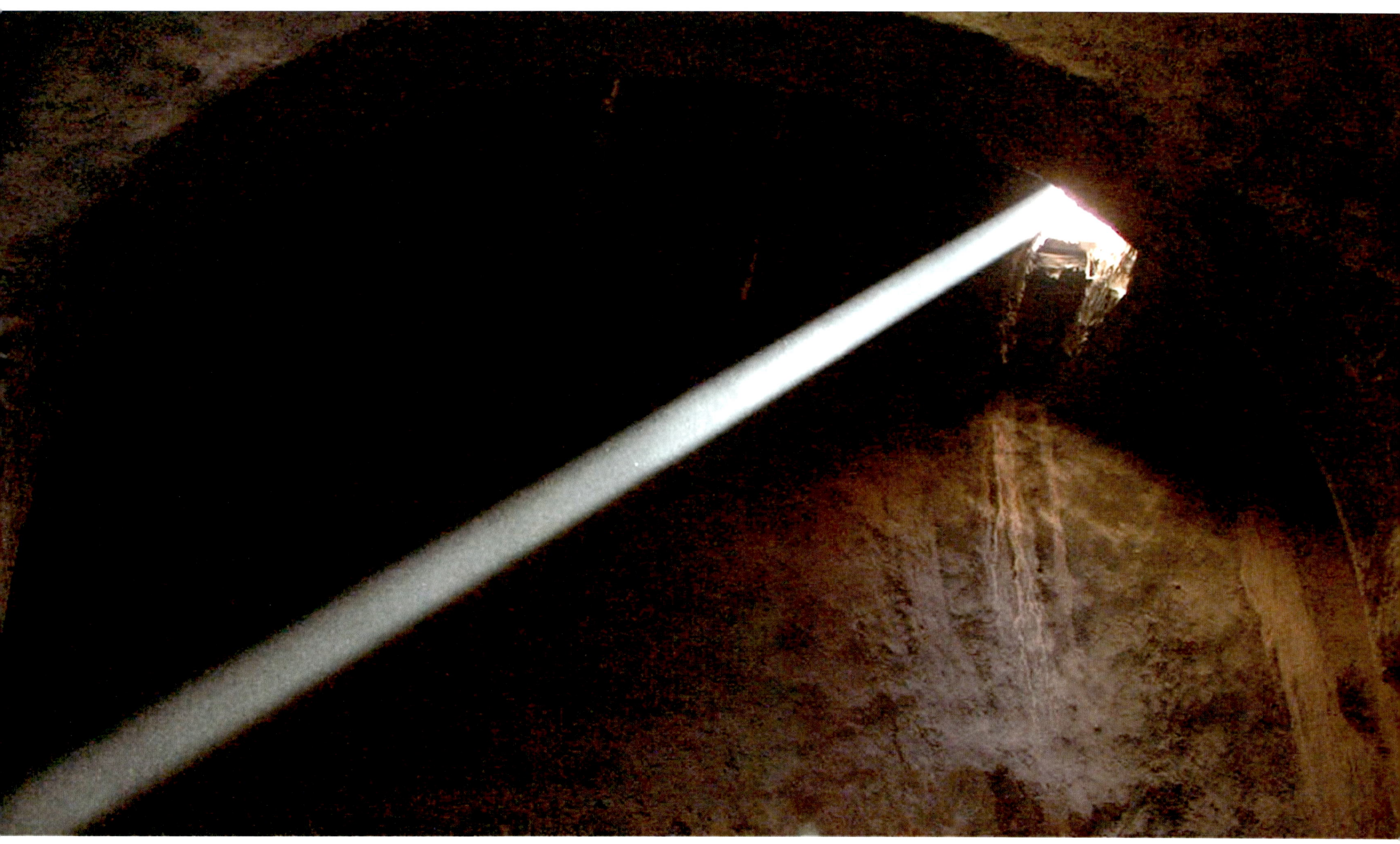

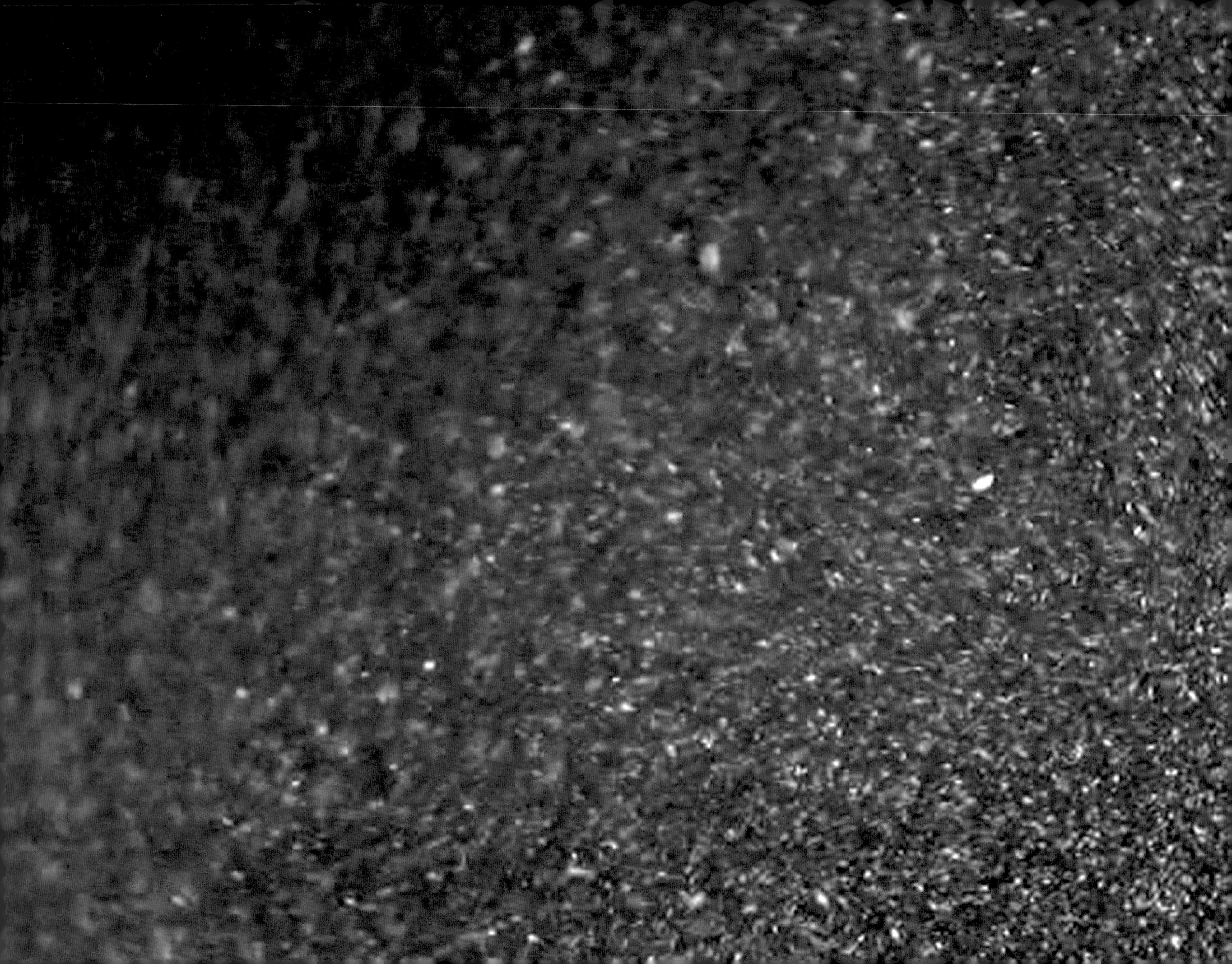

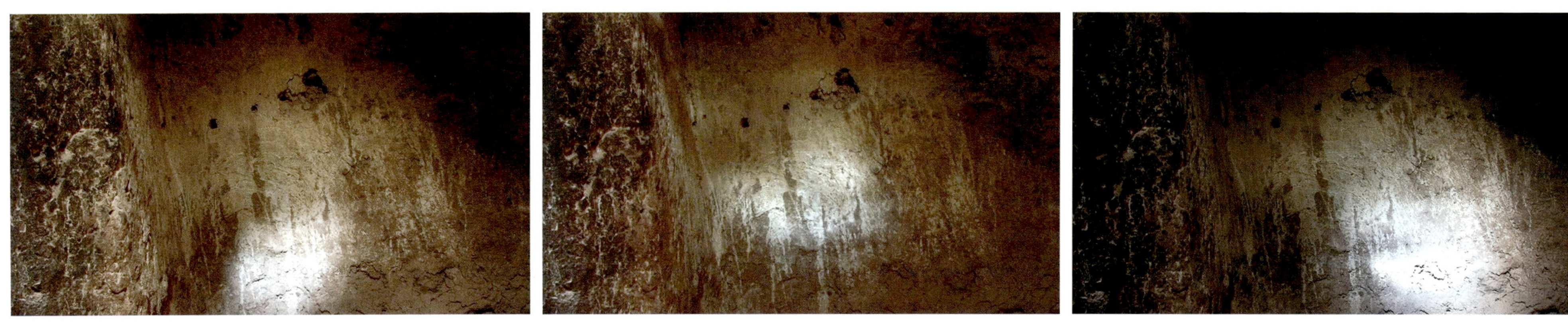

Wall: A Triptych (2009) [50.1], video stills

Previous spread: Dust and Light (2009) [47], video still

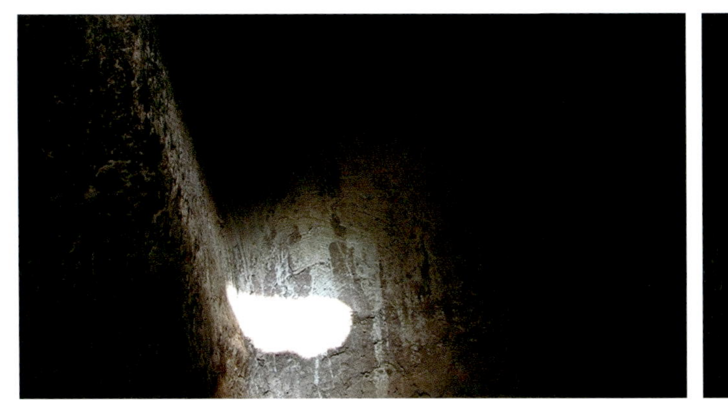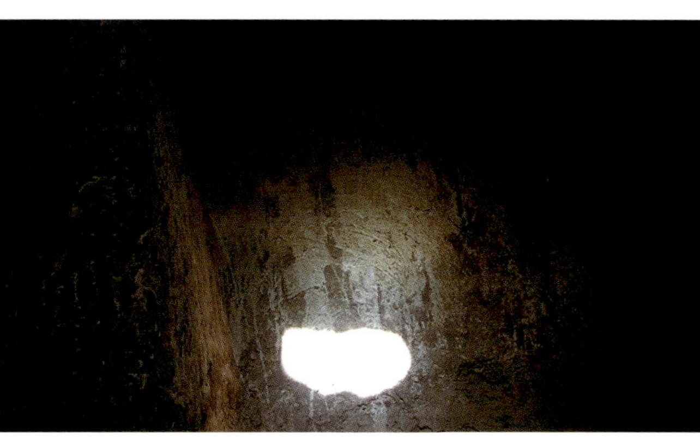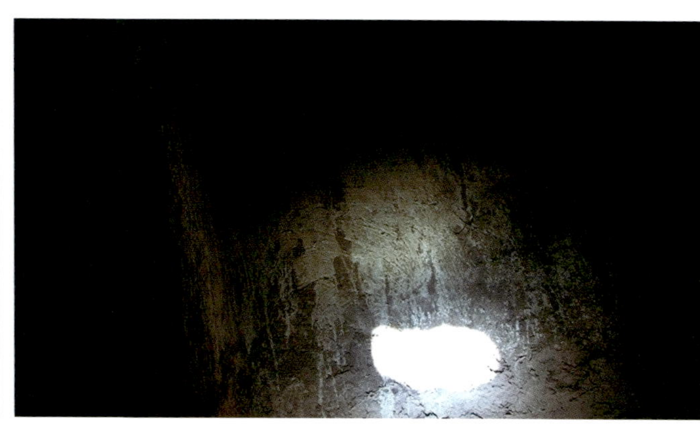

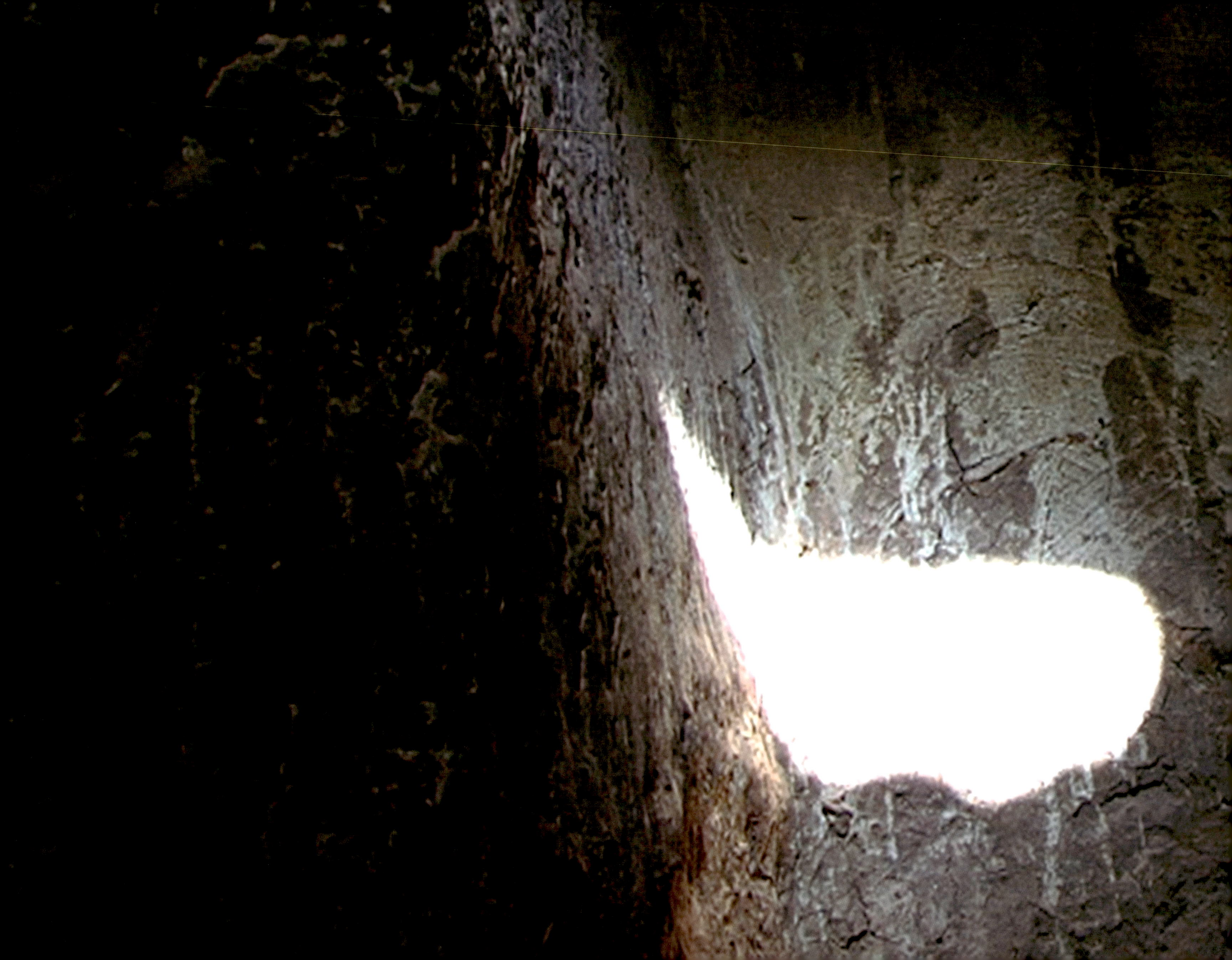

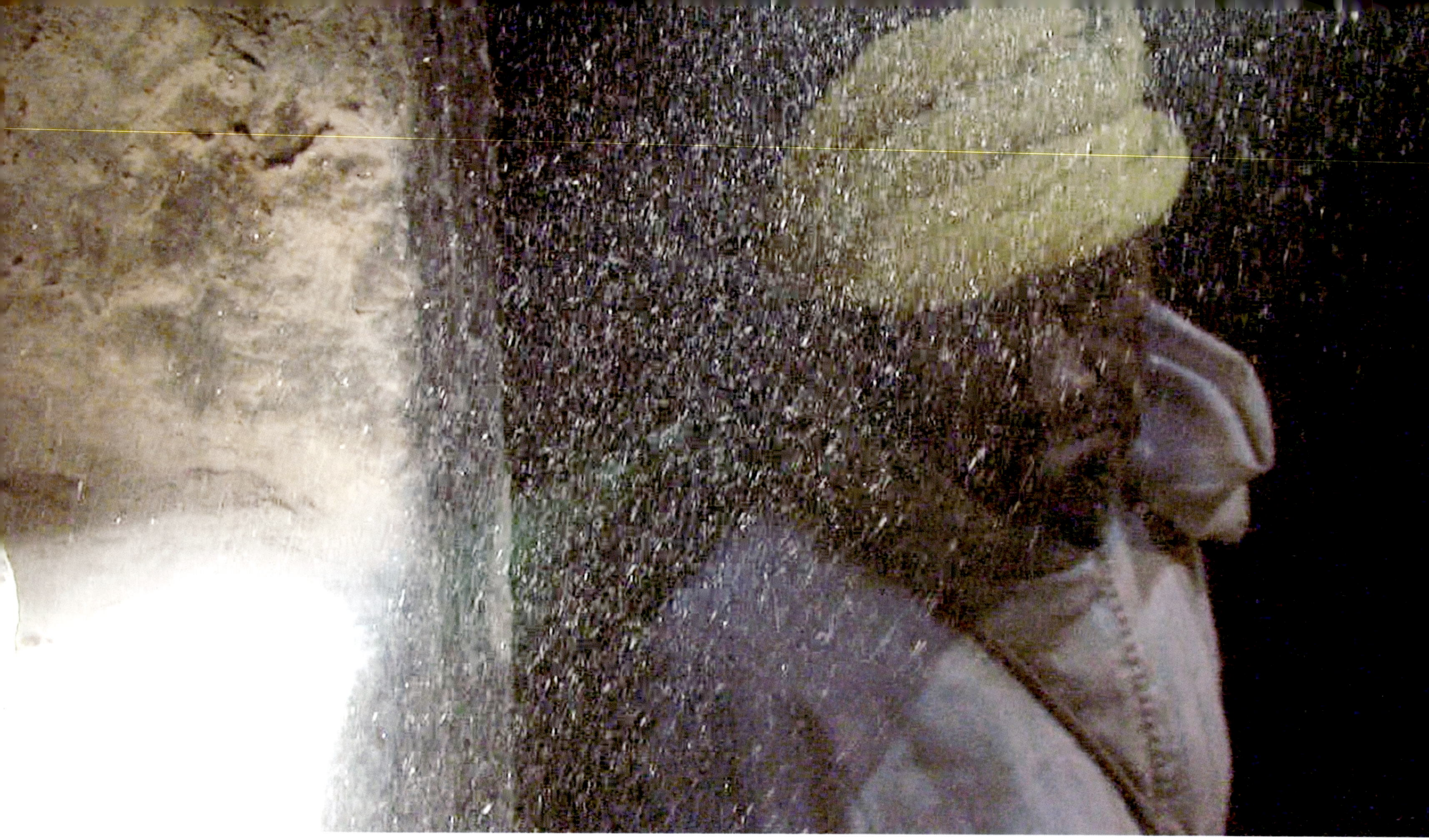

The Guardian (2009) [51], diptych, video stills

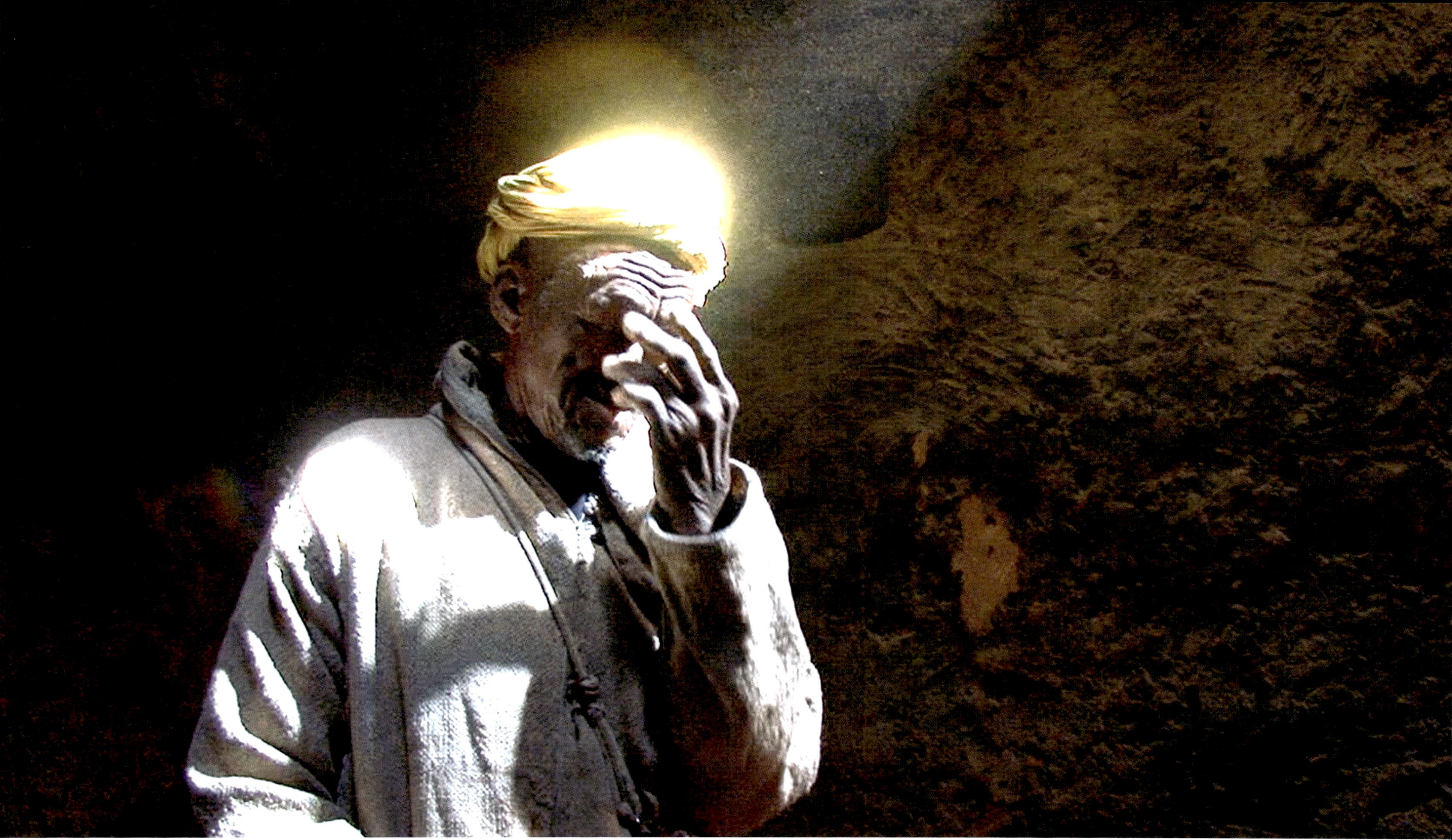

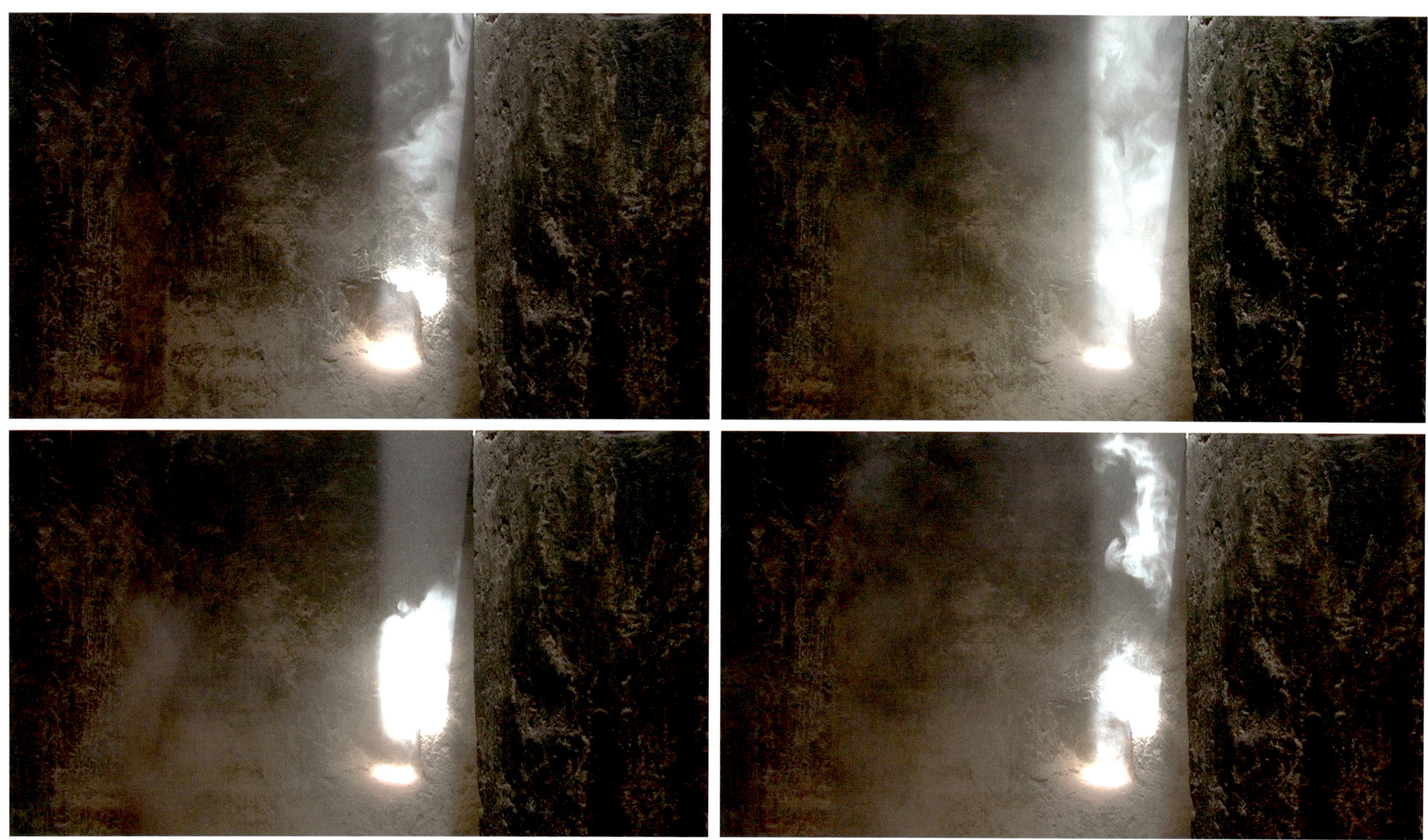

Dust (2009) [45], video stills

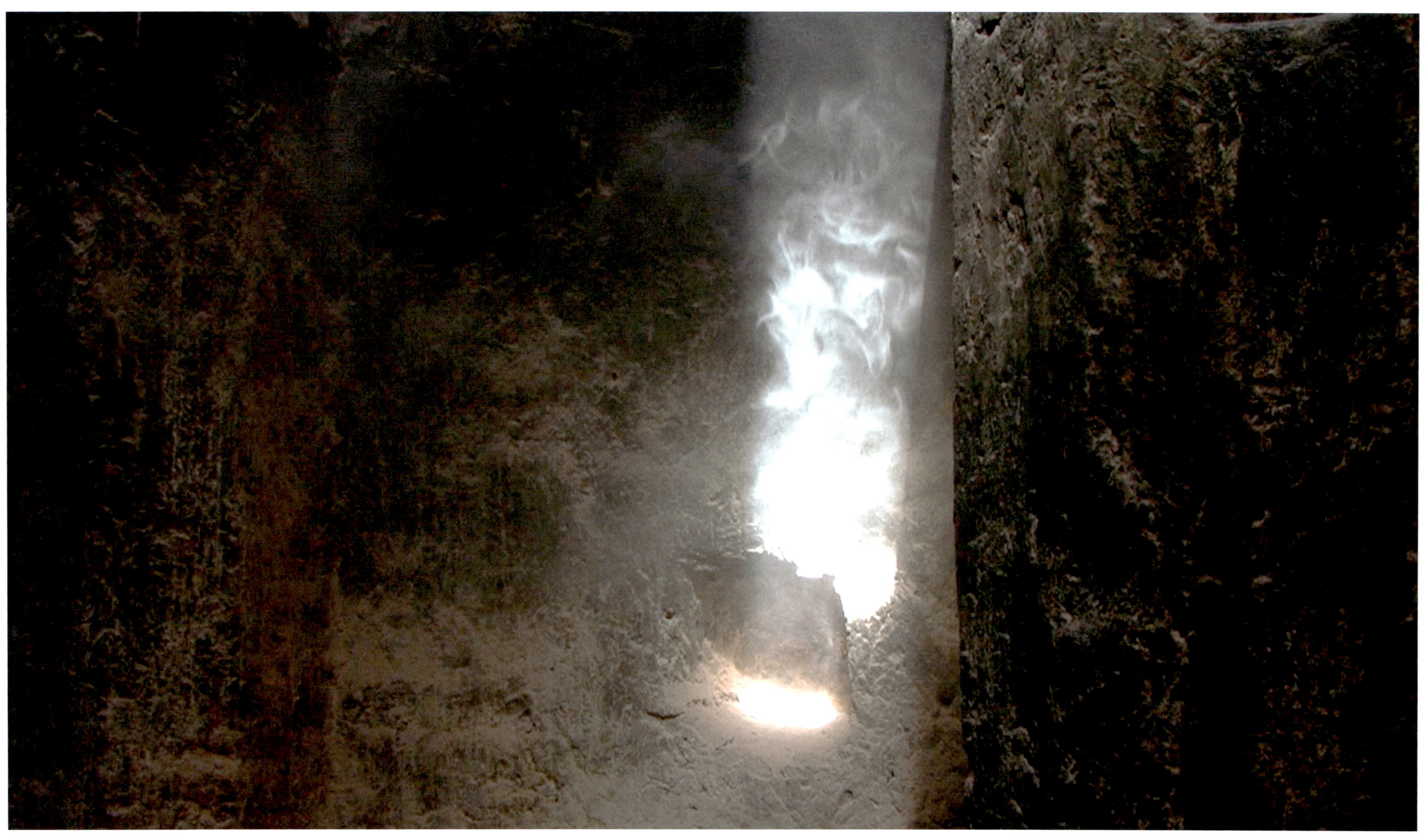

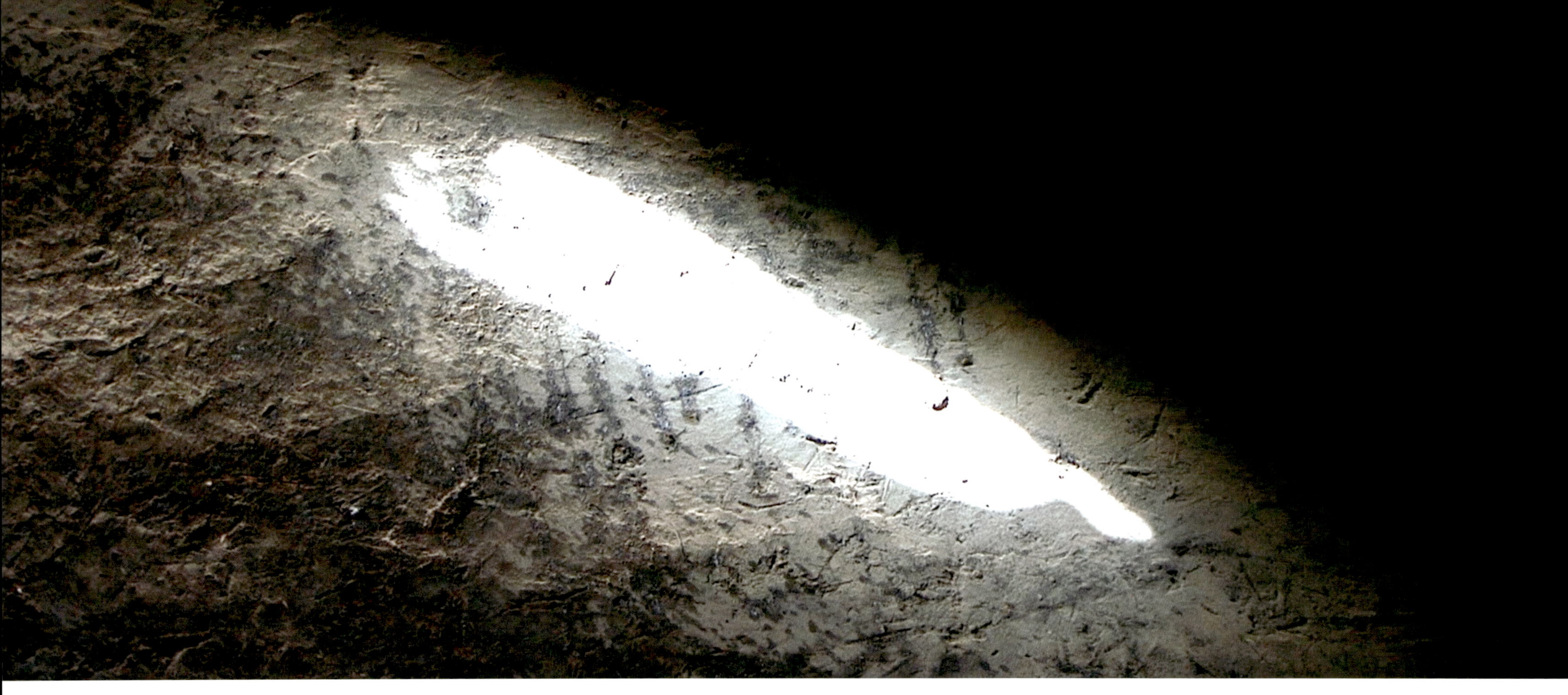

Presence (2009) [45], video stills

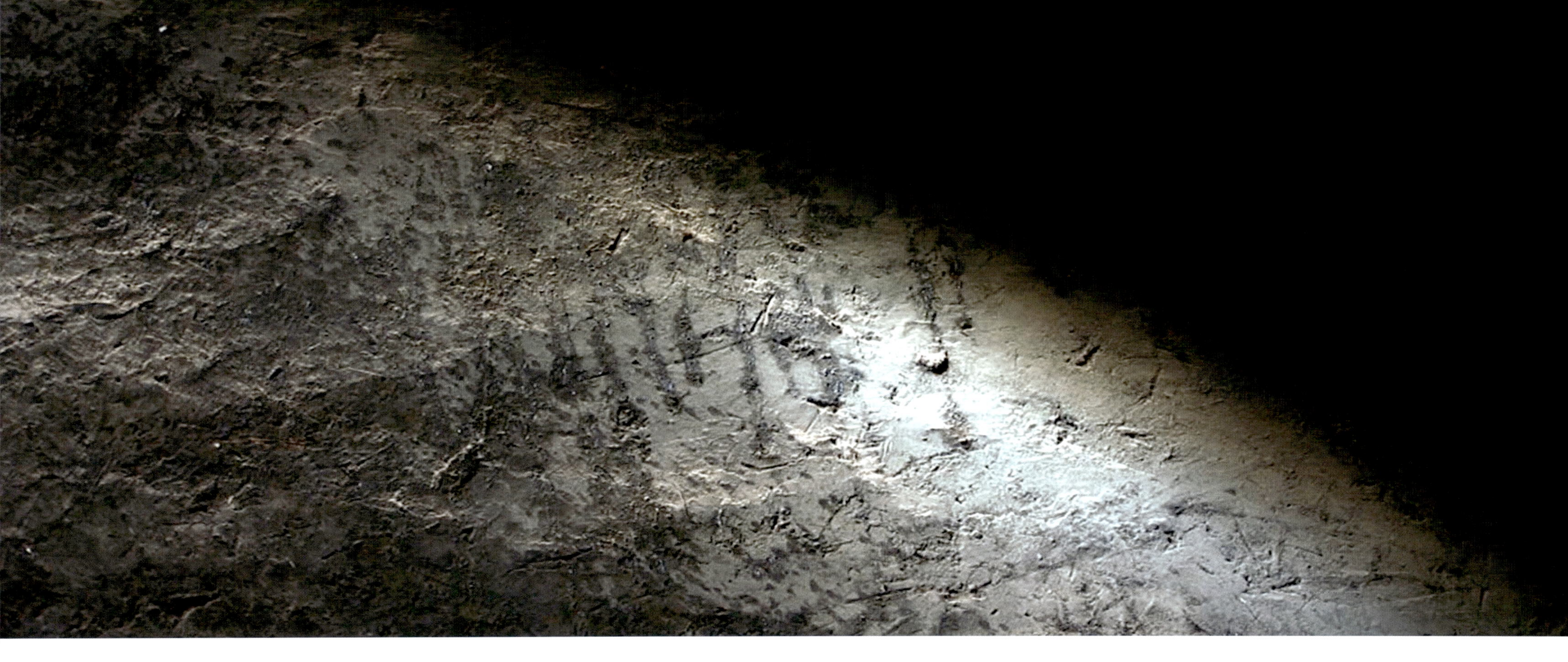

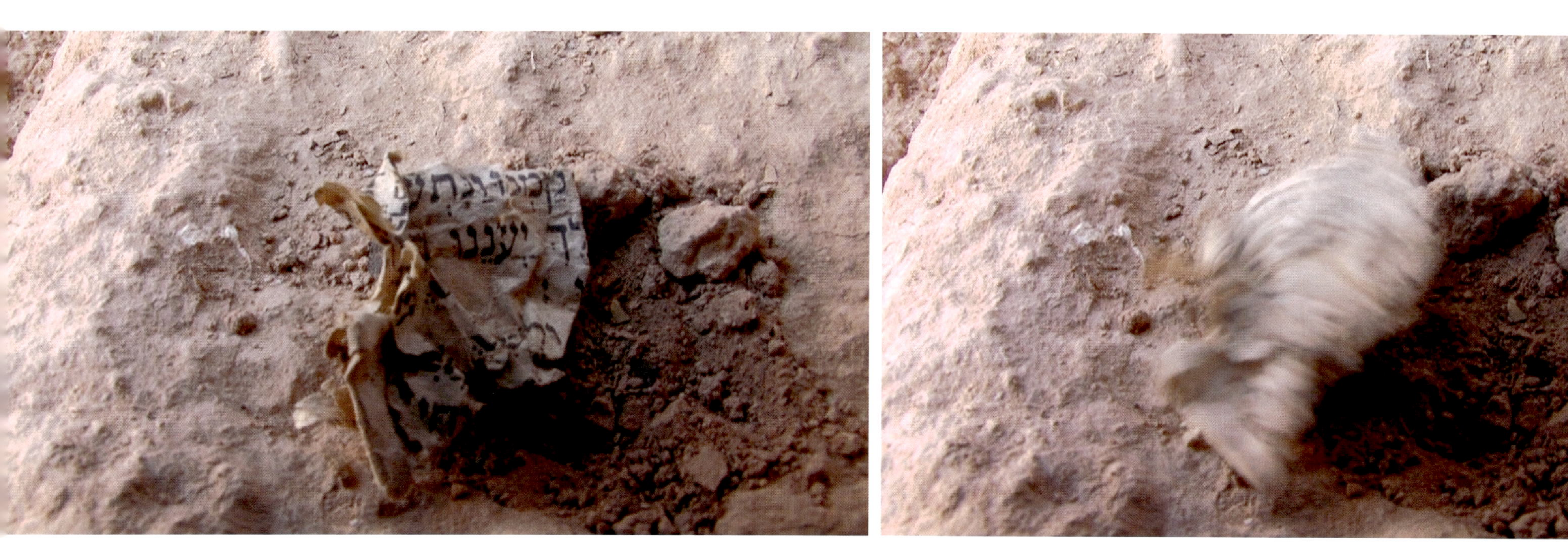

Fragment, No. 3 (2009) [59.3], video stills

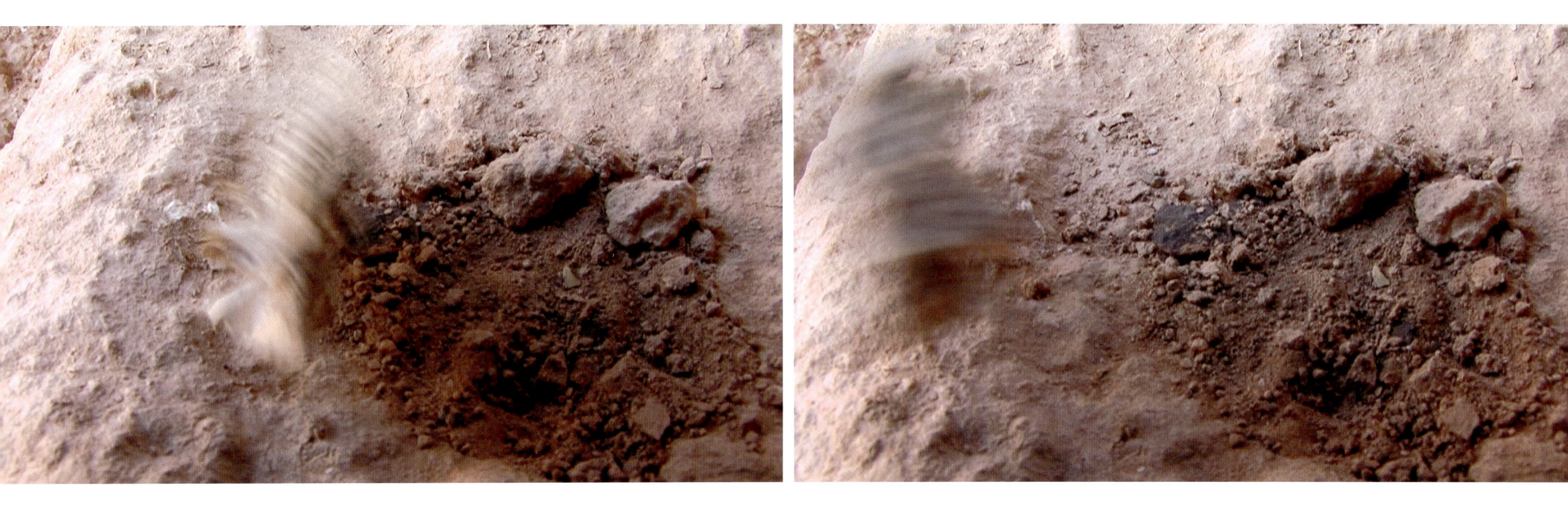

and to permanently destroy. In this sense Auschwitz can be seen as a powerful symbol of all that is opposed to Safdie's own art practices, focused as they are on the animating force of breath and animation more generally. By confronting Auschwitz Safdie was confronting a place that was inimical to her as a Jew and as an artist. That she was able to transform the untransformable, to counter its own essence and turn it into a memorial to itself, is perhaps her greatest accomplishment. The videos that document and effect this transformation are haunting and moving.

Safdie's journey to Auschwitz was motivated by the wish to accompany her friend, the photographer Marie-Jeanne Musiol, who shot the photographs from her *Black Holes* series there.[7] Safdie immediately felt compelled to accompany Marie-Jeanne, "It was not that I wanted to go, but that I *had* to go." Safdie, so long sensitive to what places can tell us about their occupants and events, needed to witness this place for herself, to see and hear the stories it might tell, and to improvise with it in an attempt to understand it. Regarding her visit, she said "It is one thing to bear witness through statistics, documentaries, literature, and art in general ... it is another to experience the place itself." What she found, and what she was able to create from these sounds and images, serves as a monument to the souls and bodies destroyed there. Her exploration of the themes of soul, body, memory, and redemption (long central to her artistic project) culminate powerfully in the Auschwitz series. Neither trite, maudlin, preachy, angry, nor visibly horrifying, these videos let Auschwitz itself speak.

7. Musiol is herself an accomplished artist who has produced important work on the Holocaust.

Safdie was not certain she would be able or want to film when she visited Auschwitz. She first had to discover what it meant to be in a place that embodies death and negation. She needed to see if she understood the place, why she was there, and what she could take away from it. Having moved from literally collecting seeds, earth, and rocks, to memorial stones, and then video footage through her many journeys, what could she metaphorically take back from Auschwitz? "There is a responsibility which comes with using this material," says Safdie, "a series about Auschwitz forces one to interpret it in certain ways." Putting the point bluntly, Safdie said, "I felt this responsibility as an artist not to fail."

Safdie's earlier works are, in many ways, preparations for the Auschwitz series. Water, stone, light, and reflection, all feature in these videos, with the addition of spider webs, which she found everywhere at Auschwitz. The spider web is of course a powerful metaphor: "You cannot escape the symbolism of the web," says Safdie, adding, "you cannot escape the web."

Spider webs are an obvious symbol of entrapment and death – they are sites of death. However, the videos of webs at Auschwitz do more than mark this disturbing affinity. The webs flutter in a breeze, "like a last breath," and are luminously beautiful. In *Web/Auschwitz* (2011) [80] the web comes into focus very slowly. In Stoicism the spider web is an analogy for the soul – both are sensitive to changes within themselves and their bodies by means of the vibrations that travel along them. Auschwitz, a universal symbol of death, is transformed by Safdie's work into a symbol of life, of souls moving, breathing, and generating new life. Again the particular and universal co-inhabit these video images, which are both about the particular souls lost here and, more generally, about humanity's persistence as a vital force.

Safdie animates this space, or, more properly, conspires with the space to animate it: "It takes time to absorb the image, to make it work to its potential in that place." She does not have control over her environment, but improvises with it. Crucially, it is nature that becomes her partner in improvisation, revealing the luminous spirit-souls residing in the darkest of places. In a sense these videos are akin to the ritual purifications of polluted places that have always formed an essential part of shamanistic practices. Tellingly, Safdie states, "You have no control over nature – this image would not have happened without the rain and the sun. It took the chance of nature to create this image. Luckily I was there." Light and water, against a backdrop of stone, all conspire under Sadfie's gaze to bring life back to a place of death.

And so this memorial to the departed souls of Auschwitz is created as much by nature, as by Safdie herself. She says, "Images find me as much as I find them. The circumstances are very interesting: why was I there just then?" Safdie manages to see a way that Auschwitz creates a memorial to itself, so that, in a symbolic sense, the souls of those who died there can reclaim the space. Herein lies perhaps the core artistic strength of this series. In the context of a vast tradition of Holocaust memorial art, this series transforms a potent site of the Holocaust itself into a Holocaust memorial to make a powerful statement of the ultimate inviolability of the souls lost there.

This distillation of memorial culminates in the video series *Reflection/Auschwitz I–III* (2011) [77–79]. It was filmed in the former latrines of the woman's barracks in Sector Bla of Auschwitz II, Birkenau. A more depersonalizing place can hardly be imagined. Safdie states:

It is a place where we leave excrement – what the body rejects and leaves behind. This is extremely symbolic in terms of both the Nazis and the concentration camps because that is what the Nazis decided to do – to exterminate those they thought were no longer fit for society. It is in this place where thousands of people left their waste before dying of hunger, torture, sickness, or extermination that I found these images.

In the midst of a long concrete building with broken windows and a puddle-filled floor sits a long row of raised toilets, all opening into a sewer filled with unctuous water that runs beneath them. Under these urinals, Safdie finds a bright light floating on the surface of the cesspool. In the darkest of places, at its lowest point, Safdie sees this flame, this spark of the soul, once again produced by water and light, moving by means of an invisible breath. It is as though the eternal flame, the most ubiquitous memorial symbol of the lost souls of the Holocaust, recreated at Holocaust memorials around the world, has inhabited Auschwitz itself all along. It is worth comparing this image with Safdie's sculptural installation *Lehav* (1993) which also uses flame and reflection to powerful effect. Where *Lehav* can be seen as a memorial to the Holocaust, *Reflection/Auschwitz* captures Auschwitz's memorial to itself. While some artists have treated Auschwitz as a symbol of the end of time, Safdie moves in the opposite direction, treating the place as a symbol of the eternal survival of humanity.

These themes are approached differently in the series *Pond/Auschwitz I–III* [74–76], which was filmed at the remains of a pool at Auschwitz that was once a site for disposing of bones and corpses, its surface still marred by an ashen film. Here Safdie employs metaphors

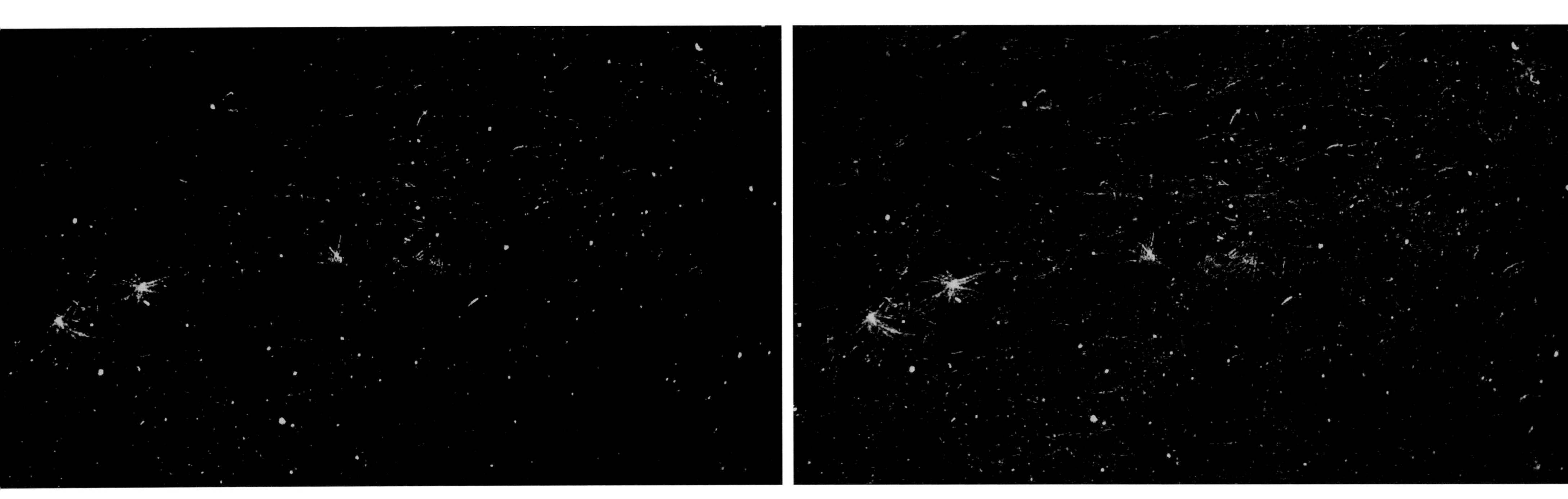

Web/Auschwitz Series 1, No. 2 (2011) [80.2], video stills

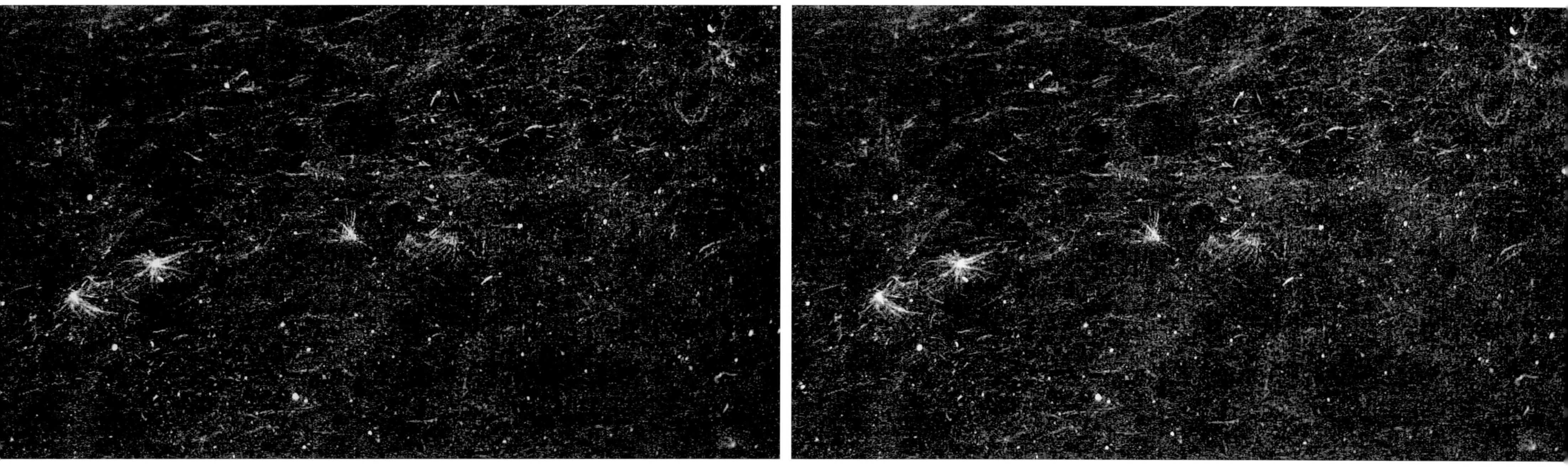

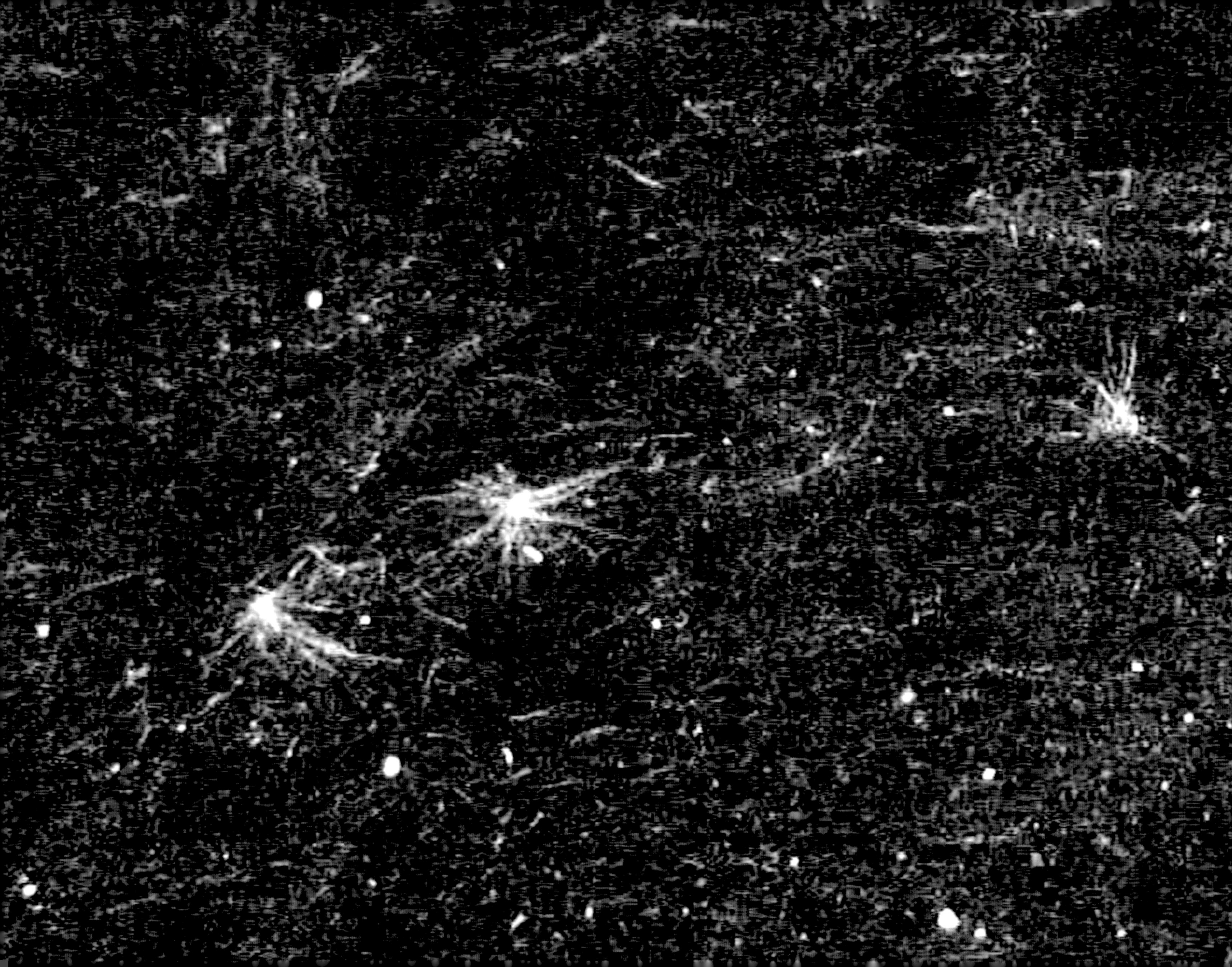

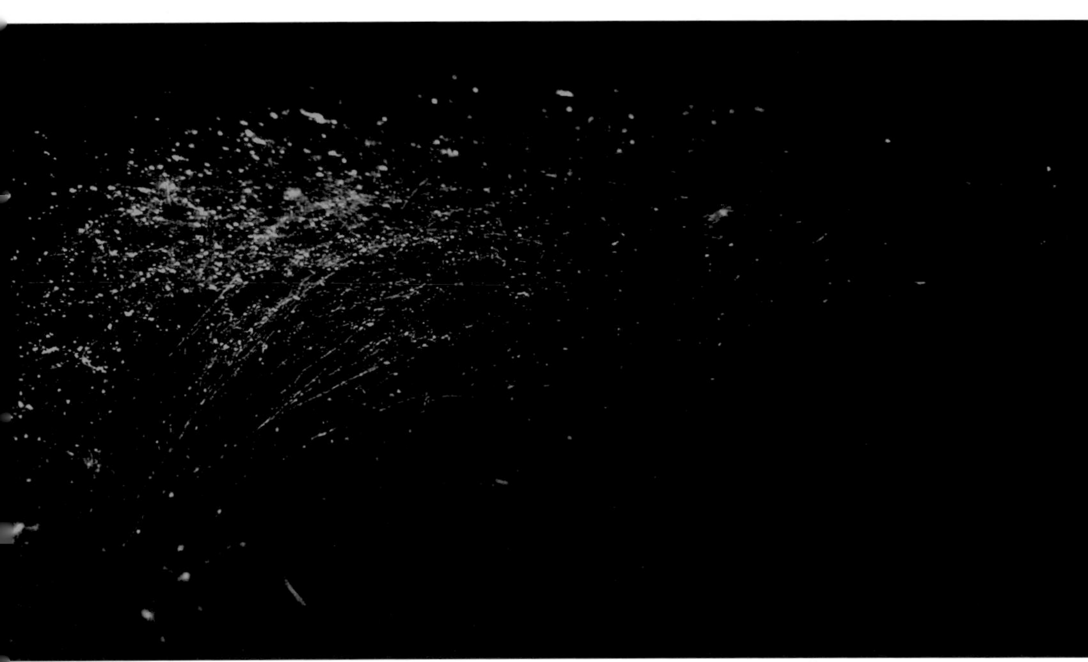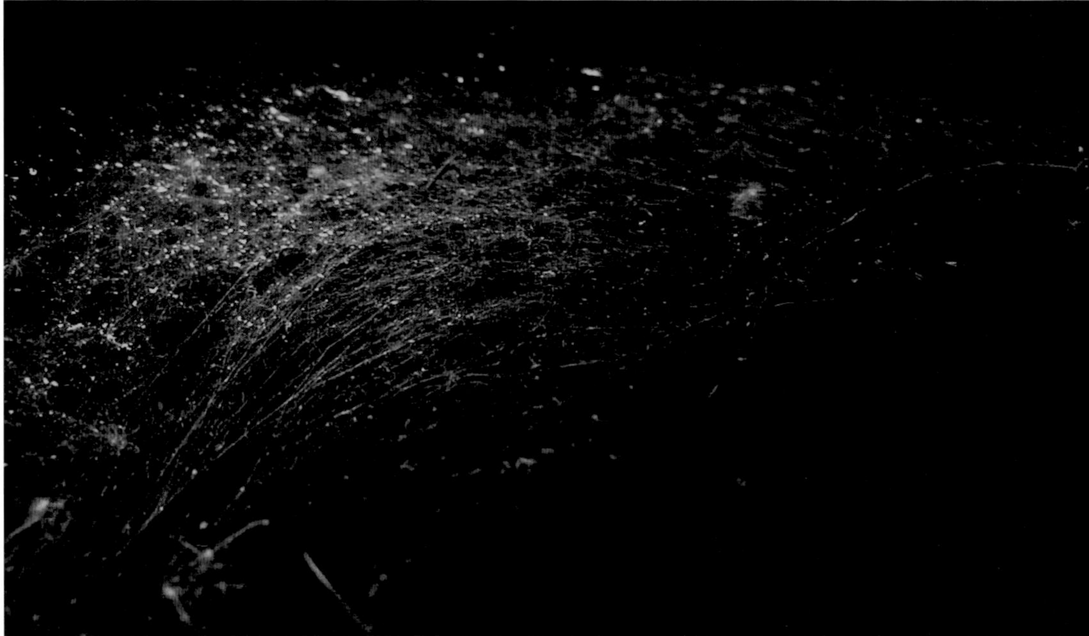

Web/Auschwitz Series 1, No. 4 (2011) [80.4], video stills

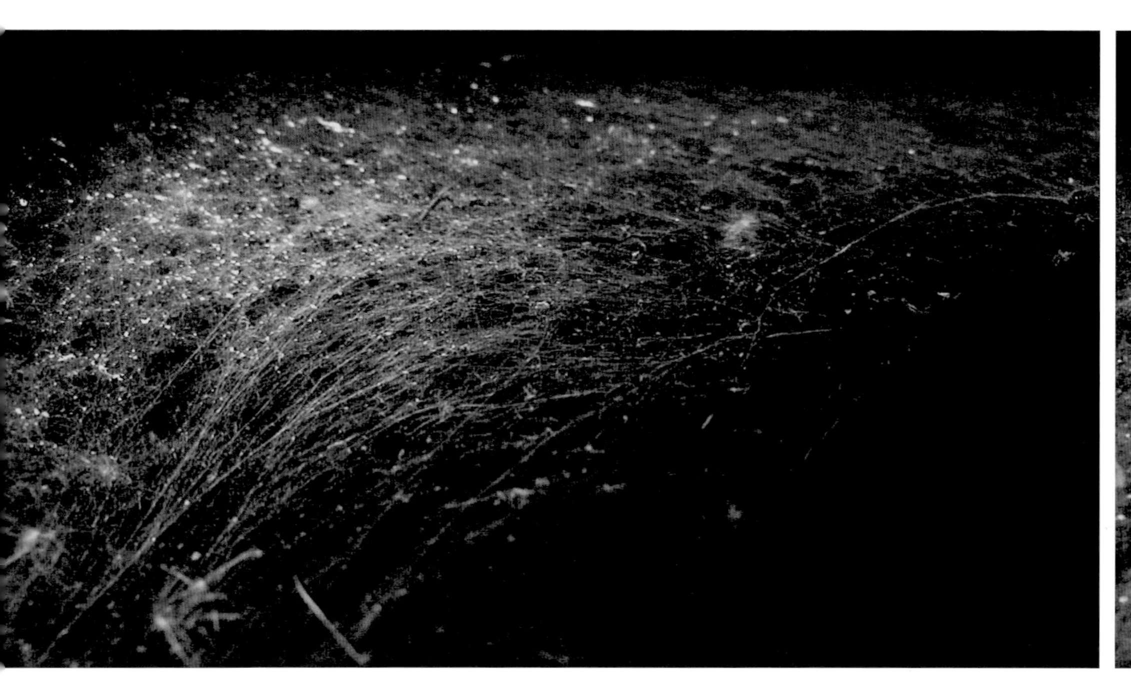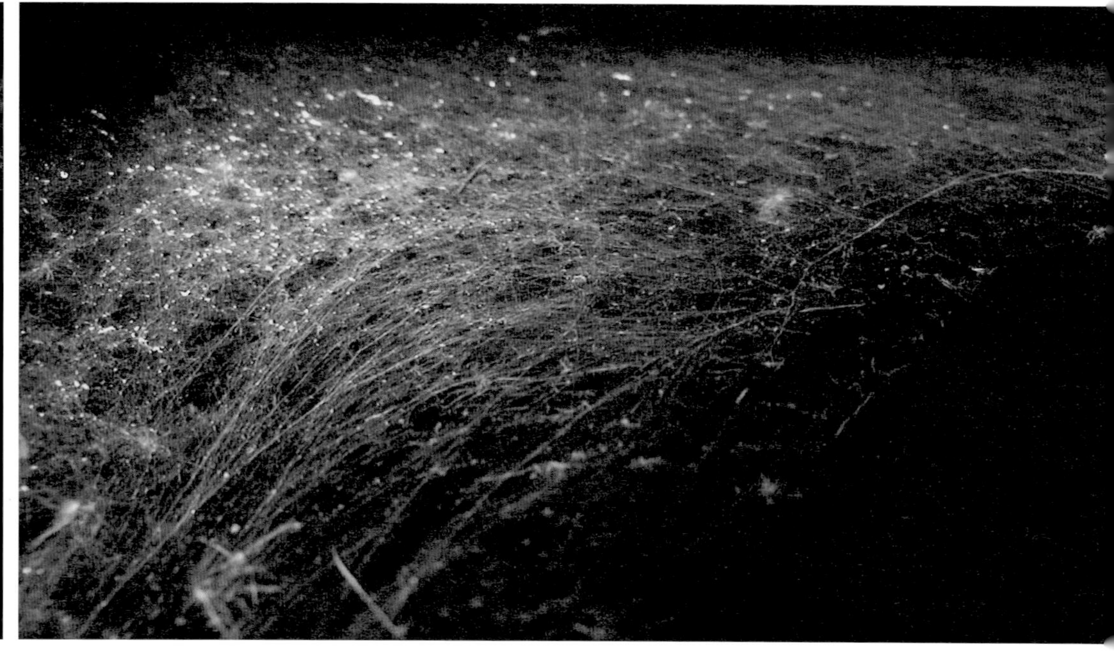

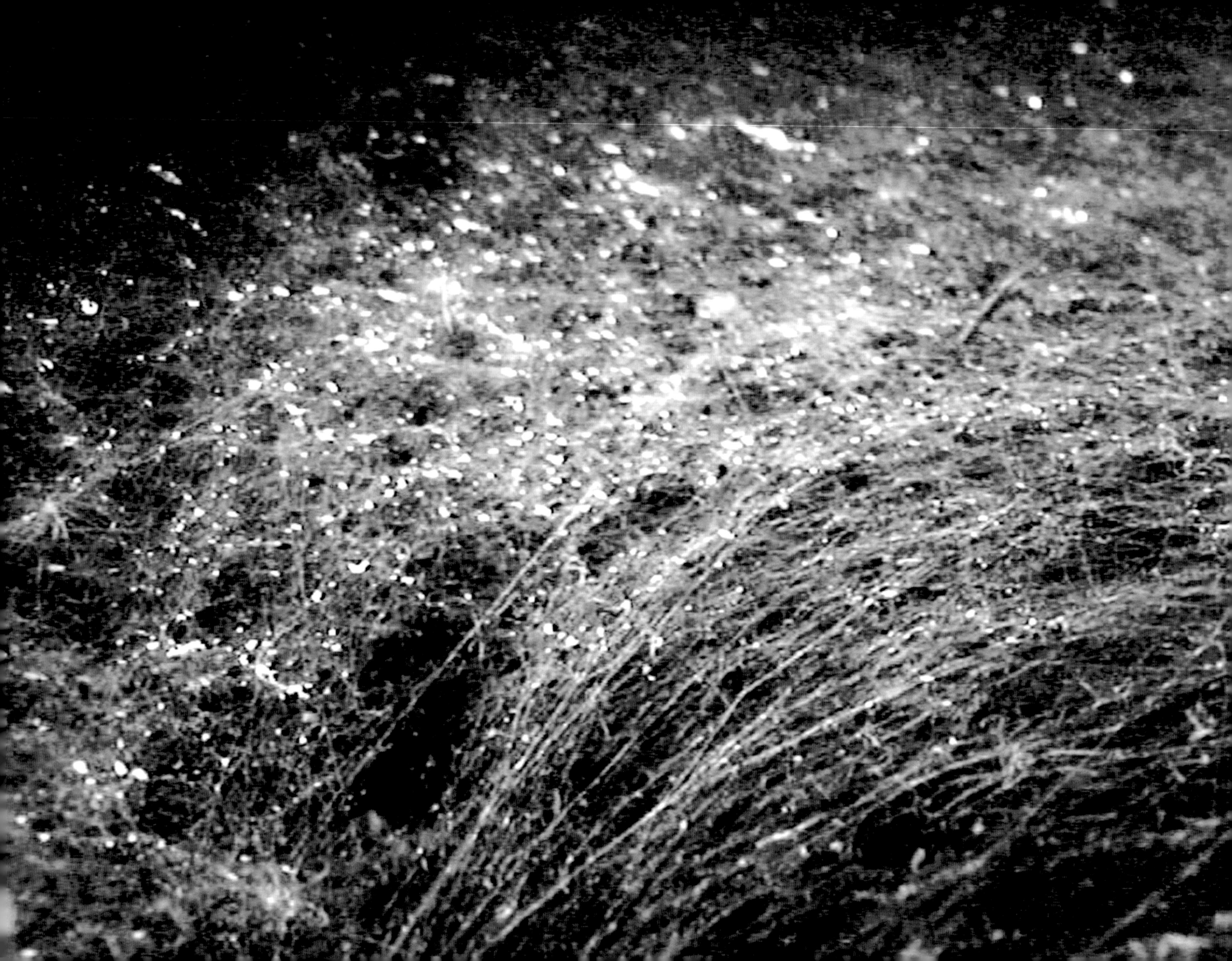

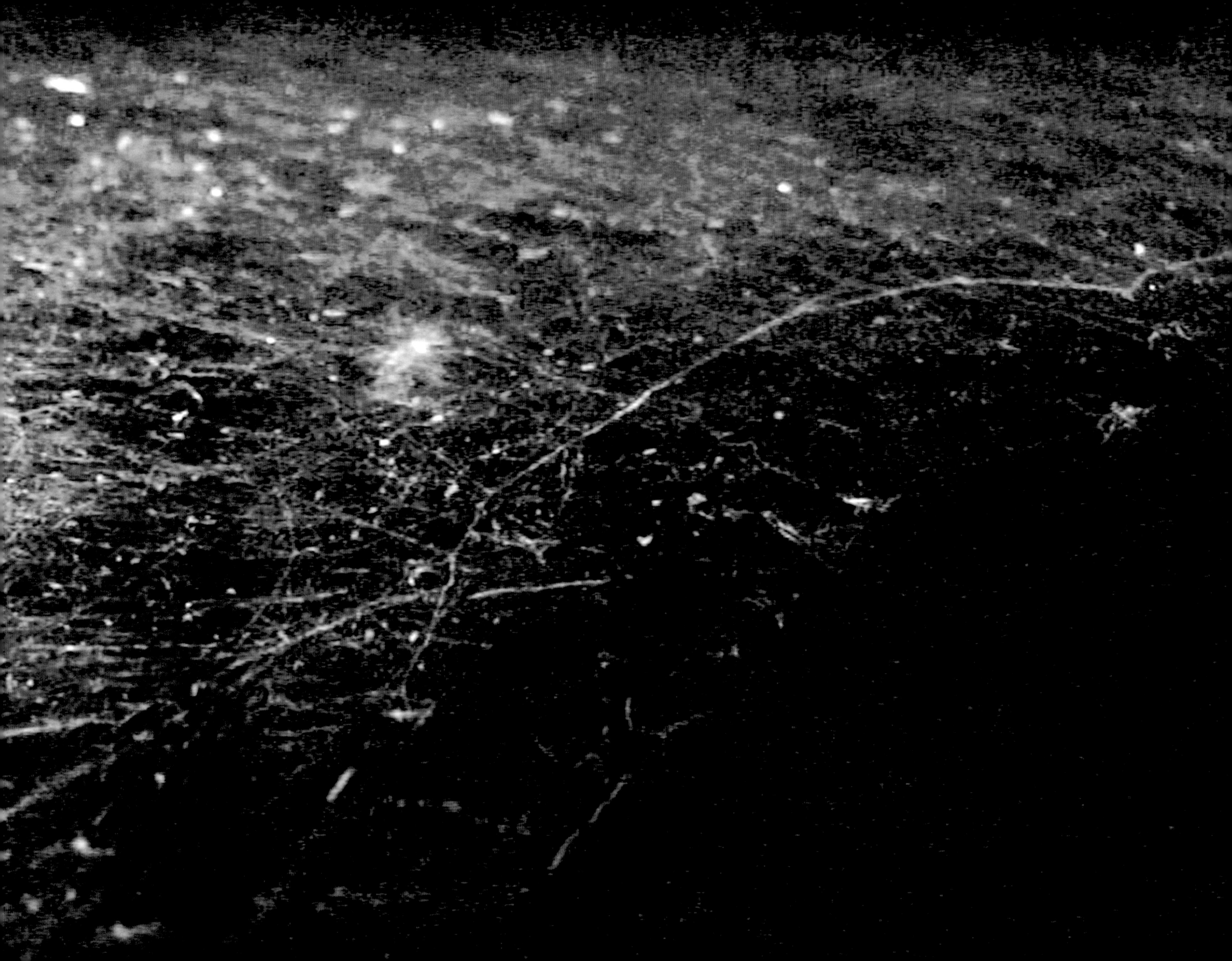

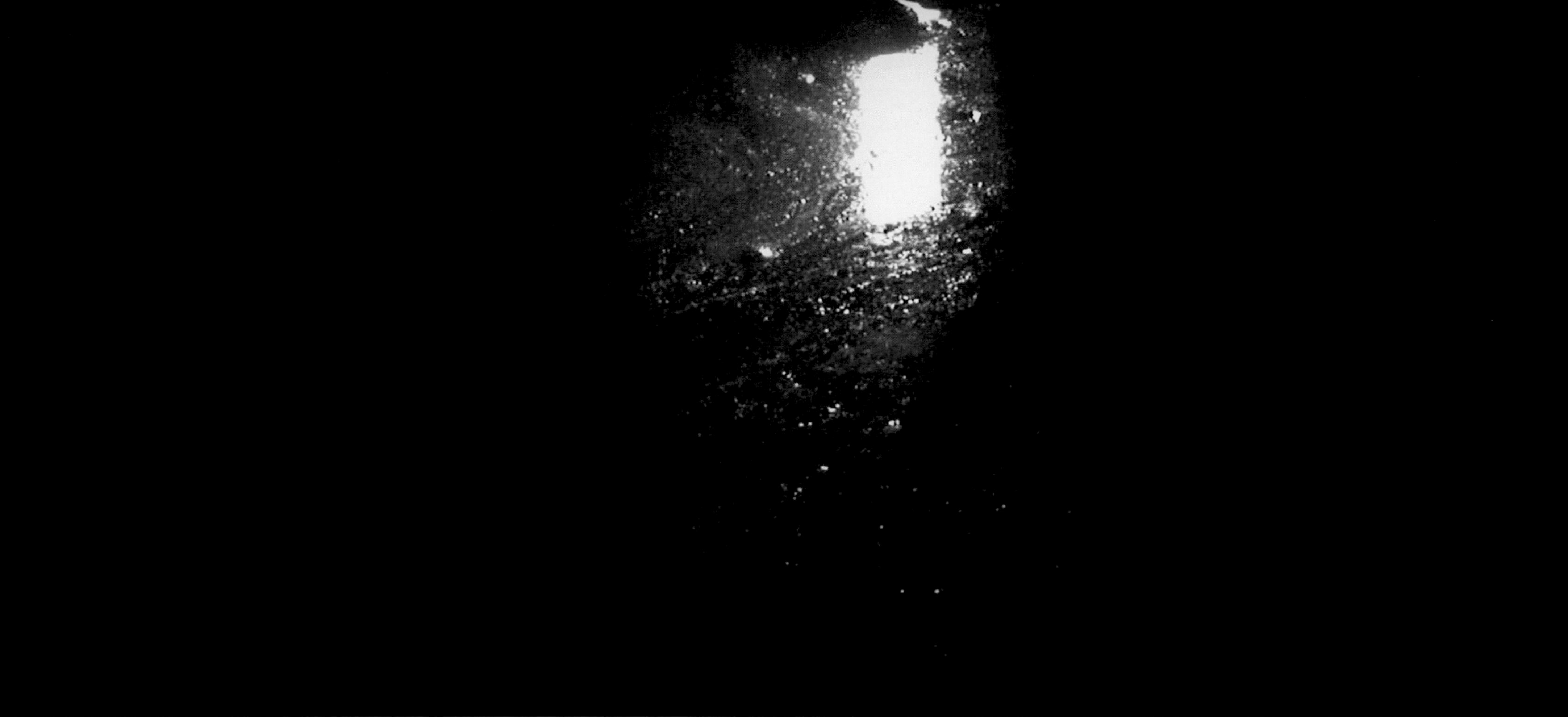

Reflection/Auschwitz II (2011) [78], video still

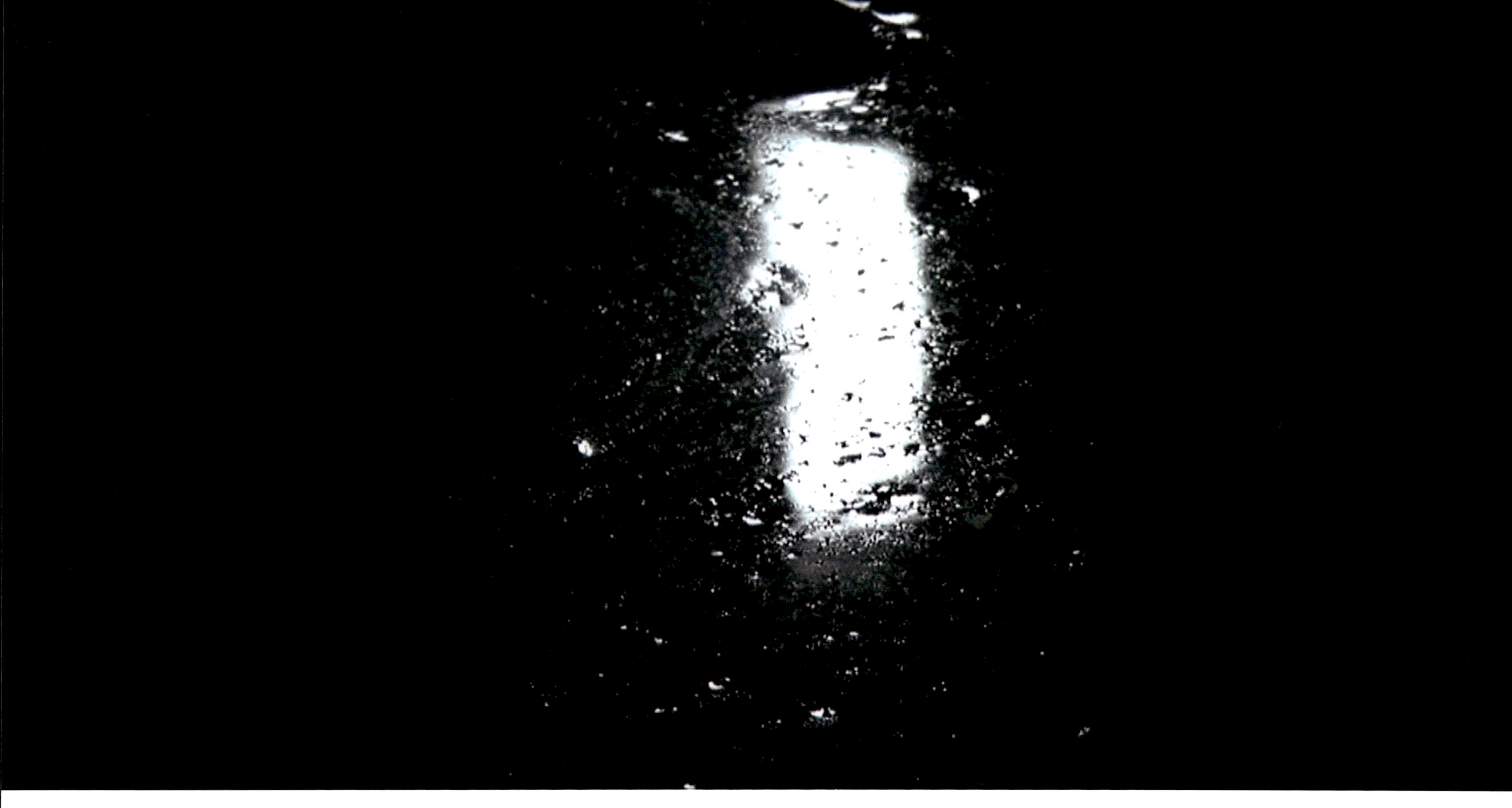

Reflection/Auschwitz I (2011) [77], video still

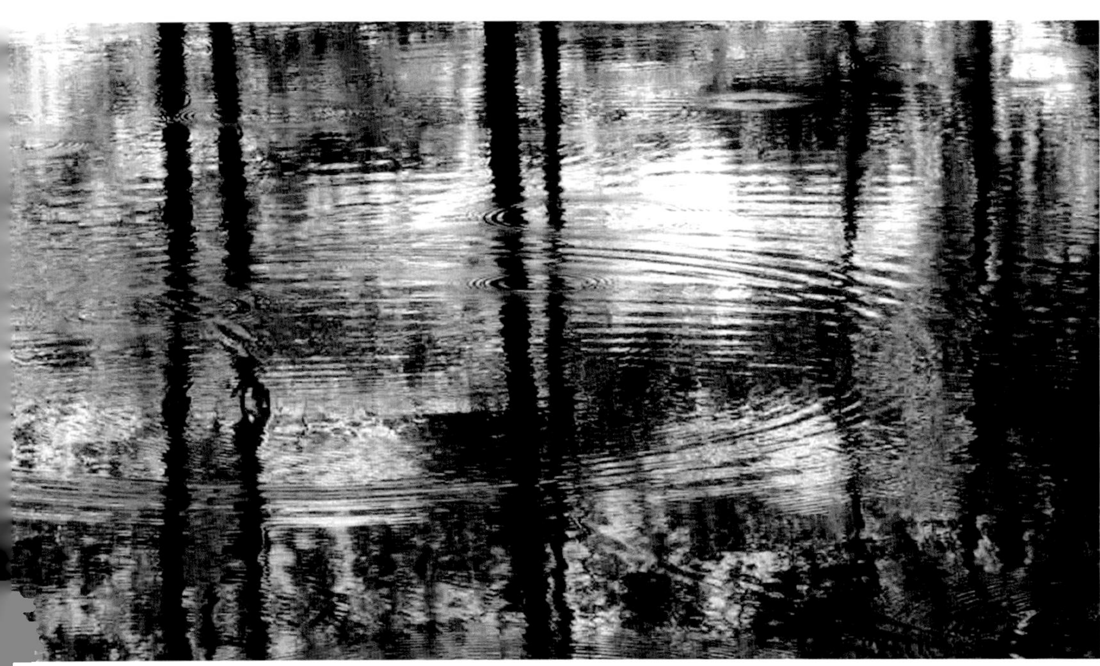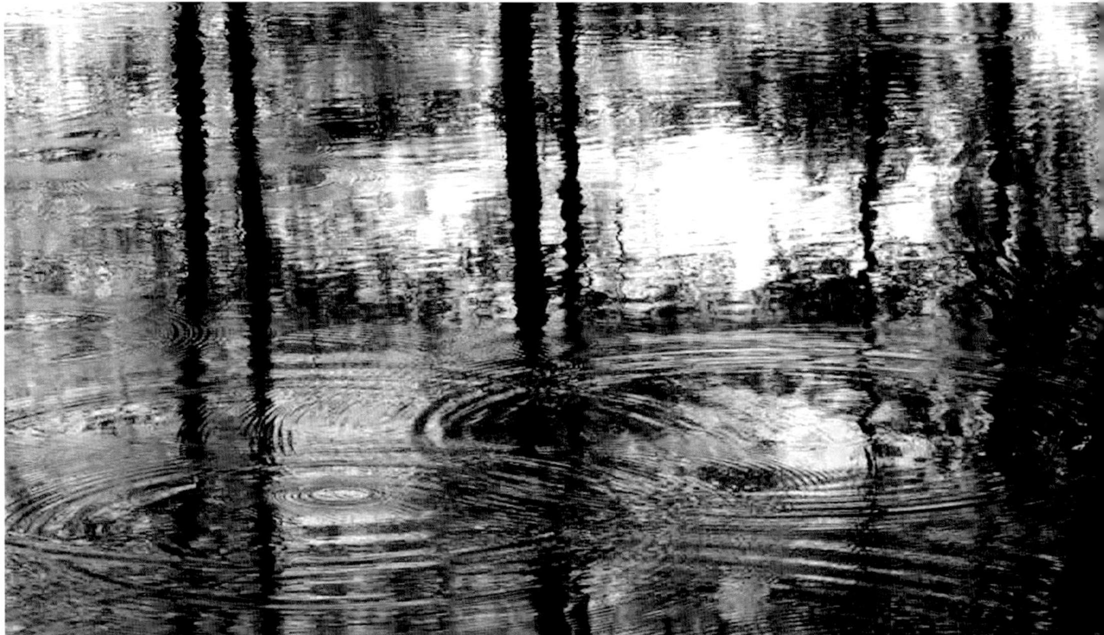

Pond/Auschwitz I (2011) [74], video stills

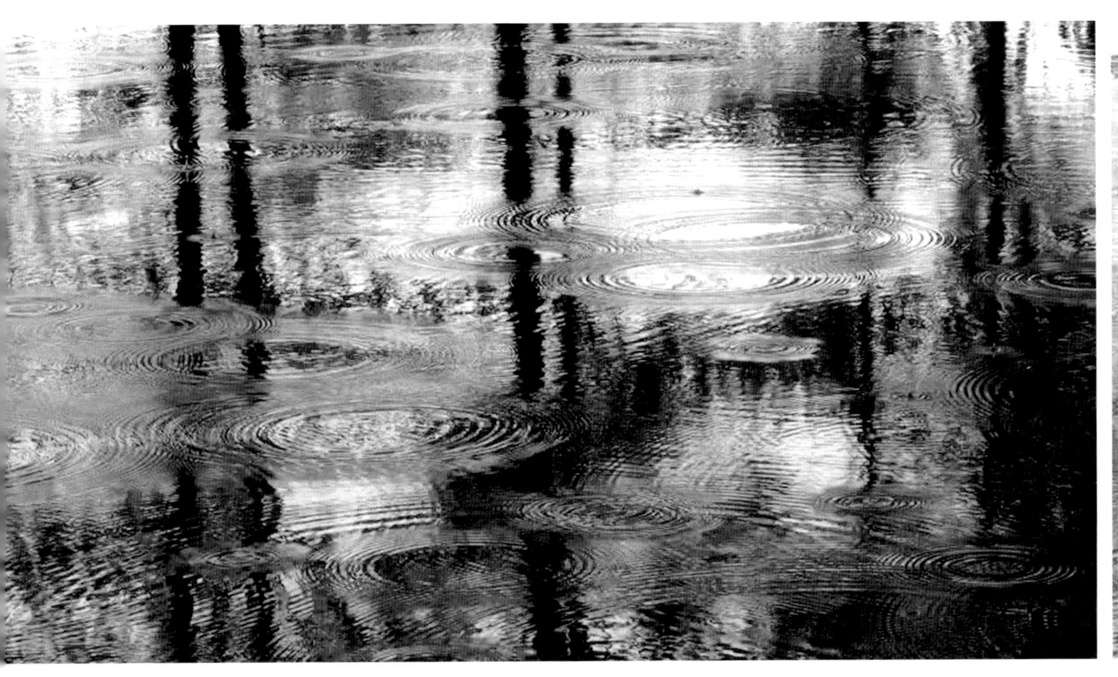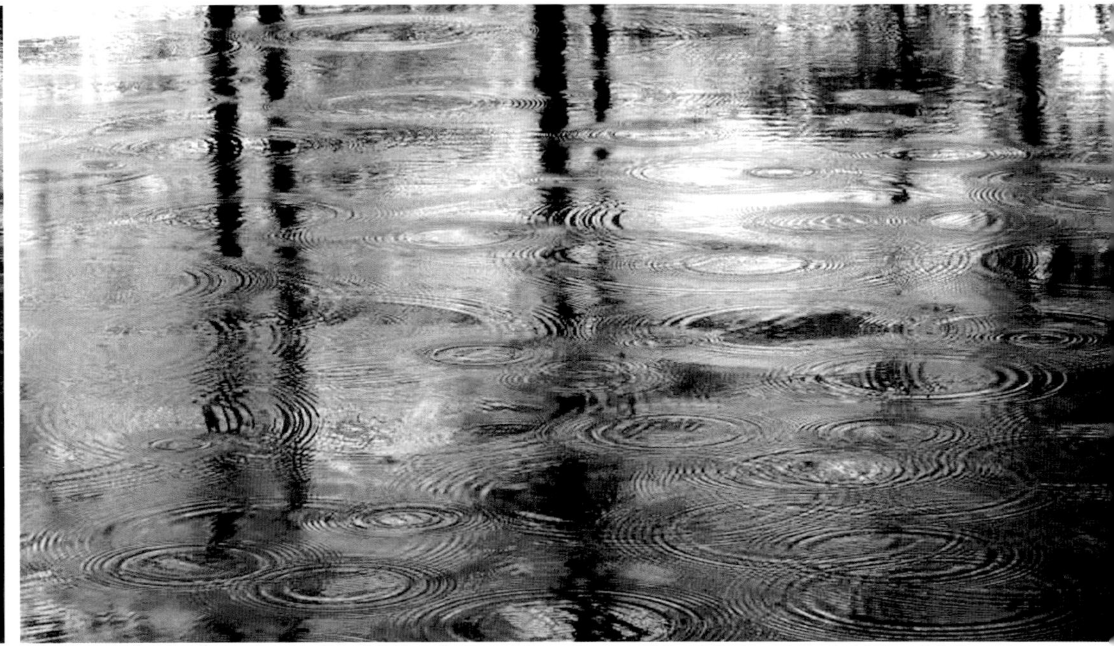

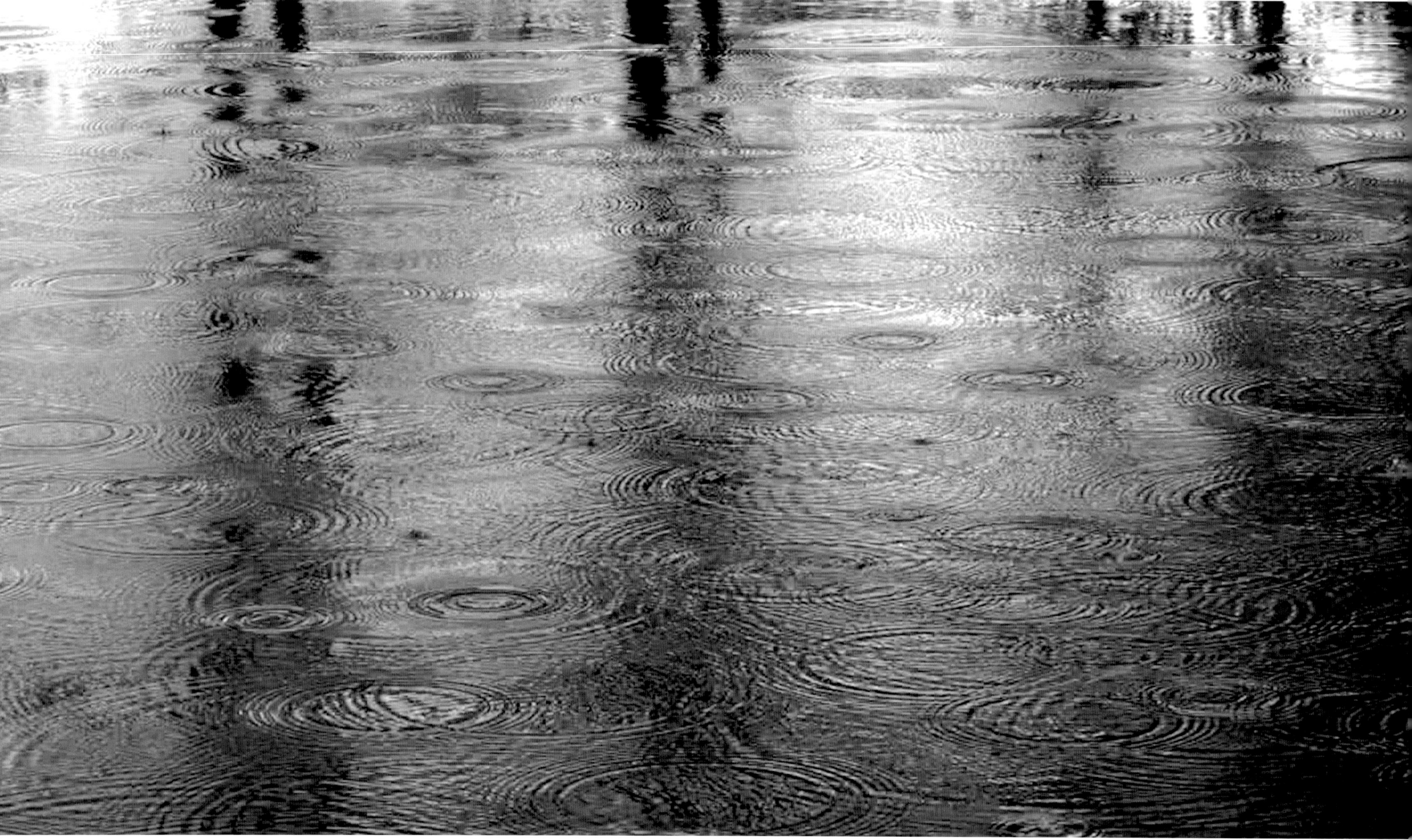

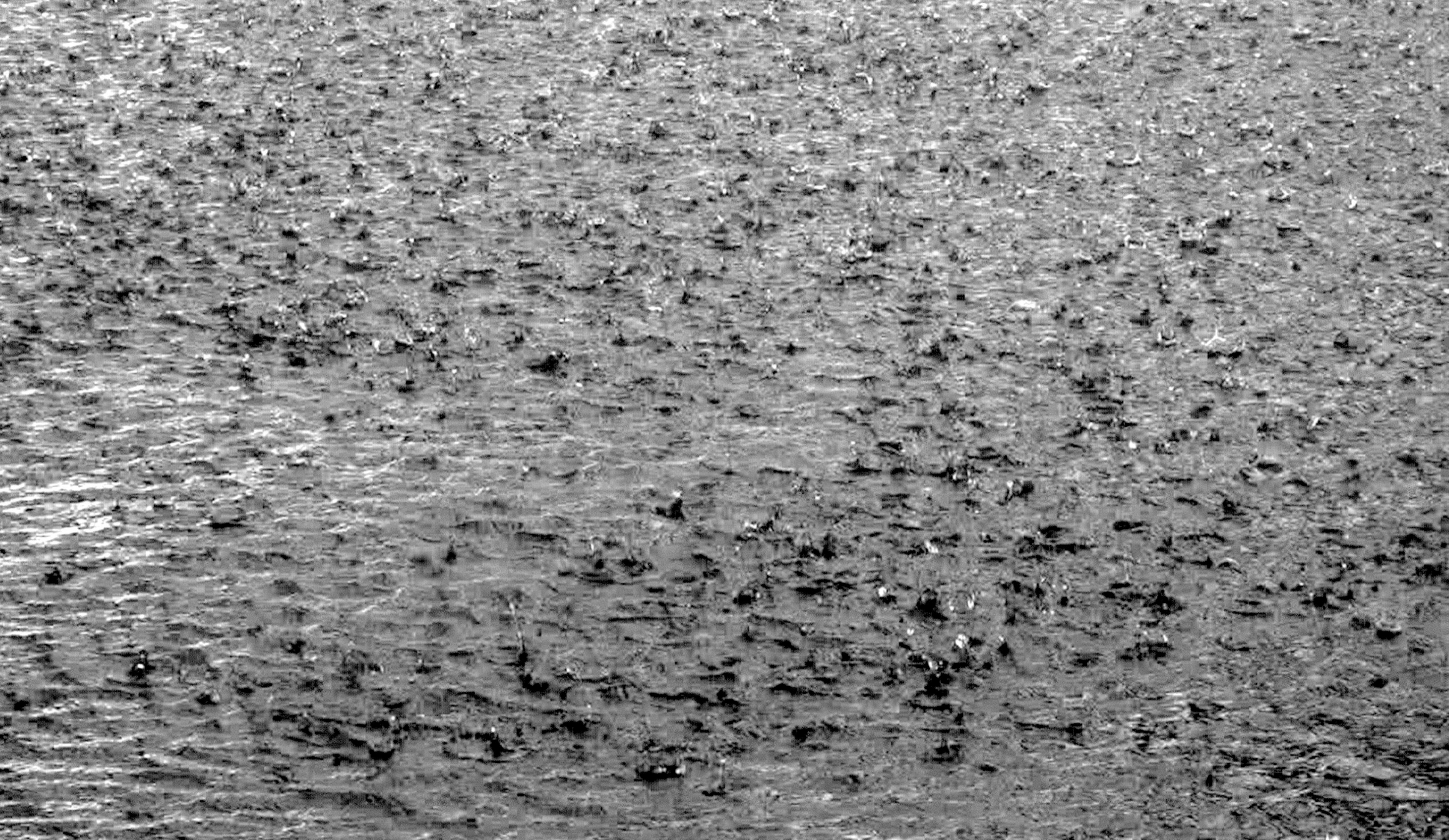

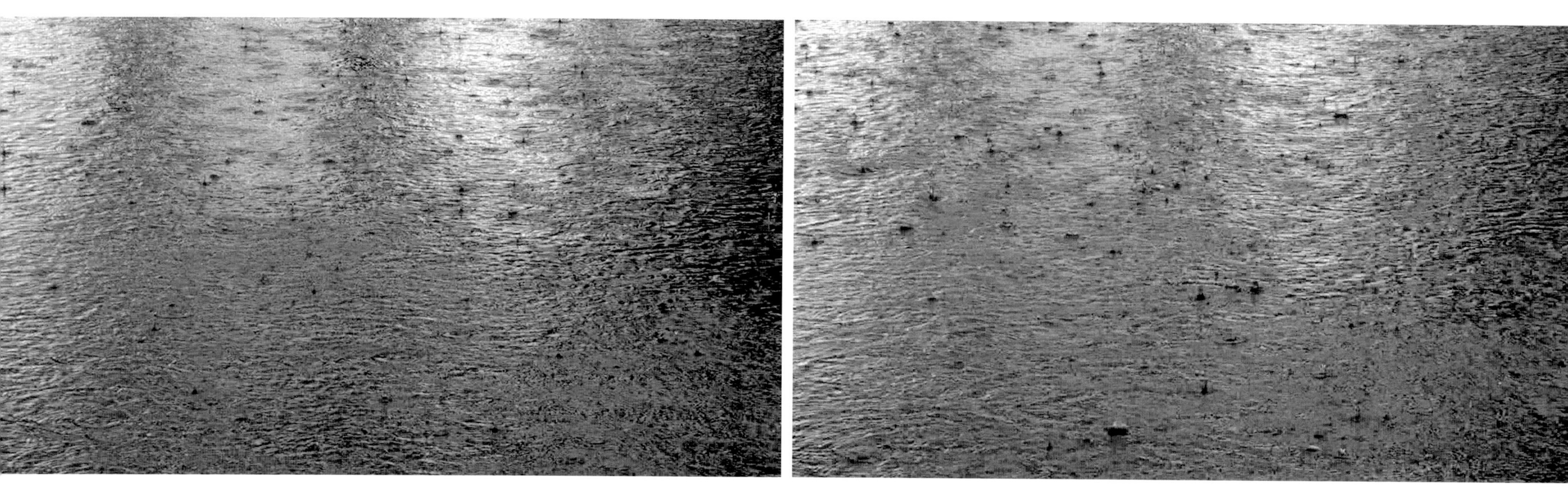

Beginning previous page: Pond/Auschwitz II (2011) [75], video stills

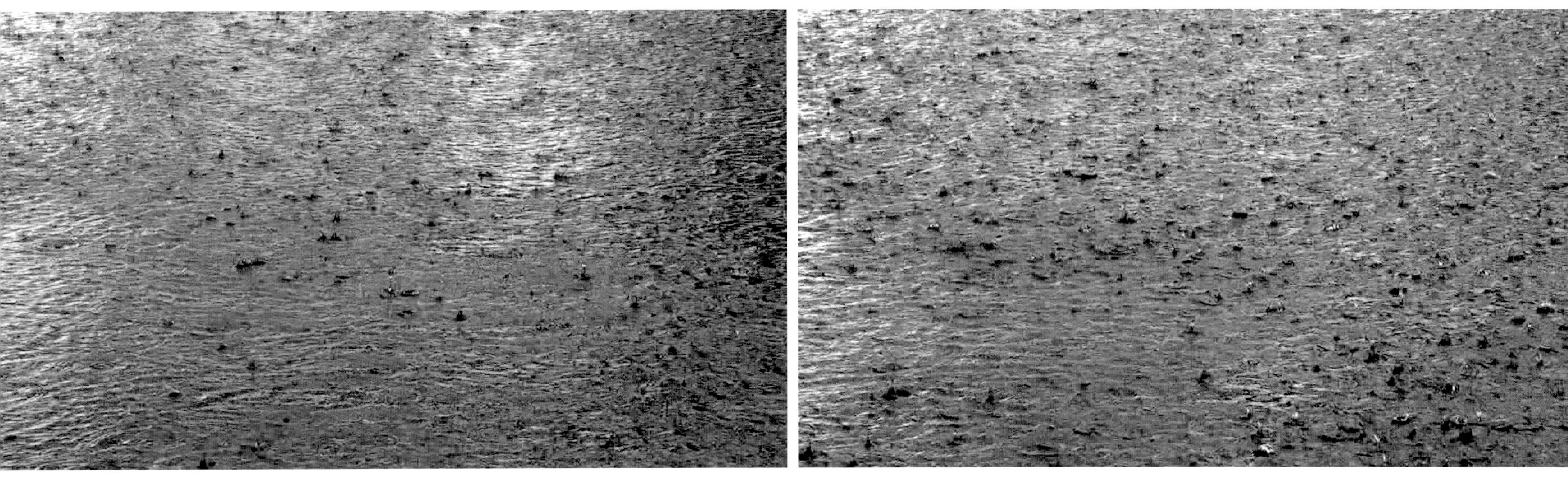

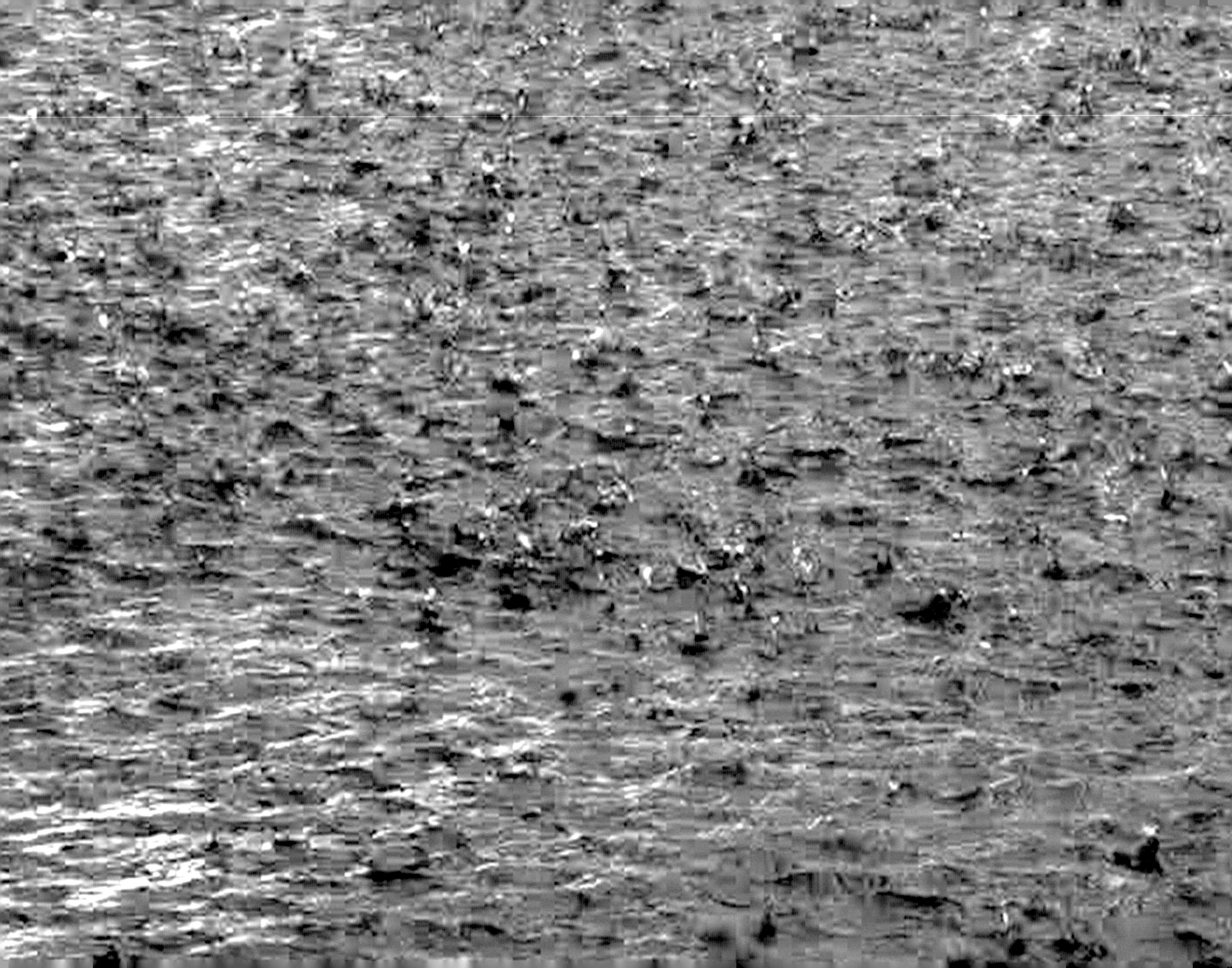

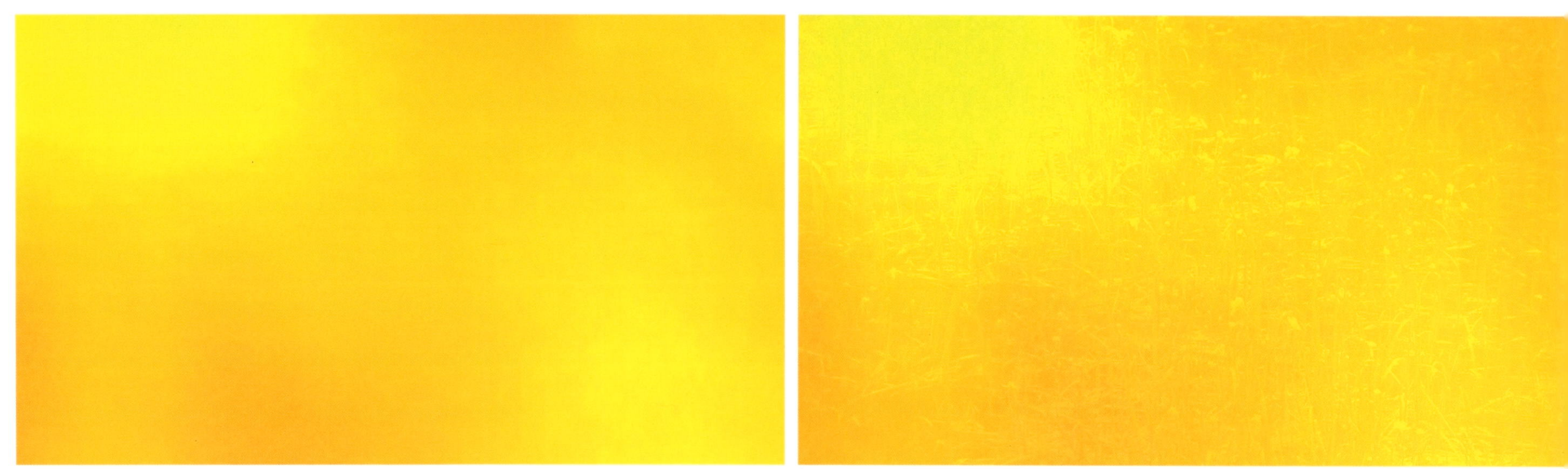

Pond/Auschwitz III (2011) [76], video stills

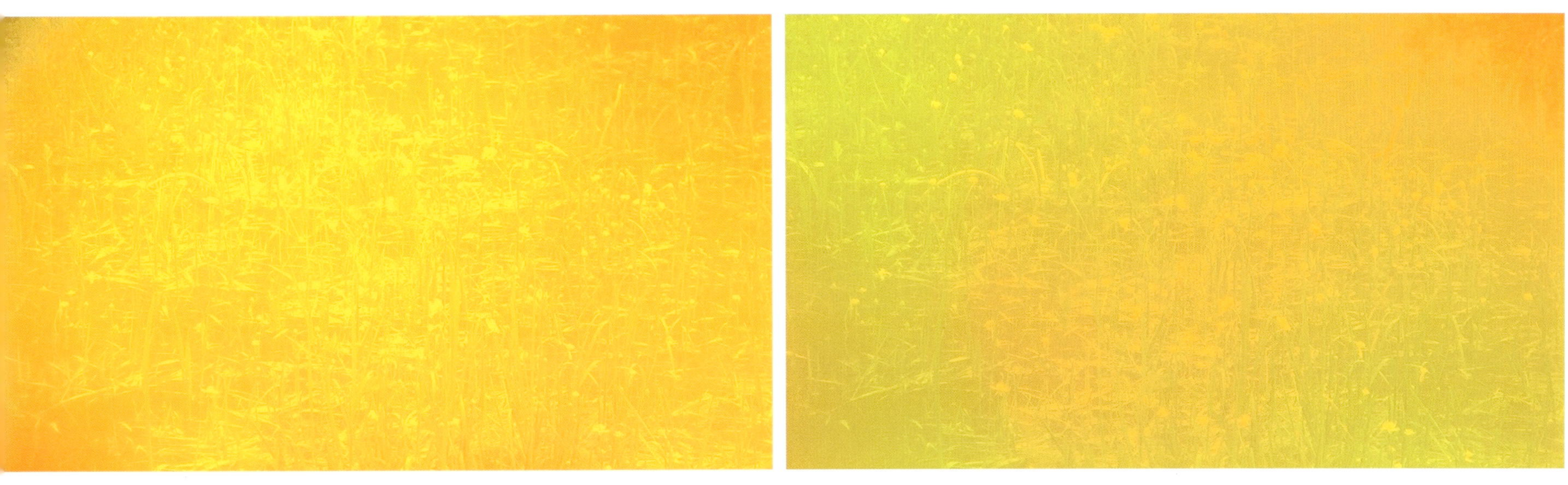

for soul and spirit that pervade her work – music and breath. *Pond/Auschwitz I* [74], while silent, is musical. However, the music is found in the image, when rain falls rhythmically on the pond. The pattern of raindrops performs a musical dance on the water's surface, a music you see. The images develop like a musical composition with their own internal logic. The harmonious unfolding of the work evokes the Platonic soul as musical harmony. Where the ashes of the slaughtered were once thrown Safdie see the traces of their spirits, made apparent through the improvisation between Safdie and nature.

In *Pond/Auschwitz II* [75], circular waves created by the drops are like sound waves made visible, suggesting the cries of the departed. The interference of the waves, forming moiré patterns, is highly musical, with rhythm, dynamics, and something akin to pitch contours. Just as many of Safdie's videos are like moving paintings, this video is like a moving score – a score performing itself through its physical representation as sound. These waves are both interacting sounds and interacting spirits, spectral improvisers bringing a community back to that place which attempted to permanently erase all sense of community.

Pond/Auschwitz III [76], the last in this series, begins with a bright yellow burst of colour filling the screen. Slowly, glyph-like marks appear on this surface. Appearing at first like finger-painted marks made on a yellow canvas, it is revealed that they are pond grasses and flowers. The bright yellow was taken from an extreme close-up of a pond flower – a symbol of life and beauty. The suggested manual work of the artist is elided with the works of nature – artist as nature, nature as artist. Safdie is able to enter into the environment even at Auschwitz to find affinity with such a place and to paint *with* it – the result of a long journey during which she became more aware of her relationship to nature and her status as a soul in a temporary and transforming body.

The journey began with a spirit – a pneumatic breath, out of reach and personified by the body of a hovering bird. It ends with this same spirit found even within and beneath Auschwitz, now formed by nature itself. As we read in the Hebrew Bible, Psalm 51, "Restore unto me the joy of salvation, and uphold me with a free spirit." This psalm, with its mention of the pneuma as spirit, seems to be a cipher for Safdie's video work. It tells us that "truth be in the hidden places" (51.8), and that wisdom is found where things are most concealed. It speaks of hearing joy and sadness, and, at the same time as this rejoicing, one's body has been broken. The Psalm, preoccupied with being cast from God's presence due to transgression and sin, is responded to by Safdie: to open yourself up to nature is to discover that the divinity is always within, it is the music of our very life.

[A]rt constantly challenges the process by which the individual person is reduced to anonymity. A person is not just a fluid particle caught up in violent historical processes, but a microcosm, which desperately seeks not only its rightful place in the world, but also its own rehabilitation.

Aharon Appelfeld, *Beyond Despair*, 23

There is never any end, there are always new sounds to imagine, new feelings to get at. And always, there is the need to keep purifying these feelings and sounds so that we can really see what we've discovered in its pure state. So that we can see more and more clearly what we are. In that way, we can give to those who listen the essence, the best of what we are. But to do that at each stage, we have to keep on cleaning the mirror.

John Coltrane, *Meditations* liner notes, Impulse A-9110, 1966

Videography

This is a complete catalogue of the video works of Sylvia Safdie up to July 2012. The thumbnail images correspond to the aspect ratios of the videos themselves. The numbering corresponds to the numbering used throughout this book. Titles of each video, and if it is a diptych, triptych, split screen, part of a series, or one video but in multiple parts, represent Safdie's decisions, and so represent how the works are intended to be shown and viewed. The degree of temporal specificity concerning when the original footage was shot reflects the relative importance Safdie gives to the precise events depicted in the videos. When there is a "subjective" account of the video, this too represents Safdie's opinion of the video's intent.

Notes:
• Videos that are labeled "Continuous loop" may also be shown as a single sequence.
• An asterisk (*) after the label "audio" indicates that the video may also be shown as a silent piece.
• Except where otherwise indicated, the different parts of a video series may be shown either on their own, or simultanously in the same space on separate screens.

[1] **Walter/Leaves**   CONTINUOUS LOOP
2002 / 6:25 MINUTES / FORMAT SD / COLOUR
CAMERA Sylvia Safdie
EDITING Brigitte Dajczer, Sylvia Safdie
AUDIO Silent

Reflections of moving leaves are projected onto
Walter's face through a glass window. Walter,
a ninety-seven-year-old man, is in a state of
sleep/awakening.

[2] **Gulls**   CONTINUOUS LOOP
2002 / 1:10 MINUTES / FORMAT SD / COLOUR
CAMERA Sylvia Safdie
EDITING Marielle Quesney, Sylvia Safdie
AUDIO Silent

Hovering time is resonant in this short video,
which focuses attention on the flight of a gull.

[3] **Providence Island**   CONTINUOUS LOOP
2002 / 10:18 MINUTES / FORMAT SD / COLOUR
CAMERA Sylvia Safdie
EDITING Marielle Quesney, Sylvia Safdie
AUDIO Silent

A still frame of a moving landscape becomes a
meditation on transformation.

[4] **Water over Stone**   CONTINUOUS LOOP
2002 / 5 MINUTES / FORMAT SD / COLOUR
CAMERA Sylvia Safdie
EDITING Marielle Quesney, Sylvia Safdie
AUDIO Silent

A close-up reveals the rhythmic movements of
water falling at varying speeds over a stone in a
lake. We are able to closely observe the organic
transformation that is occurring.

[5] **Owl's Head**   CONTINUOUS LOOP
2002 / 37 MINUTES / FORMAT SD / COLOUR
CAMERA Sylvia Safdie
EDITING Marielle Quesney
AUDIO Silent

A still frame of a moving landscape becomes a
meditation on transformation.

[6] **Juan**   CONTINUOUS LOOP
2002 / 2:30 MINUTES / FORMAT SD / COLOUR
CAMERA Sylvia Safdie
EDITING Marielle Quesney, Sylvia Safdie
AUDIO Silent

A portrait of artist Juan Guer is superimposed
with the rhythmic flow of water.

[7] **Ben**   CONTINUOUS LOOP
2002 / 4:30 MINUTES / FORMAT SD / COLOUR
CAMERA Sylvia Safdie
EDITING Brigitte Dajczer, Sylvia Safdie
AUDIO Silent

A portrait of choreographer Benjamin Harkarvy
is superimposed with the rhythmic flow of
water.

[8] **Sam**   CONTINUOUS LOOP
2002 / 3:14 MINUTES / FORMAT SD / COLOUR
CAMERA Sylvia Safdie
EDITING Marielle Quesney, Sylvia Safdie
AUDIO Silent

A portrait of Sam is superimposed with rain
gently falling on water.

[9] **Stone Cutter**   CONTINUOUS LOOP
2003 / 11 MINUTES / FORMAT SD / COLOUR
CAMERA Sylvia Safdie
EDITING Adad Hannah, Sylvia Safdie
AUDIO Silent

The rhythmic movements of a stone carver's
hand are observed as he chisels a stone. The
video was recorded in Mamallapuram, India.
Note: this video was designed to be shown in
the same space as *Foot*.

[10] **Foot**   CONTINUOUS LOOP
2003 / 2:30 MINUTES / FORMAT SD / COLOUR
CAMERA Sylvia Safdie
EDITING Adad Hannah, Sylvia Safdie
AUDIO Silent

The rhythmic movements of a stone carver's
foot are observed as he chisels a stone. The
video was recorded in Mamallapuram, India.
Note: this video was designed to be shown in
the same space as *Stone Cutter*.

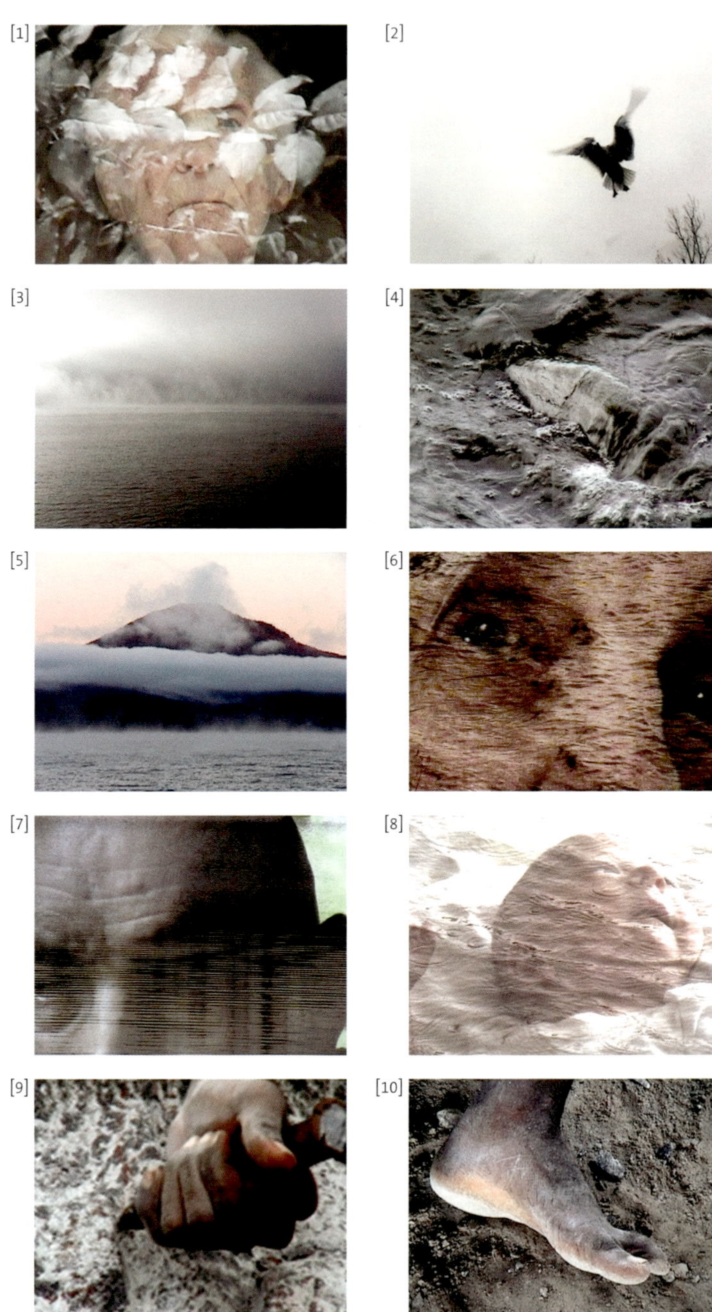

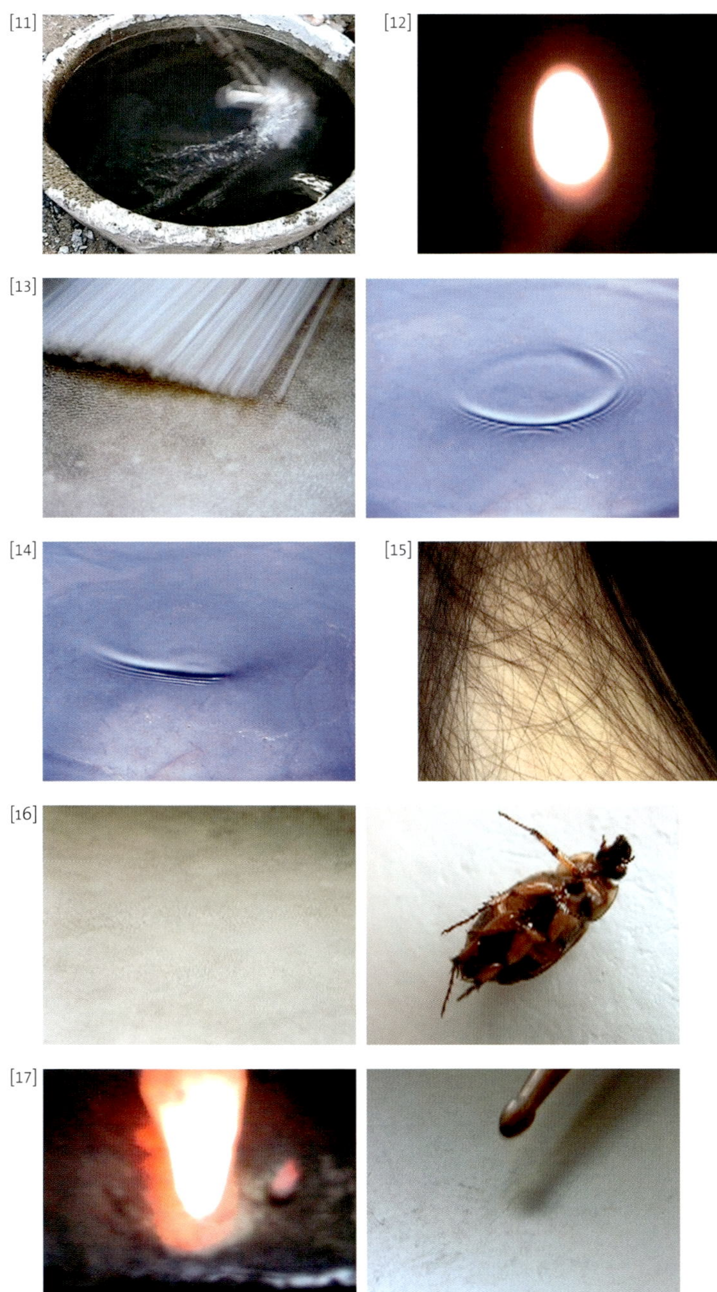

[11] **Well** CONTINUOUS LOOP
2003 / 3:45 MINUTES / FORMAT SD / COLOUR
CAMERA Sylvia Safdie
EDITING Adad Hannah, Sylvia Safdie
AUDIO Silent

After being forged, metal tools used for stone cutting are rapidly passed through water for cooling.

[12] **Flame** CONTINUOUS LOOP
2003 / 1:05 MINUTES / FORMAT SD / COLOUR
CAMERA Sylvia Safdie
EDITING Adad Hannah, Sylvia Safdie
AUDIO Silent

A meditation on a burning flame, recorded at Thanjavur Temple, India.

[13] **Circle I** DIPTYCH
2004 / 1:39 MINUTES / FORMAT SD / COLOUR
CAMERA Sylvia Safdie
EDITING Brigitte Dajczer, Sylvia Safdie
AUDIO John Heward, percussion

In this diptych, continuous circular ripples of water dialogue with the image and sound of drums.

[14] **Circle II**
2004 / 1:39 MINUTES / FORMAT SD / COLOUR
CAMERA Sylvia Safdie
EDITING Brigitte Dajczer, Sylvia Safdie
AUDIO* John Heward, percussion

Continuous circular ripples of water and the sound of drums interact.

[15] **Movements**
2005 / 6:24 MINUTES / FORMAT SD / COLOUR
CAMERA Sylvia Safdie
EDITING Brigitte Dajczer
AUDIO Liu Fang, pipa

Gestural movements gain drama through the relationship between image, movement, and sound. This video features Liu Fang improvising with the pipa (a Chinese string instrument) to a heron's slow walk.

[16] **Dance** DIPTYCH
2005 / 5:09 MINUTES / FORMAT SD / COLOUR
CAMERA Sylvia Safdie
EDITING Adad Hannah, Sylvia Safdie
AUDIO John Heward, percussion

Just before its death, a beetle flips onto its back, its movement becoming slower and slower, until it dies. John Heward watched *Dance* and improvised the accompanying music.

[17] **Solo** DIPTYCH
2005 / 7:22 MINUTES / FORMAT SD / COLOUR
CAMERA Sylvia Safdie
EDITING Adad Hannah, Brigitte Dajczer, Sylvia Safdie
AUDIO John Heward, percussion

In this diptych, an Indian metal worker making tools is juxtaposed with the steady rhythms of a drummer. The pairing of sound and image becomes a meditation on the energies of making.

[18] **Gilberthe**
2005 / 10:57 MINUTES / FORMAT SD / COLOUR
CAMERA Sylvia Safdie
EDITING Marielle Quesney, Sylvia Safdie
AUDIO Silent

Portrait of Gilberthe Asselin at age ninety-four.

[20] **Time Passing**   DIPTYCH
CONTINUOUS LOOP
2005 / 9:40 MINUTES / FORMAT SD / COLOUR
CAMERA Sylvia Safdie
EDITING Brigitte Dajczer, Sylvia Safdie
AUDIO Silent

On one screen, ninety-five-year-old Gladys
Barnes' hands are captured as she engages in
conversation. On the other screen, six-month-
old Anais' hand is captured as she lies in her
chair observing her surroundings.

[21] **Hands**   DIPTYCH
2005 / 2:48 MINUTES / FORMAT SD / COLOUR
CAMERA Sylvia Safdie
EDITING Brigitte Dajczer, Sylvia Safdie
AUDIO John Heward, percussion

On one screen, John Heward's hands as he
drums, on the other, ninety-five-year-old Gladys
Barnes' hands as she engages in conversation.
The combination shows how hand movement
is both instinctive and intentional.

[22] **Dana/Ben**   DIPTYCH
2005 / 4:08 MINUTES / FORMAT SD / COLOUR
CAMERA Sylvia Safdie
EDITING Brigitte Dajczer, Sylvia Safdie
AUDIO Dana Reason, John Heward

Two unrelated videos are shown
simultaneously: one, of Dana Reason's face as
he improvises on piano; the other, slowed down
superimposed footage of Ben Harkarvy.

[23] **Wind**
2006 / 7:56 MINUTES / FORMAT SD / COLOUR
CAMERA Sylvia Safdie
EDITING Brigitte Dajczer, Sylvia Safdie
AUDIO Joe McPhee, alto saxophone
John Heward, drums

Sound improvised by two musicians encounters
the interplay of light and shadow created by
the movement of leaves.

[19] **Gladys: A Life**
2005 / 5:20 MINUTES / FORMAT SD / COLOUR
CAMERA Sylvia Safdie
EDITING Brigitte Dajczer, Sylvia Safdie
AUDIO Silent

This portrait of Gladys Barnes, a ninety-five-
year-old native of Trout River, Newfoundland,
was captured while spending hours in
conversation and silence as Gladys passed in
and out of states of sleep and awakening.

[24] **Reed**   CONTINUOUS LOOP
2006 / 3:48 MINUTES / FORMAT SD / COLOUR
CAMERA Sylvia Safdie
EDITING Brigitte Dajczer, Sylvia Safdie
AUDIO Silent

A reed is reflected in water.

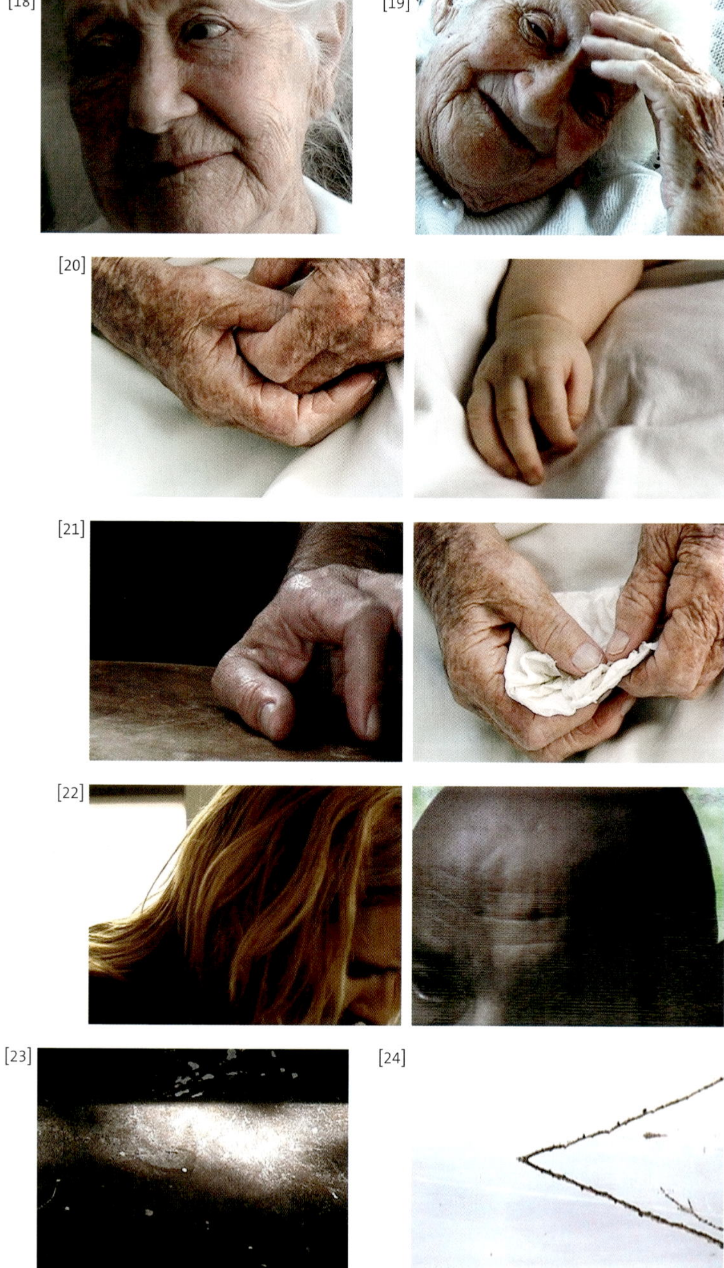

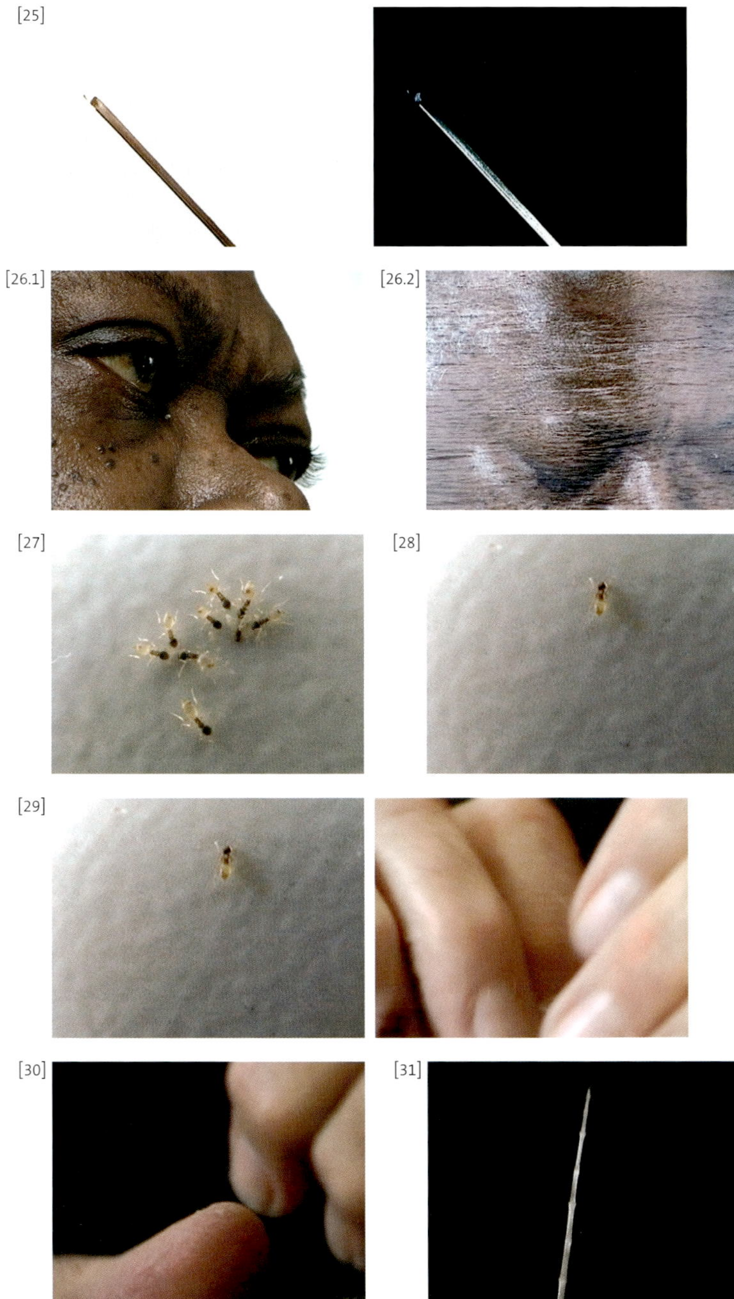

[25] **Act / Shadow**   DIPTYCH
2006 / 11:03 MINUTES / FORMAT SD / COLOUR
CAMERA Sylvia Safdie
EDITING Brigitte Dajczer, Sylvia Safdie
AUDIO Malcolm Goldstein, composition, violin
and voice

Malcolm Goldstein performs his composition
"Gentle Rain Preceding Mushrooms" (in
memoriam John Cage). What is shown is the
bow and the image's negative.

[26.1] **Joe (Part I: Breath)**
2007 / 3:22 MINUTES / FORMAT SD / COLOUR
CAMERA Sylvia Safdie
EDITING Brigitte Dajczer, Sylvia Safdie
AUDIO Joe McPhee, pocket trumpet

For the hundredth anniversary of his father's
birth and the tenth anniversary of his death,
Joe McPhee, using the pocket trumpet, explores
the birth of sound. The result is a two-part
video, *Breath* and *Sound*.

[26.2] **Joe (Part II: Sound)**
2007 / 4:01 MINUTES / FORMAT SD / COLOUR

[27] **Gathering**
2007 / 5:42 MINUTES / FORMAT SD / COLOUR
CAMERA Sylvia Safdie
EDITING Brigitte Dajczer, Sylvia Safdie
AUDIO John Heward, percussion

A group of ants in constant movement are
involved in a mysterious activity. With the
accompaniment of sound, the viewer becomes
involved in their ritual.

[28] **Touch I**
2007 / 4:55 MINUTES / FORMAT SD / COLOUR
CAMERA Sylvia Safdie
EDITING Brigitte Dajczer, Sylvia Safdie
AUDIO John Heward, percussion

The rhythmic movements of an ant's gestures
are amplified and transformed by the sound
of drums.

[29] **Touch II**   DIPTYCH
2007 / 4:55 MINUTES / FORMAT SD / COLOUR
CAMERA Sylvia Safdie
EDITING Brigitte Dajczer, Sylvia Safdie
AUDIO John Heward, percussion

The rhythmic movement of an ant is
juxtaposed with hands drumming. Through
sight and sound, the viewer becomes involved
in their rhythmic movements.

[30] **Touching**
2007 / 4:54 MINUTES / FORMAT SD / COLOUR
CAMERA Sylvia Safdie
EDITING Brigitte Dajczer, Sylvia Safdie
AUDIO John Heward, percussion

A close-up reveals the subtle gestures of John
Heward's hands as he plays a drum.

[31] **Line**
2007 / 8:26 MINUTES / FORMAT SD / COLOUR
CAMERA Sylvia Safdie
EDITING Brigitte Dajczer, Sylvia Safdie
AUDIO Malcolm Goldstein, violin

A fragment of a branch can be seen through
a windowpane as its linear form becomes
distorted by the blurring of raindrops. What
is left is an image of a line both forming and
dissolving as it encounters movement and
light, reflection and refraction.

Reflections: A Trilogy
2007 / FORMAT SD / COLOUR
[32.1] **Part 1** 5:44 MINUTES
[32.2] **Part 2** 3:33 MINUTES
[32.3] **Part 3** 5:15 MINUTES
CAMERA Sylvia Safdie
EDITING Patrick Andrew Boivin, Sylvia Safdie
AUDIO Malcolm Goldstein, violin

A branch's reflection in the water is erased by
the transforming patterns made by falling rain.

[33] **Reflections** TRIPTYCH
2007 / 14:26 MINUTES / FORMAT SD
BLACK AND WHITE / CAMERA Sylvia Safdie
EDITING Patrick Andrew Boivin, Sylvia Safdie
AUDIO Malcolm Goldstein, violin

In this meditation on impermanence, a branch's
reflection in the water is slowly erased by the
transforming patterns created by falling rain. The
three sections enable the viewer to experience
the event in the past, present, and future,
accompanied by one soundtrack.

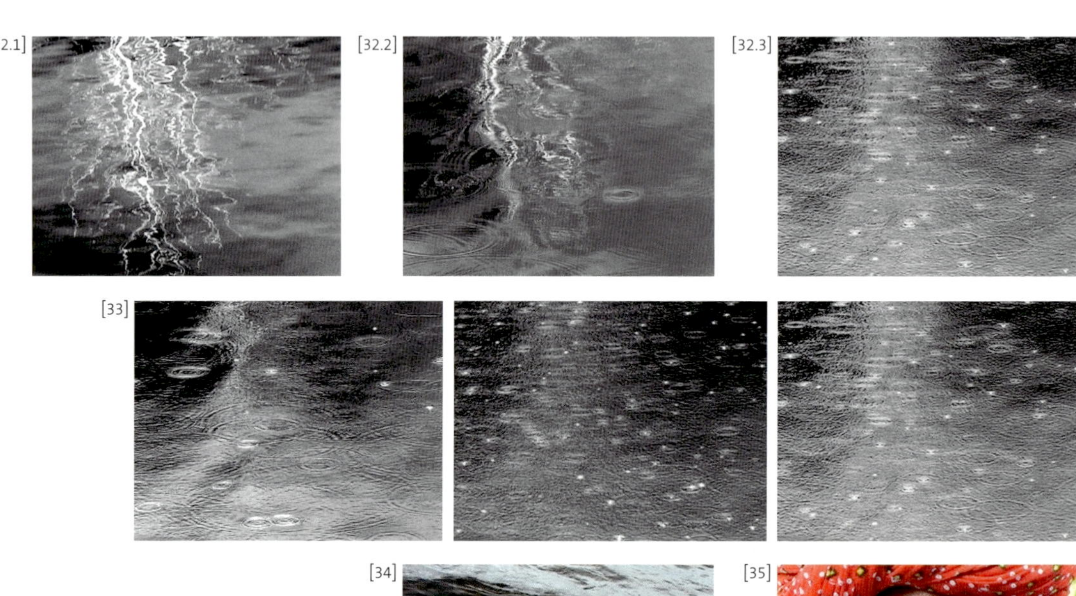

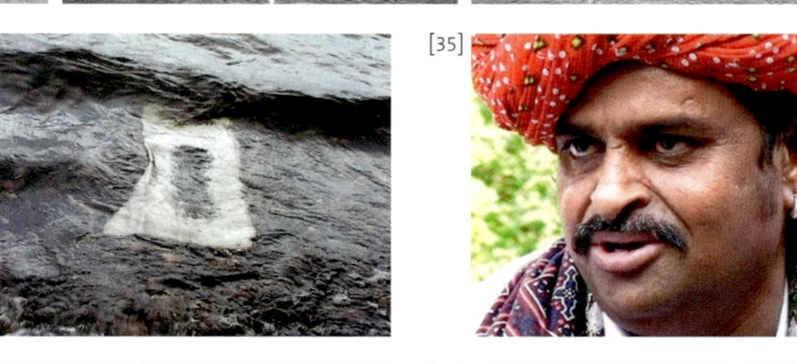

[34] **John Heward: A Portrait**
2008 / 19:47 MINUTES / FORMAT SD / COLOUR
ENGLISH AND FRENCH VERSIONS
CAMERA Sylvia Safdie / EDITING Brigitte Dajczer,
Sylvia Safdie / AUDIO John Heward, percussion;
Joe McPhee, alto saxophone
AUDIO DESIGN Brigitte Dajczer

The camera follows Canadian painter and
musician John Heward as he is immersed in the
process of construction and deconstruction.

[35] **Hayat Mohammed**
2008 / 9:00 MINUTES / FORMAT SD / COLOUR
CAMERA Sylvia Safdie
EDITING Brigitte Dajczer, Sylvia Safdie
AUDIO Mubarak Khan Langa Group

The camera focuses on Hayat Mohammed's
face as he sings with the Mubarak Khan
Langa Group during the 2007 Rajasthan
International Folk Festival. His voice, facial
expressions, and physical gestures reveal the
deep inner life force behind his singing.

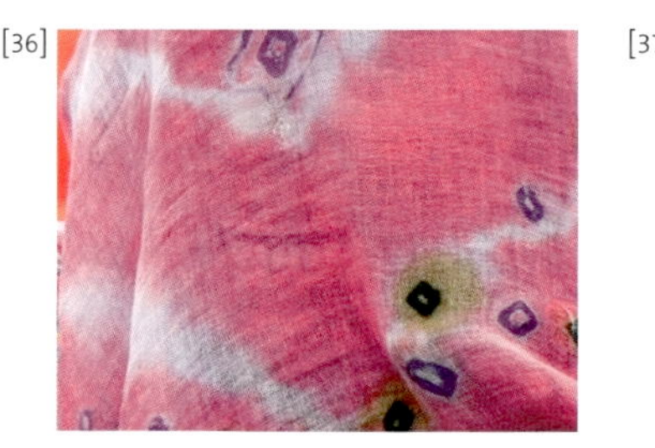

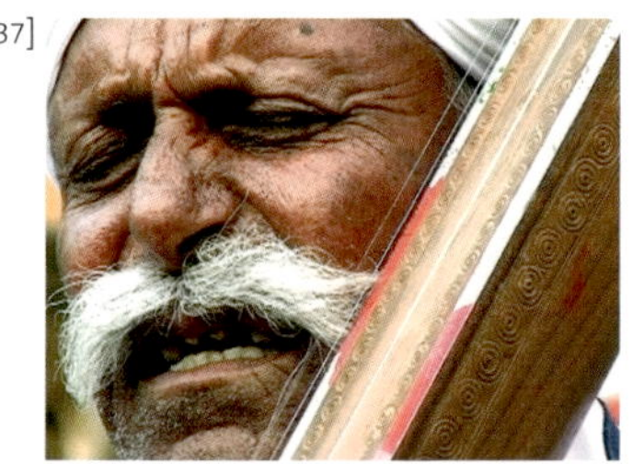

[36] **Sumitra Maina**
2008 / 5:58 MINUTES / FORMAT SD / COLOUR
CAMERA Sylvia Safdie
EDITING Brigitte Dajczer, Sylvia Safdie
AUDIO The Mithu Khan Langa Group

Sumitra Maina sings with the Mithu Khan
Langa Group during the 2007 Rajasthan
International Folk Festival. The repetition of
the verse and melody become haunting as her
piercing voice is heard from behind a veil.

[37] **Padmaran**
2008 / 4:44 MINUTES / FORMAT SD / COLOUR
CAMERA Sylvia Safdie / EDITING Brigitte
Dajczer, Sylvia Safdie / AUDIO Padmaran
performing with the Mithu Khan Langa Group

The camera focuses on Padmaran's face as
he sings with the Manganiyar group from
western Rajasthan during the 2007 Rajasthan
International Folk Festival. His face reveals his
deep connection to the music and the intensity
of his emotion.

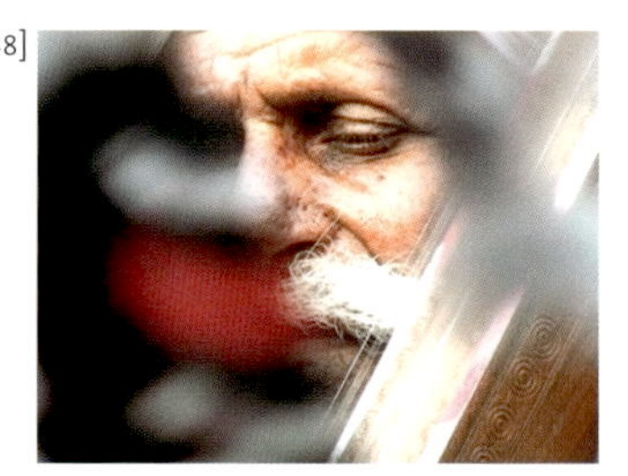

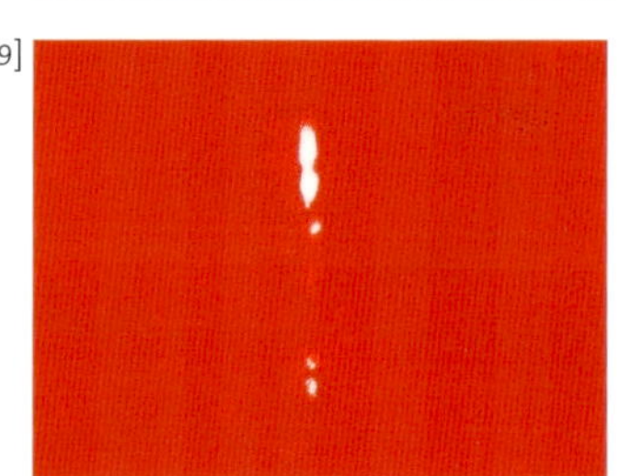

[38] **Song**
2008 / 5:20 MINUTES / FORMAT SD / COLOUR
CAMERA Sylvia Safdie / EDITING Brigitte Dajczer
AUDIO A performance that included the
following groups: Kamad, Bohpa, Kalbeilya,
Natnayat, Langa, Manganiyar

During the 2007 Rajasthan International Folk
Festival, several groups performed at the end of
the concert. In this video, the camera focuses
on Padmaran's face, one of the musicians, as he
absorbs and responds to the music.

[39] **Rajasthan (Red)**
2008 / 5:48 MINUTES / FORMAT SD / COLOUR
CAMERA Sylvia Safdie / EDITING Brigitte
Dajczer, Sylvia Safdie / AUDIO unknown

Light flickering on a red ground heightens the
pulsating and edgy sound of the music. The
song was performed by a Rajasthan folklore
group whose style originated in the Nayak
tradition. The video and music were recorded
on location during the 2007 Rajasthan
International Folk Festival.

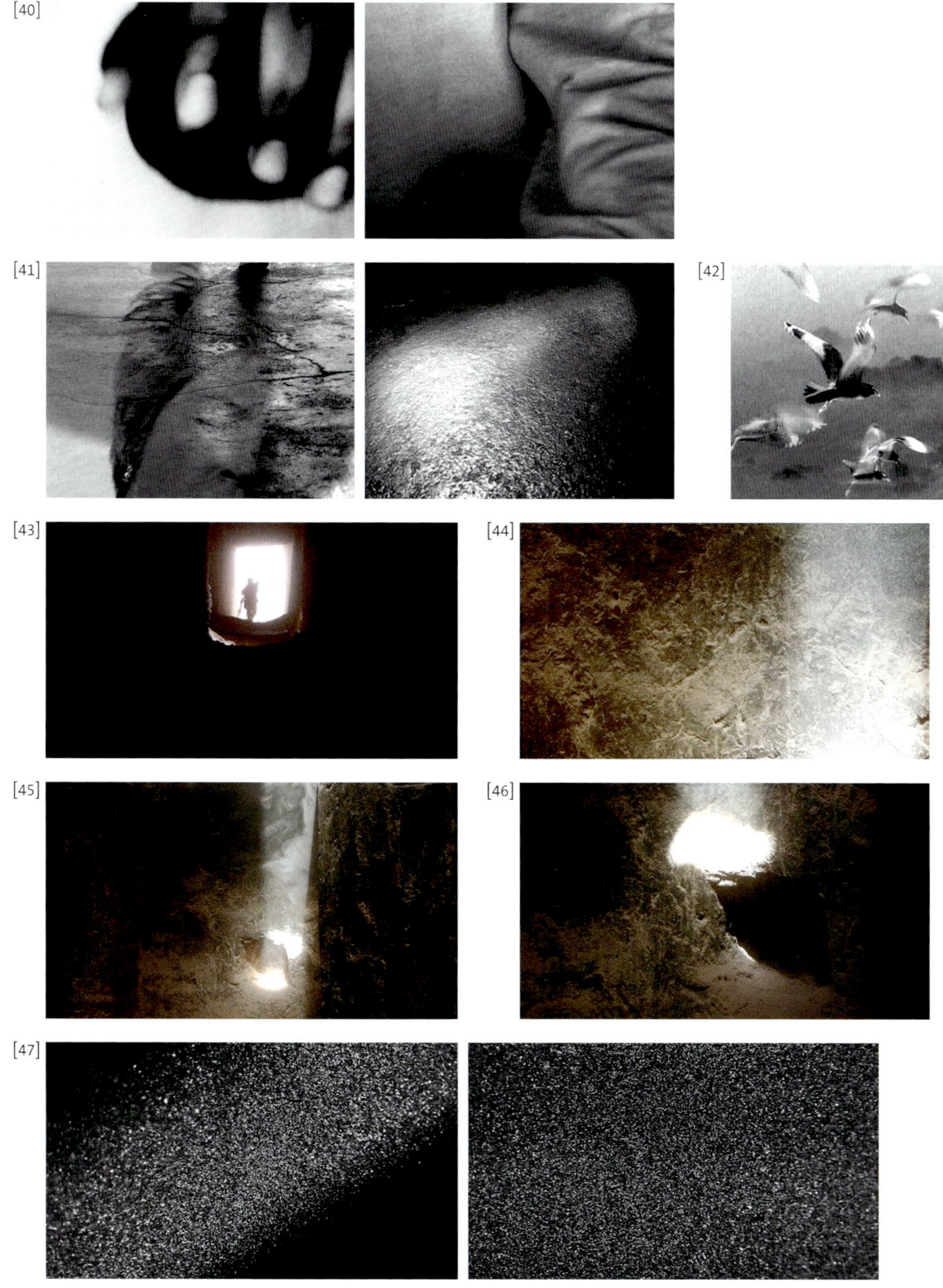

[40] **Late Afternoon Raga**   DIPTYCH
2008 / 5:15 MINUTES / FORMAT SD
BLACK AND WHITE / CAMERA Sylvia Safdie
EDITING Brigitte Dajczer, Sylvia Safdie
AUDIO Faiyaz Ali Kahn on the Sarangi, Babalu
Varma on the Tabla

In this diptych, the relationship between sound
and image extends the rhythm and pulse of
the music of a traditional classical raga. The
music was recorded live on a late October 2007
afternoon in Varanasi, India.

[41] **Lori**   DIPTYCH
2008 / 4:15 MINUTES / FORMAT SD
BLACK AND WHITE
CAMERA Sylvia Safdie
EDITING Brigitte Dajczer, Sylvia Safdie
AUDIO Lori Freedman, bass clarinet

In this diptych, music, light, shadow, and
reflection come together to create a dialogue
between image and sound.

[42] **Nightbirds**
2008 / 4:00 MINUTES / FORMAT SD
BLACK AND WHITE
CAMERA Sylvia Safdie
EDITING Patrick Andrew Boivin, Sylvia Safdie
AUDIO Dominic Duval, bass

Dominic Duval's composition "Nightbird
Invention" becomes one with the flight of
seagulls.

[43] **Morning**
2009 / 1:33 MINUTES / FORMAT HD / COLOUR
CAMERA Sylvia Safdie
EDITING Patrick Andrew Boivin, Sylvia Safdie
AUDIO DESIGN* Patrick Andrew Boivin

In a light-filled opening, the silhouette of a
woman with a child on her back appears as she
empties a pail of water and then disappears
into light. This video was recorded at the
entrance to the mellah (the old Jewish quarter
in Amzrou), a kasbah in southern Morocco.

[44] **Particles**
2009 / 3:56 MINUTES / FORMAT HD / COLOUR
CAMERA Sylvia Safdie
EDITING Patrick Andrew Boivin, Sylvia Safdie
AUDIO* David Prentice, violin

Dust, light, and a wall are the elements in this
video. The location is an abandoned synagogue
in Amzrou, a kasbah in southern Morocco.

[45] **Dust**
2009 / 4:50 MINUTES / FORMAT HD / COLOUR
CAMERA Sylvia Safdie
EDITING Patrick Andrew Boivin, Sylvia Safdie
AUDIO* Malcolm Goldstein, violin and voice

Dust, light, and a wall are the elements in this
video. The location is an abandoned synagogue
in Amzrou, a kasbah in southern Morocco.

[46] **Opening**
2009 / 4:02 MINUTES / FORMAT HD / COLOUR
CAMERA Sylvia Safdie
EDITING Patrick Andrew Boivin, Sylvia Safdie
SOUND DESIGN* Patrick Andrew Boivin

An opening in a wall in an abandoned synagogue
in Amzrou provides the setting for a meditation
on dust and light. The audio consists of Muslim
prayers recorded while filming the synagogue
and of Jewish prayers recorded in Moulai Ighir,
Morocco, in November 2009.

[47] **Dust and Light**   DIPTYCH
CONTINUOUS LOOP
2009 / 6:12 MINUTES / FORMAT HD
BLACK AND WHITE / CAMERA Sylvia Safdie
EDITING Patrick Andrew Boivin, Sylvia Safdie
AUDIO Silent

Dust illuminated by light floats in space in an
abandoned synagogue in Amzrou, a kasbah in
southern Morocco. Note: for installation each
panel will be viewed on a separate projector.

Amzrou Synagogue Interiors, Series I
CONTINUOUS LOOPS
2009 / FORMAT HD / COLOUR
[48.1] **Interior 1** 1:16 MINUTES
[48.2] **Interior 2** 1:07 MINUTES
[48.3] **Interior 3** 0:58 MINUTES
[48.4] **Interior 4** 1:10 MINUTES
[48.5] **Interior 5** 1:28 MINUTES
[48.6] **Interior 6** 0:58 MINUTES
[48.7] **Interior 7** 0:46 MINUTES
CAMERA Patrick Andrew Boivin, Sylvia Safdie
EDITING Patrick Andrew Boivin, Sylvia Safdie
AUDIO Silent

Seven different perspectives reveal and explore
the interior of a synagogue in Amzrou, a kasbah
in southern Morocco.

Amzrou Synagogue Interiors, Series II
CONTINUOUS LOOPS
2009–2011 / FORMAT HD / COLOUR
[49.1] **No. 1** 2:09 MINUTES
[49.2] **No. 2** 2:09 MINUTES
CAMERA Sylvia Safdie
EDITING Patrick Andrew Boivin, Sylvia Safdie
AUDIO Silent

Explorations of the interior of a synagogue in
Amzrou, a Kasbah in southern Morocco.
Note: these works can be shown as a diptych.

[50.1] **Wall: A Triptych**
2009 / 6:37 MINUTES / FORMAT HD / COLOUR
CAMERA Sylvia Safdie / EDITING Patrick Andrew
Boivin, Sylvia Safdie / AUDIO* Arthur Bull,
harmonica / AUDIO DESIGN Patrick Andrew Boivin

A light patch travels through time on the wall of
an abandoned synagogue in Amzrou, a kasbah in
southern Morocco. The original sequence in real
time is 22 minutes. For this triptych, it has been
divided into three sections, enabling the viewer
to experience it in the past, present, and future.

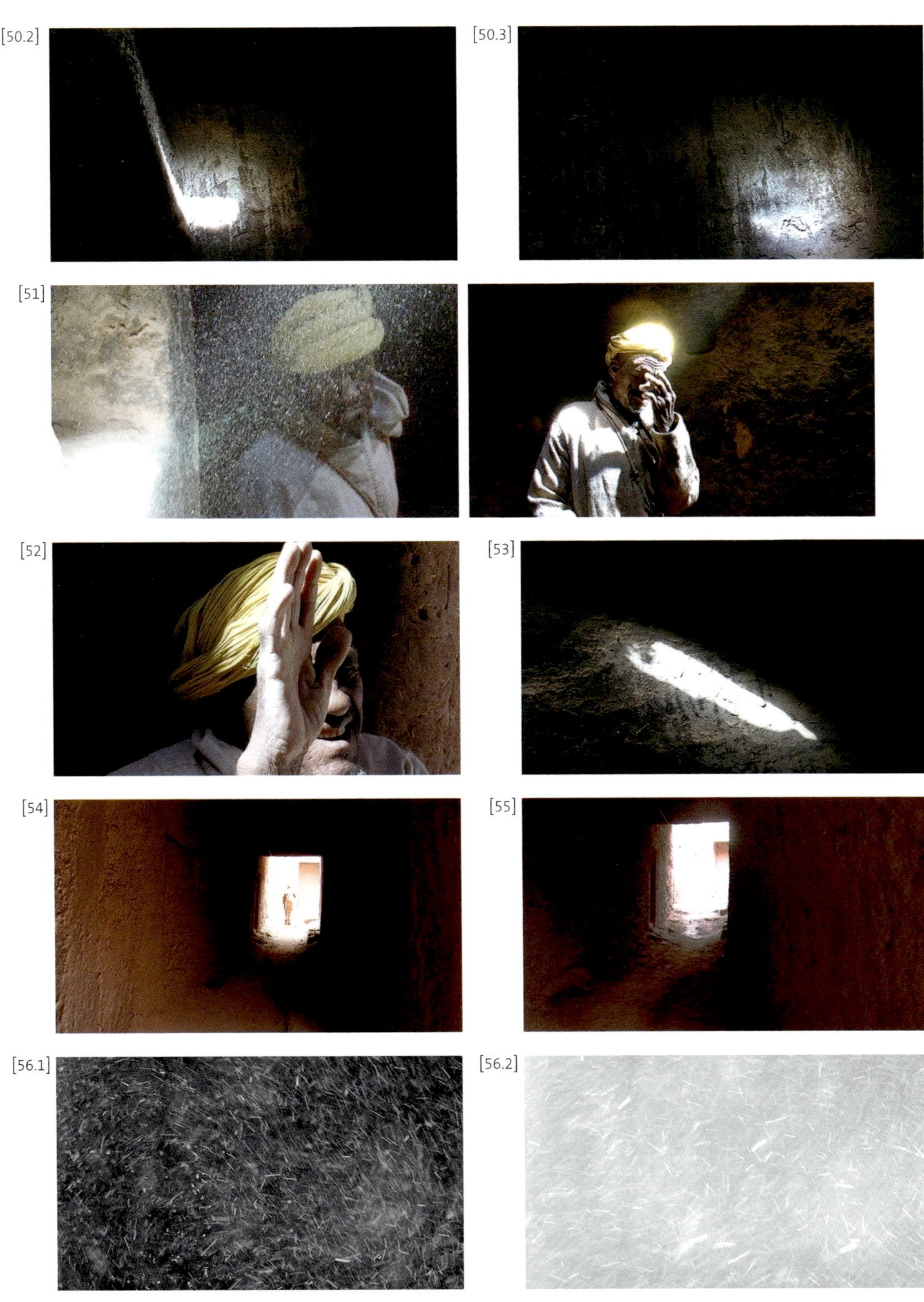

[50.2] **Wall**
2009 / 23:53 MINUTES / FORMAT HD / COLOUR
CAMERA Sylvia Safdie
EDITING Patrick Andrew Boivin, Sylvia Safdie
AUDIO* Arthur Bull, harmonica
AUDIO DESIGN Patrick Andrew Boivin

Light reveals and conceals. A light patch travels across the wall of an abandoned synagogue in Amzrou, a kasbah in southern Morocco.

[50.3] **Wall (excerpt)**
2009 / 8:59 MINUTES / FORMAT HD / COLOUR
CAMERA Sylvia Safdie
EDITING Patrick Andrew Boivin, Sylvia Safdie
AUDIO* Arthur Bull, harmonica
AUDIO DESIGN Patrick Andrew Boivin

Light reveals and conceals. A light patch travels across the wall of an abandoned synagogue in Amzrou, a kasbah in southern Morocco.

[51] **The Guardian** DIPTYCH
2009 / 3:26 MINUTES / FORMAT HD / COLOUR
CAMERA Sylvia Safdie
EDITING Patrick Andrew Boivin, Sylvia Safdie
AUDIO DESIGN Patrick Andrew Boivin

Mbark Hedioui, the caretaker, stands in the interior of an abandoned synagogue in Amzrou, a kasbah in southern Morocco. His recitations of the names of the Jewish families who used to live in the area act as markers to a community that no longer exists in its place of origin.

[52] **Mbark Hedioui**
2009 / FORMAT HD / COLOUR
Portrait 1 2:09 MIN. **Portrait 2** 2:22 MIN.
Portrait 3 2:29 MIN. **Portrait 4** 2:29 MIN.
CAMERA Sylvia Safdie
EDITING Patrick Andrew Boivin, Sylvia Safdie
AUDIO Silent
A portrait in four parts of Mbark Hedioui, the caretaker of the synagogue in Amzrou, a kasbah in southern Morocco.

[53] **Presence**
2009 / 29:33 MINUTES / FORMAT HD / COLOUR
CAMERA Sylvia Safdie
EDITING Patrick Andrew Boivin, Sylvia Safdie
AUDIO* Malcolm Goldstein, violin

A patch of light travels in real time across a wall in an abandoned synagogue in Amzrou, a kasbah in southern Morocco.

[54] **Pathway/Amzrou I**
CONTINUOUS LOOP
2009 / 0:28 MINUTES / FORMAT HD / COLOUR
CAMERA Sylvia Safdie
EDITING Patrick Andrew Boivin, Sylvia Safdie
AUDIO Silent

A pathway in Amzrou, a kasbah in southern Morocco.

[55] **Pathway/Amzrou II**
CONTINUOUS LOOP
2009 / 0:45 MINUTES / FORMAT HD / COLOUR
CAMERA Sylvia Safdie
EDITING Patrick Andrew Boivin, Sylvia Safdie
AUDIO Silent

Mbark Hedioui, the caretaker of an abandoned synagogue, walks along a pathway in Amzrou, a kasbah in southern Morocco.

[56.1] **Dispersion (black)**
[56.2] **Dispersion (white)**
2009 / 8:04 MINUTES / FORMAT HD
BLACK AND WHITE / CAMERA Sylvia Safdie
EDITING Patrick Andrew Boivin, Sylvia Safdie
AUDIO* Malcolm Goldstein, violin

The rhythmic movement of dust floating in an abandoned synagogue in Amzrou, a kasbah in southern Morocco, is amplified and transformed by sound.

[57.1] **Marrakech: Jewish Cemetery**
TRIPTYCH
CONTINUOUS LOOP
2009 / 18:08 MINUTES / FORMAT HD / COLOUR
CAMERA Sylvia Safdie
EDITING Patrick Andrew Boivin, Sylvia Safdie
AUDIO DESIGN Patrick Andrew Boivin

This triptych is a meditation on the Jewish
cemetery in Marrakech.

[57.2] **Marrakech: Jewish Cemetery**
CONTINUOUS LOOP
2009 / 8:23 MINUTES / FORMAT HD / COLOUR
CAMERA Sylvia Safdie
EDITING Patrick Andrew Boivin, Sylvia Safdie
AUDIO DESIGN Patrick Andrew Boivin

A meditation on the Jewish cemetery in
Marrakech.

[58] **Tagadirt Cemetery**   DIPTYCH
2009 / 4:00 MINUTES / FORMAT HD / COLOUR
CAMERA Sylvia Safdie
EDITING Patrick Andrew Boivin, Sylvia Safdie
AUDIO DESIGN Patrick Andrew Boivin

This video explores an abandoned Jewish
cemetary in Tagadirt, a small village in southern
Morocco where Jews settled over 2,000 years
ago and no longer live. Today, what remains are
mounds of stones and foliage.

Fragments   CONTINUOUS LOOPS
2009 / FORMAT HD / COLOUR
[59.1] **Fragment, No. 1** 1:22 MINUTES
[59.2] **Fragment, No. 2** 0:45 MINUTES
[59.3] **Fragment, No. 3** 0:22 MINUTES
CAMERA Sylvia Safdie
EDITING Brigitte Dajczer, Sylvia Safdie,
Patrick Andrew Boivin / AUDIO Silent
These fragments from a Hebraic Bible were
found on the ground of the synagogue in
Tagadirt, a small village in southern Morocco.

[60] **Adib Hamad**   DIPTYCH
2009 / 5:25 MINUTES / FORMAT HD /COLOUR
CAMERA Patrick Andrew Boivin, Sylvia Safdie
EDITING Patrick Andrew Boivin, Sylvia Safdie
AUDIO DESIGN Patrick Andrew Boivin

A portrait of Adib Hamad, a seventy-four-year-
old imam in his home in the mellah, in the old
Jewish quarter in Tagadirt, a small village in
southern Morocco.

[57.1]
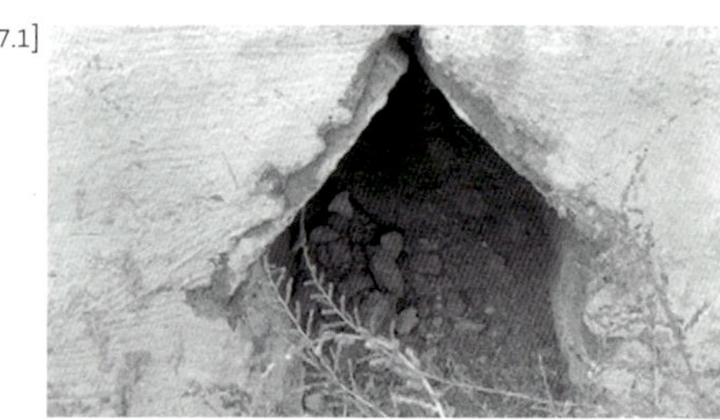
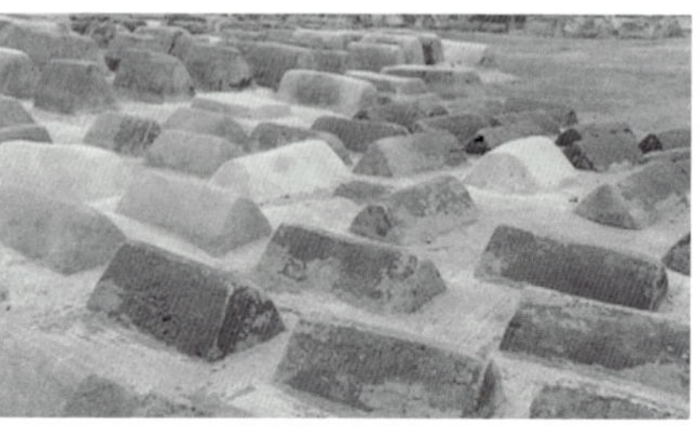
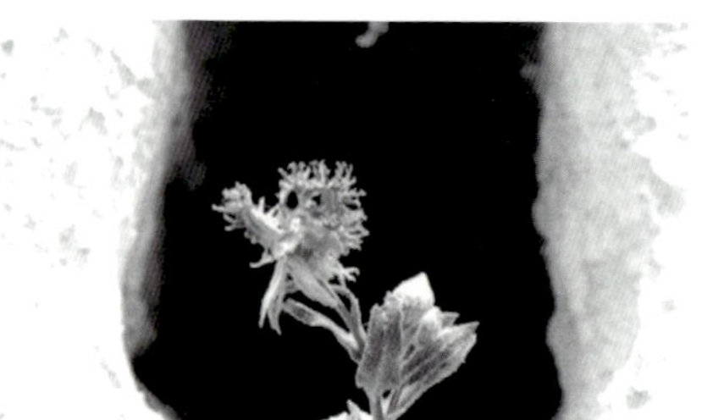

[57.2]
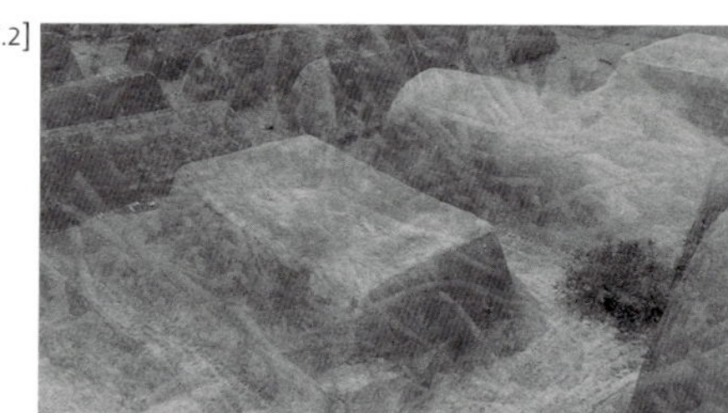

[58]
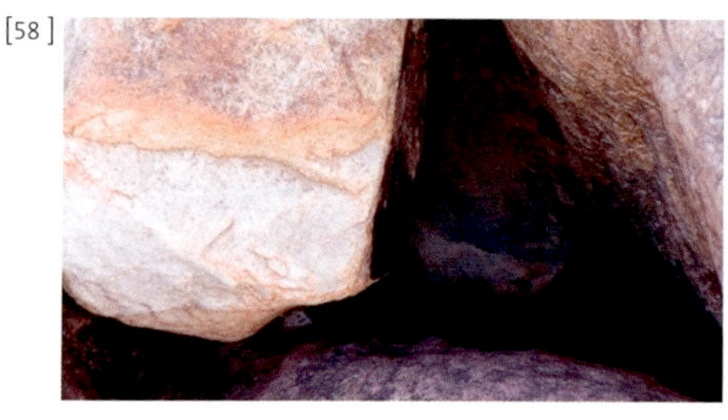
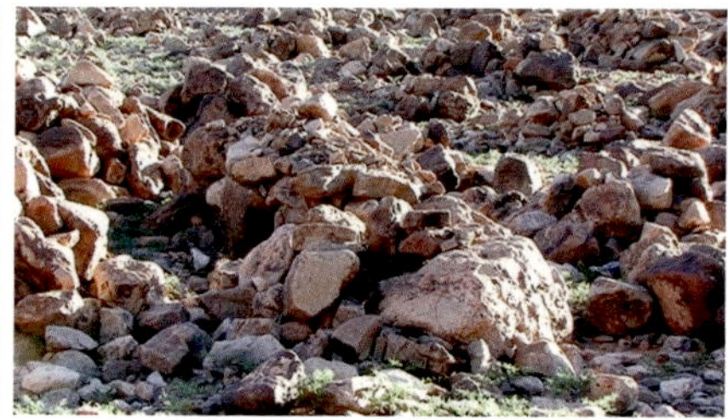

[59.1]
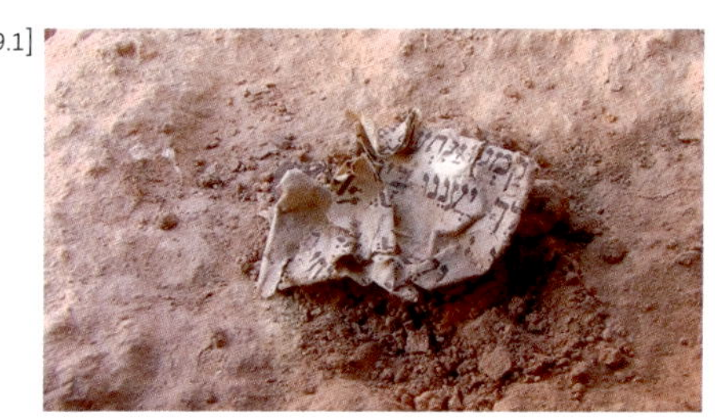
[59.2]
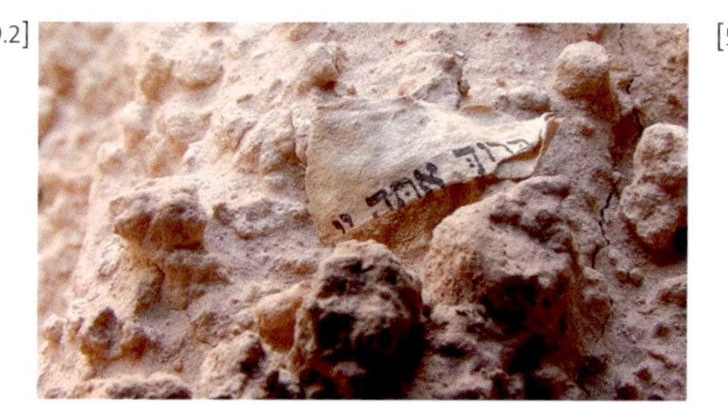
[59.3]
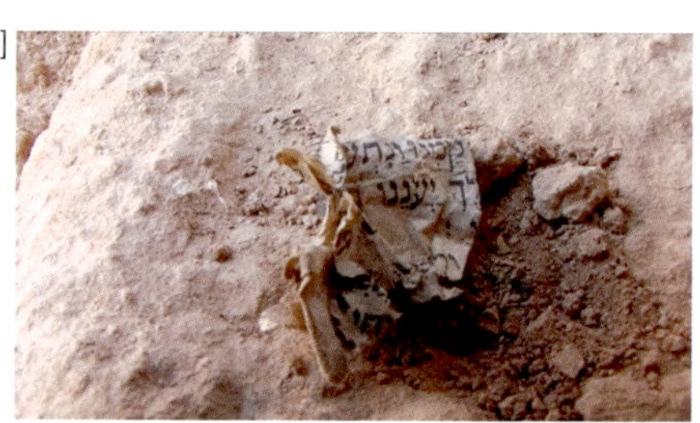

[60]
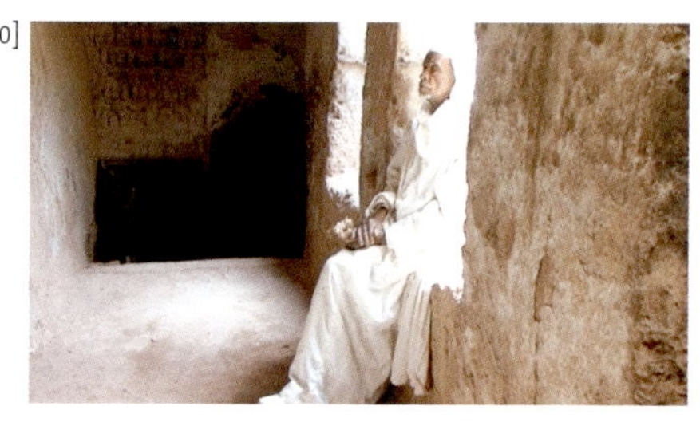
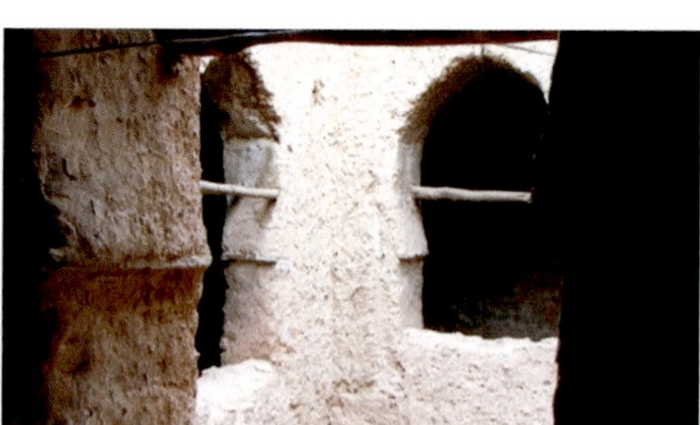

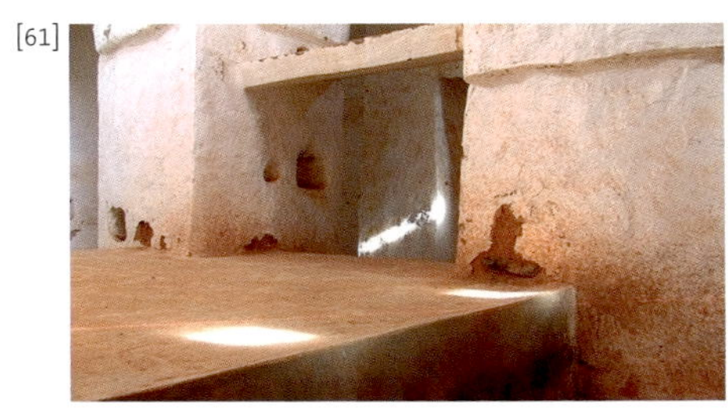

[61]

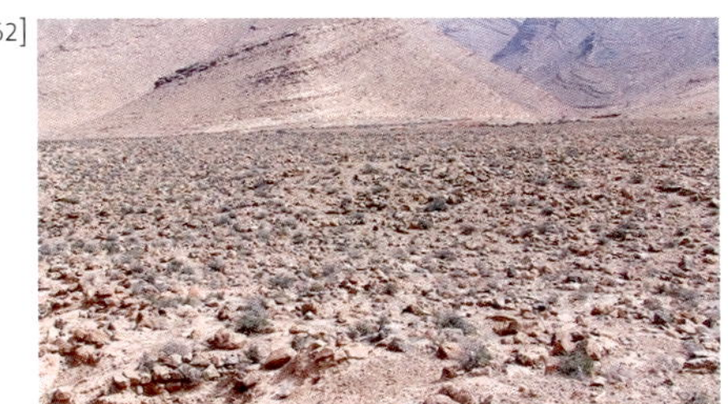

[62]

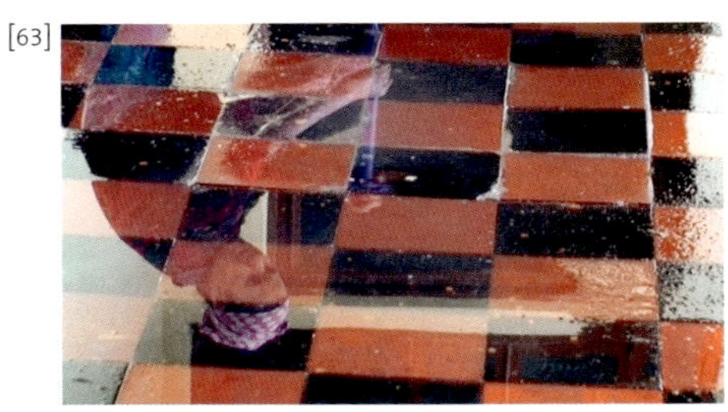

[63]

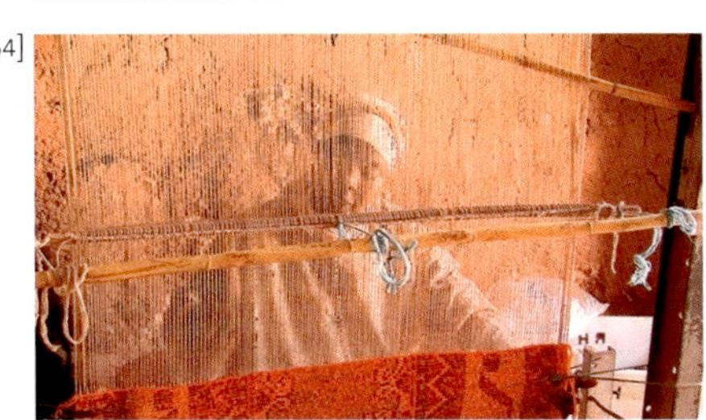

[64]

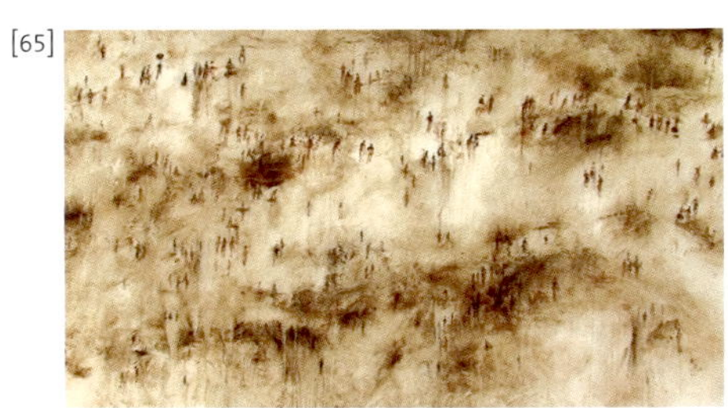

[65]

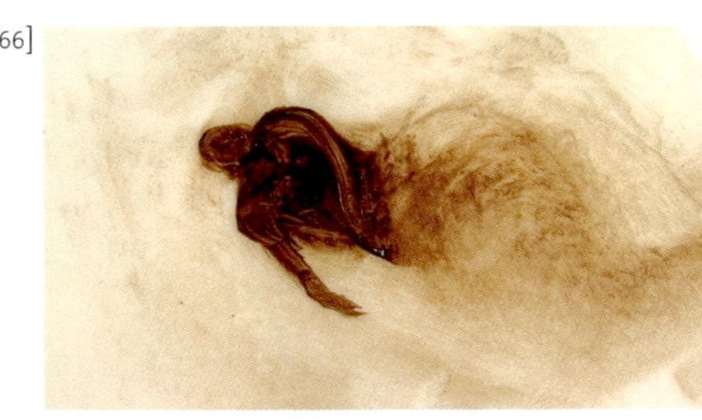

[66]

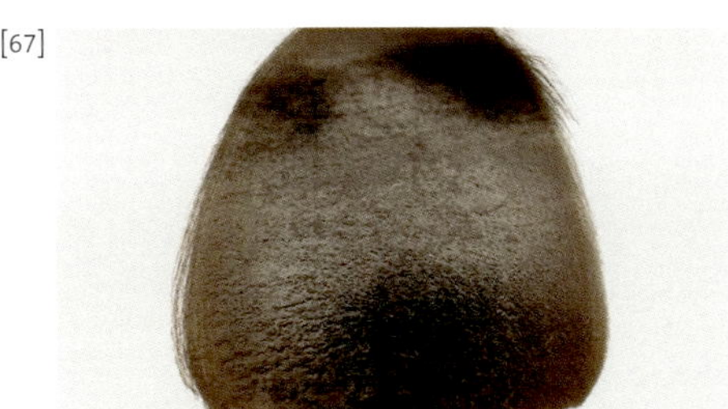

[67]

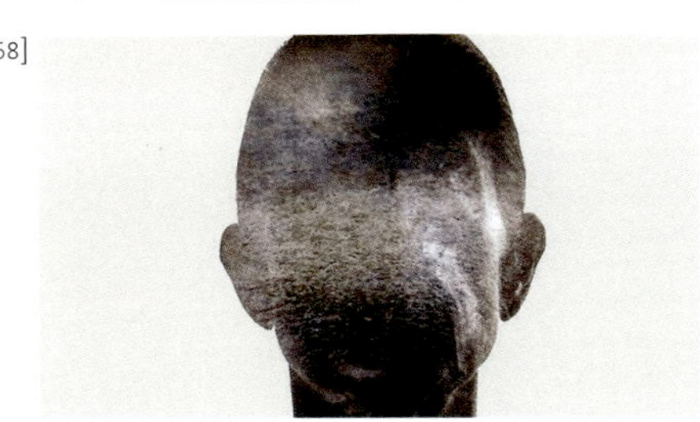

[68]

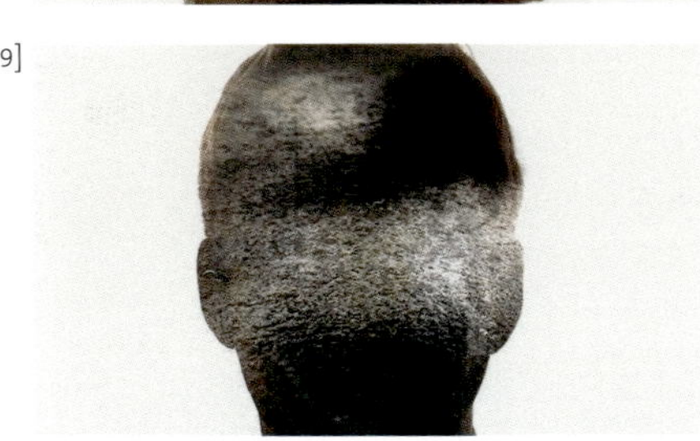

[69]

[61] Prayers

2009 / 7:13 MINUTES / FORMAT HD / COLOUR
CAMERA Sylvia Safdie
EDITING Patrick Andrew Boivin, Sylvia Safdie
AUDIO DESIGN Patrick Andrew Boivin

The relationship between sound and place is explored in the synagogue of Oufran, southern Morocco. The audio consists of Muslim prayers recorded while filming the synagogue, and of Jewish prayers recorded in Moulai Ighir, Morocco, in November 2009.

[62] Oufran, Cemetery

2009 / 2:55 MINUTES / FORMAT HD / COLOUR
CAMERA Sylvia Safdie
EDITING Sylvia Safdie, Patrick Andrew Boivin
AUDIO DESIGN Patrick Andrew Boivin

A meditation on the Jewish cemetery in Oufran in southern Morocco, which contains tombs that are almost 2,000 years old. Today what remains are shards of stone. It is only by chance that you will turn over a stone that will reveal Hebraic script.

[63] Cleansing

2009 / 6:50 MINUTES / FORMAT HD / COLOUR
CAMERA Sylvia Safdie
EDITING Brigitte Dajczer, Sylvia Safdie
AUDIO DESIGN Brigitte Dajczer

Mona, a servant, is washing the floor on a Friday afternoon in preparation for the Sabbath in a home in the mellah, the old Jewish quarter in Marrakech. The sound of the muezzin chanting Muslim prayers accompanies her activity.

[64] Jeannine Fadma

2009 / 2:53 MINUTES / FORMAT HD / COLOUR
CAMERA Sylvia Safdie
EDITING Patrick Andrew Boivin, Sylvia Safdie
AUDIO DESIGN Jeannine Fadma, singing

Jeannine Fadma is a weaver who lives in Ait Ben Haddou, a small town in the Atlas Mountains of Morocco. She sings as she weaves. There is a strong relationship between the gestures that she makes in the weaving and the rhythm of the song.

[65] Figures and Ground II

2009 / 5:31 MINUTES / FORMAT HD / COLOUR
PAINTING Sylvia Safdie / CAMERA Sylvia Safdie
EDITING Patrick Andrew Boivin, Brigitte Dajczer, Sylvia Safdie / AUDIO* John Heward, percussion

The transformation of the human gesture is explored through the process of painting and the use of earth and oil as foundational materials.

[66] Figures and Ground III

2009 / 7:03 MINUTES / FORMAT HD / COLOUR
PAINTING Sylvia Safdie / CAMERA Sylvia Safdie
EDITING Patrick Andrew Boivin, Brigitte Dajczer, Sylvia Safdie / AUDIO* John Heward, percussion

The transformation of the human gesture is explored through the process of painting and the use of earth and oil as foundational materials.

[67] Head I

2009 / 5:21 MINUTES / FORMAT HD / COLOUR
CAMERA Patrick Andrew Boivin, Sylvia Safdie
EDITING Patrick Andrew Boivin, Sylvia Safdie
AUDIO* John Heward, cymbal; Brian Lipson, trumpet; Patrick Andrew Boivin, synthesizer
AUDIO DESIGN* Patrick Andrew Boivin

Head, shadows, water, and sound come together in a work on transformation and meditation.

[68] Head II

2009 / 5:21 MINUTES / FORMAT HD / COLOUR
CAMERA Patrick Andrew Boivin, Sylvia Safdie
EDITING Patrick Andrew Boivin, Sylvia Safdie
AUDIO* John Heward, cymbal; Brian Lipson, trumpet; Patrick Andrew Boivin, synthesizer
AUDIO DESIGN* Patrick Andrew Boivin

Head, shadows, water, and sound come together in a work on transformation and meditation.

[69] Head III

2009 / 5:21 MINUTES / FORMAT HD / COLOUR
CAMERA Patrick Andrew Boivin, Sylvia Safdie
EDITING Patrick Andrew Boivin, Sylvia Safdie
AUDIO* John Heward, cymbal; Brian Lipson, trumpet; Patrick Andrew Boivin, synthesizer
AUDIO DESIGN* Patrick Andrew Boivin

Head, shadows, water, and sound come together in a work on transformation and meditation.

[70] Untitled I
2009 / 8:30 MINUTES / FORMAT HD / COLOUR
CAMERA Patrick Andrew Boivin, Sylvia Safdie
EDITING Patrick Andrew Boivin, Sylvia Safdie
AUDIO* Thomas Buckner, vocals

Light, shadow, and water transform the body.
This video can be viewed horizontally or
vertically.

[71] Untitled III
2010 / 6:07 MINUTES / FORMAT HD / COLOUR
CAMERA Patrick Andrew Boivin, Sylvia Safdie
EDITING Patrick Andrew Boivin, Sylvia Safdie
AUDIO* John Heward, cymbals; Patrick Andrew
Boivin, synthesizer
AUDIO DESIGN Patrick Andrew Boivin

Body, water, and stones come together in this
work on the nature of transformation and
meditation.

[72] Untitled IV
2010 / 5:23 MINUTES / FORMAT HD / COLOUR
CAMERA Patrick Andrew Boivin, Sylvia Safdie
EDITING Patrick Andrew Boivin, Sylvia Safdie
AUDIO* John Heward, cymbals; Patrick Andrew
Boivin, synthesizer
AUDIO DESIGN Patrick Andrew Boivin

Body, water, and stones come together in this
work on the nature of transformation and
meditation.

Body/Stone/Water
2009 / FORMAT HD / COLOUR
[73.1] **Body/Stone/Water I** 11:32 MINUTES
[73.2] **Body/Stone/Water II** 3:27 MINUTES
[73.3] **Body/Stone/Water III** 3:34 MINUTES
[73.4] **Body/Stone/Water IV** 4:21 MINUTES
[73.5] **Body/Stone/Water V** 4:34 MINUTES
[73.6] **Body/Stone/Water VI** 6:08 MINUTES
CAMERA Patrick Andrew Boivin, Sylvia Safdie
EDITING Patrick Andrew Boivin, Sylvia Safdie
AUDIO* Thomas Buckner, vocals; Patrick Andrew
Boivin, aluminium bowl
AUDIO DESIGN Patrick Andrew Boivin

The body moves through stone, water, and light,
creating a meditative and perceptual space.

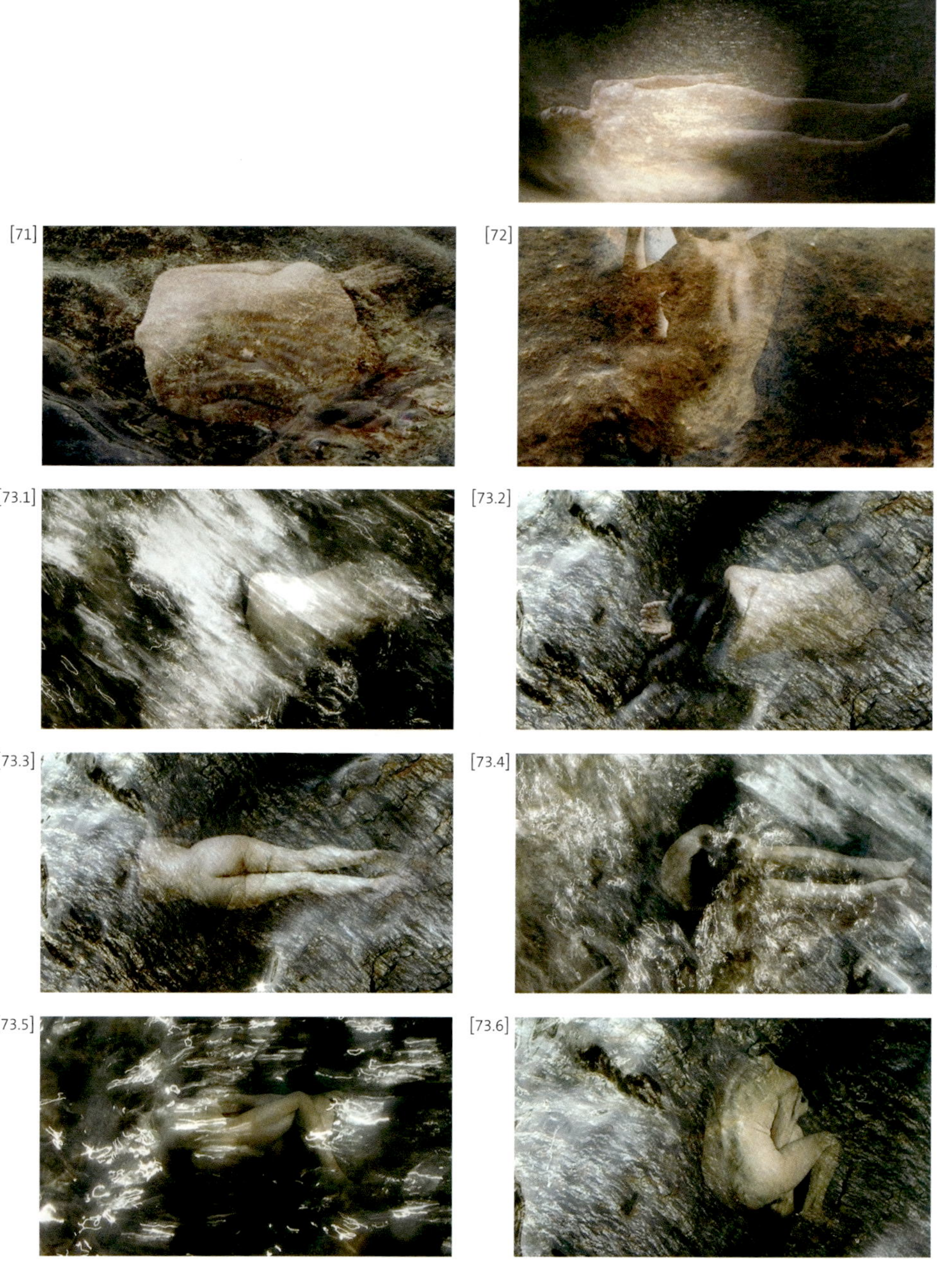

[70]

[71] [72]

[73.1] [73.2]

[73.3] [73.4]

[73.5] [73.6]

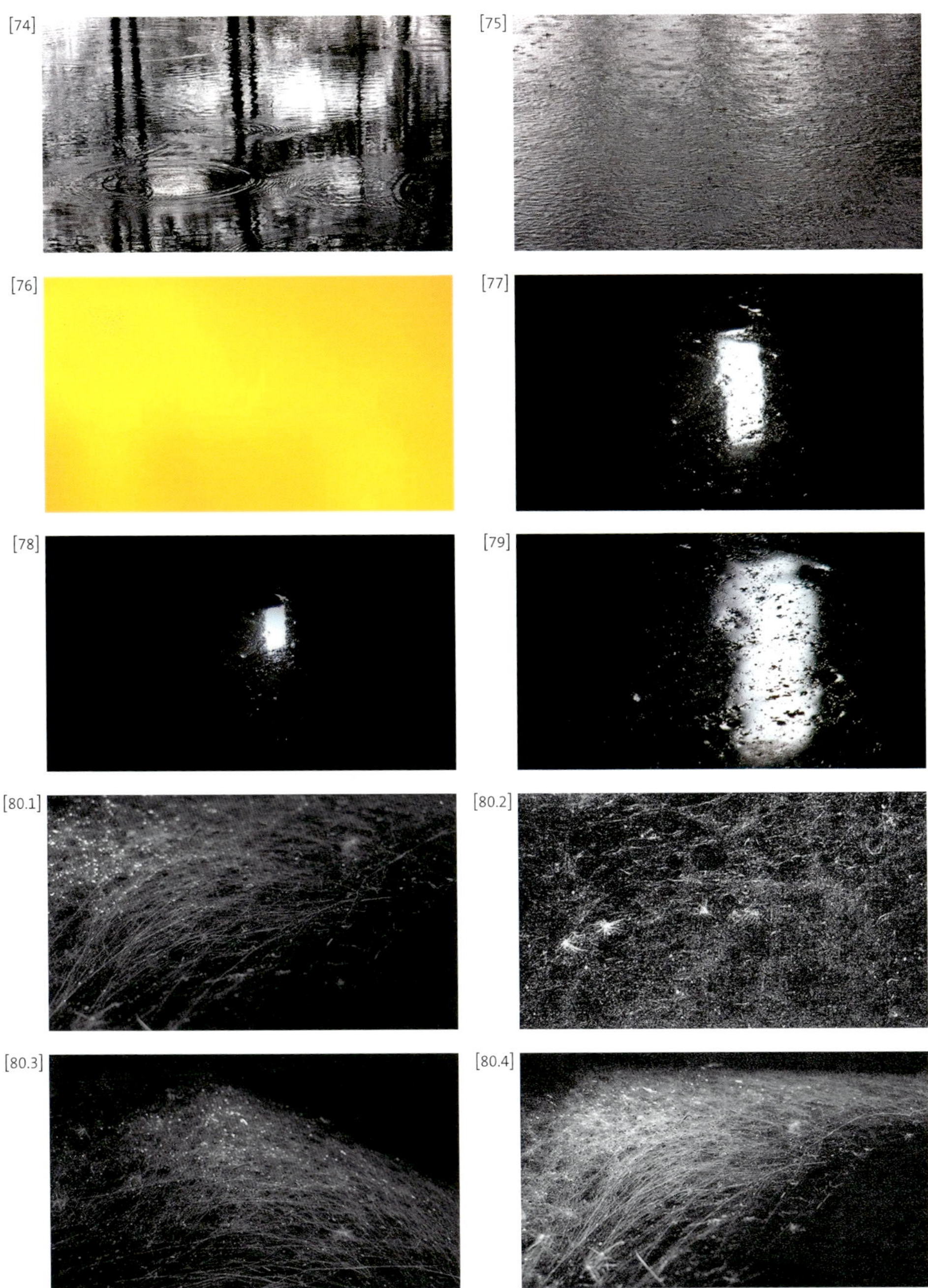

[74] **Pond/Auschwitz I**
CONTINUOUS LOOP
2011 / 1:26 MINUTES / FORMAT HD /COLOUR
CAMERA Sylvia Safdie
EDITING Patrick Andrew Boivin, Sylvia Safdie
AUDIO Silent

Auschwitz, May 2010. Reflections of trees
are transformed by rain falling on pond in
Auschwitz II, Birkenau.

[75] **Pond/Auschwitz II**
CONTINUOUS LOOP
2011 / 1:33 MINUTES / FORMAT HD / COLOUR
CAMERA Sylvia Safdie
EDITING Patrick Andrew Boivin, Sylvia Safdie
AUDIO Silent

Auschwitz, May 2010. Rain falling on pond in
Auschwitz II, Birkenau.

[76] **Pond/Auschwitz III**
CONTINUOUS LOOP
2011 / 3:58 MINUTES / FORMAT HD / COLOUR
CAMERA Sylvia Safdie
EDITING Patrick Andrew Boivin, Sylvia Safdie
AUDIO Silent

Auschwitz, May 2010. A close-up of a yellow
flower petal slowly transforms to reveal flowers
in a pond in Auschwitz II, Birkenau.

[77] **Reflection/Auschwitz I**
CONTINUOUS LOOP
2011 / 6:18 MINUTES / FORMAT HD / COLOUR
CAMERA Sylvia Safdie
EDITING Patrick Andrew Boivin, Sylvia Safdie
AUDIO Silent

Auschwitz, May 2010. Light reflected on the
water in Auschwitz II, Birkenau, Sector B1a.

[78] **Reflection/Auschwitz II**
CONTINUOUS LOOP
2011 / 5:33 MINUTES / FORMAT HD / COLOUR
CAMERA Sylvia Safdie
EDITING Patrick Andrew Boivin, Sylvia Safdie
AUDIO Silent

Auschwitz, May 2010. Light reflected on the
water in Auschwitz II, Birkenau, Sector B1a.

[79] **Reflection/Auschwitz III**
CONTINUOUS LOOP
2011 / 6:16 MINUTES / FORMAT HD / COLOUR
CAMERA Sylvia Safdie
EDITING Patrick Andrew Boivin, Sylvia Safdie
AUDIO Silent

Auschwitz, May 2010. Light reflected on the
water in Auschwitz II, Birkenau, Sector B1a.

Web/Auschwitz Series I
2011 / FORMAT HD / BLACK AND WHITE
[80.1] **Web/Auschwitz Series I, No. 1**
7:31 MINUTES
[80.2] **Web/Auschwitz Series I, No. 2**
7:31 MINUTES
[80.3] **Web/Auschwitz Series I, No. 3**
7:31 MINUTES
[80.4] **Web/Auschwitz Series I, No. 4**
7:31 MINUTES
CAMERA Sylvia Safdie
EDITING Patrick Andrew Boivin, Sylvia Safdie
AUDIO Silent

Auschwitz, May 2010. Spider webs are
illuminated by light in Auschwitz II, Birkenau,
Sector B1a.

[81] **Barre I**
2011 / 2:18 MINUTES / FORMAT HD
BLACK AND WHITE
CAMERA Sylvia Safdie
EDITING Patrick Andrew Boivin, Sylvia Safdie
AUDIO Barre Phillips, bass

Barre Phillips improvises in La Chapelle Sainte
Philomène, Puget-Ville, France, October 2010.

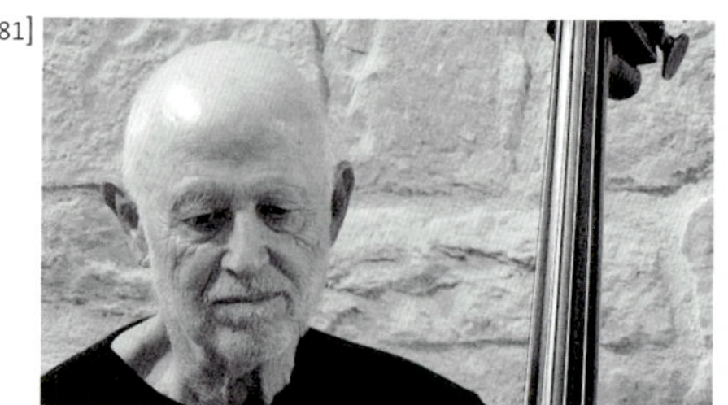

[82] **Barre II**
2011 / 2:27 MINUTES / FORMAT HD / COLOUR
CAMERA Sylvia Safdie
EDITING Patrick Andrew Boivin, Sylvia Safdie
AUDIO Barre Phillips, bass

The ocean and haze of Nova Scotia are
amplified and transformed by Barre Phillips'
improvisation recorded in La Chapelle Sainte
Philomène, Puget-Ville, France, October 2010.

[83] **Barre III**
2011 / 2:54 MINUTES / FORMAT HD
BLACK AND WHITE
CAMERA Sylvia Safdie
EDITING Patrick Andrew Boivin, Sylvia Safdie
AUDIO Barre Phillips, bass

Light and shadow are amplified and
transformed by Barre Phillips' improvisation,
recorded in La Chapelle Sainte Philomène,
Puget-Ville, France, October 2010.

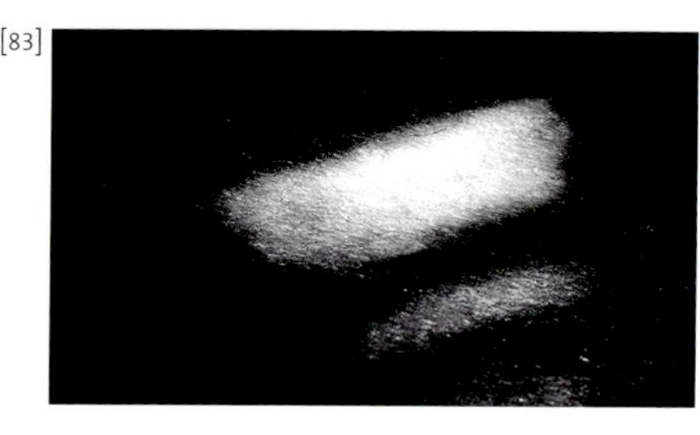

[84] **Concert**
2011 / 6:35 MINUTES / FORMAT HD
BLACK AND WHITE
CAMERA Sylvia Safdie, Nick Tsiavos
EDITING Patrick Andrew Boivin, Sylvia Safdie
AUDIO Barre Phillips, bass; John Heward,
percussion; Lionel Gorcin, saxophones

Concert recorded on location in Barjols, France,
September 2010.

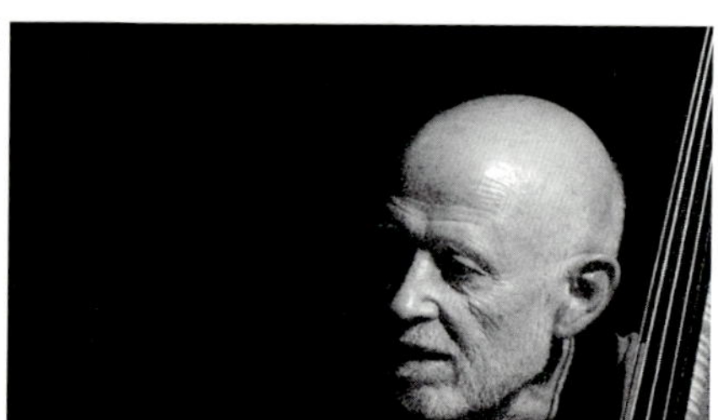

[85] **Piano I**
2011 / 8:23 MINUTES / FORMAT HD / COLOUR
CAMERA Patrick Andrew Boivin, Sylvia Safdie
EDITING Patrick Andrew Boivin, Sylvia Safdie
AUDIO Charity Chan, piano

Charity Chan coaxes a range of alternative
timbres and sounds from the piano, using
a combination of extended and prepared
techniques.

[86] **Piano II**
2011 / 5:43 MINUTES / FORMAT HD / COLOUR
CAMERA Patrick Andrew Boivin, Sylvia Safdie
EDITING Patrick Andrew Boivin, Sylvia Safdie
AUDIO Charity Chan, piano

Charity Chan coaxes a range of alternative
timbres and sounds from the piano, using
a combination of extended and prepared
techniques.

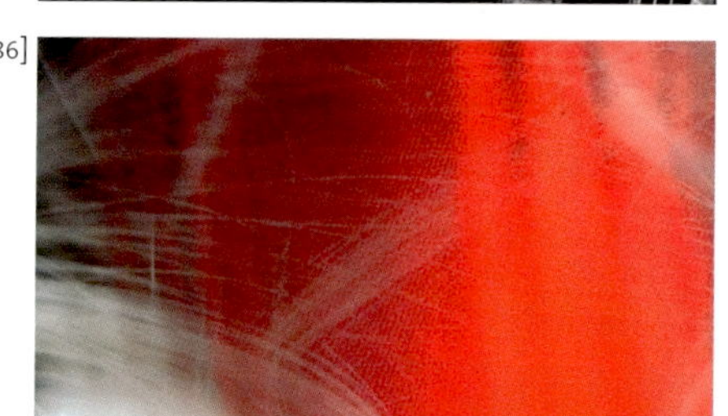

[87] **Piano III**
2011 / 5:43 MINUTES / FORMAT HD / COLOUR
CAMERA Patrick Andrew Boivin, Sylvia Safdie
EDITING Patrick Andrew Boivin, Sylvia Safdie
AUDIO Charity Chan, piano

Charity Chan coaxes a range of alternative
timbres and sounds from the piano, using
a combination of extended and prepared
techniques.

[88] **Piano IV** DIPTYCH
2011 / 5:43 MINUTES / FORMAT HD
BLACK AND WHITE
CAMERA Patrick Andrew Boivin, Sylvia Safdie
EDITING Patrick Andrew Boivin, Sylvia Safdie
AUDIO Charity Chan, piano

Charity Chan coaxes a range of alternative
timbres and sounds from the piano, using
a combination of extended and prepared
techniques.

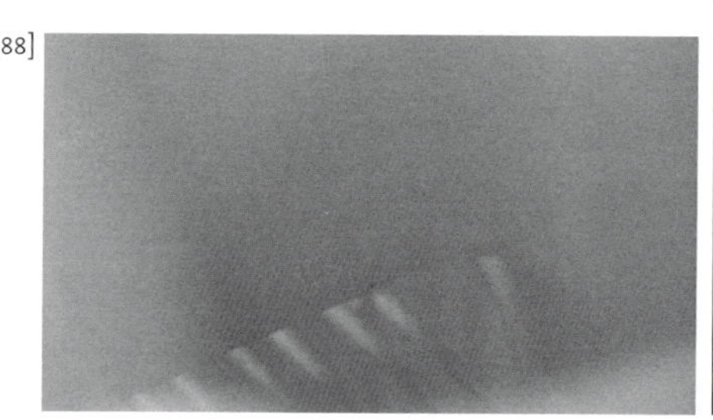

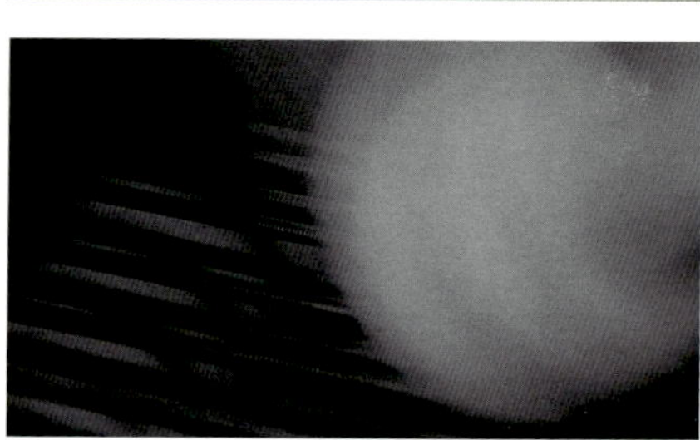

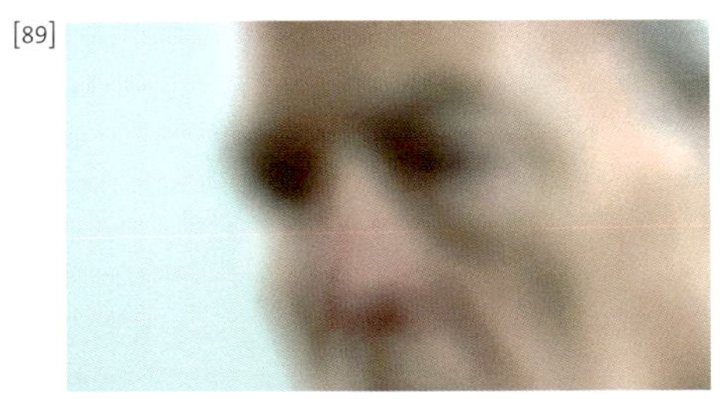

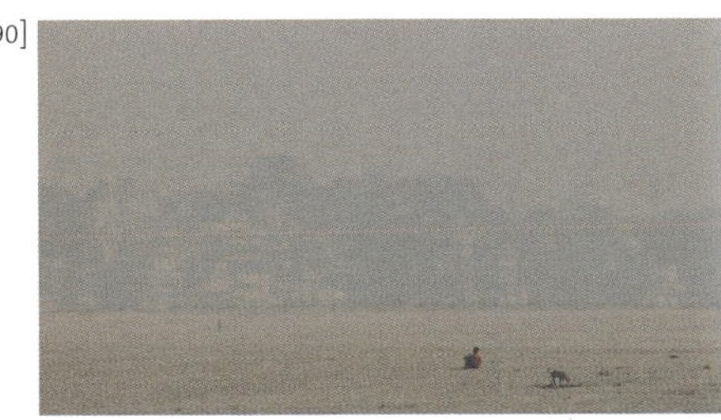

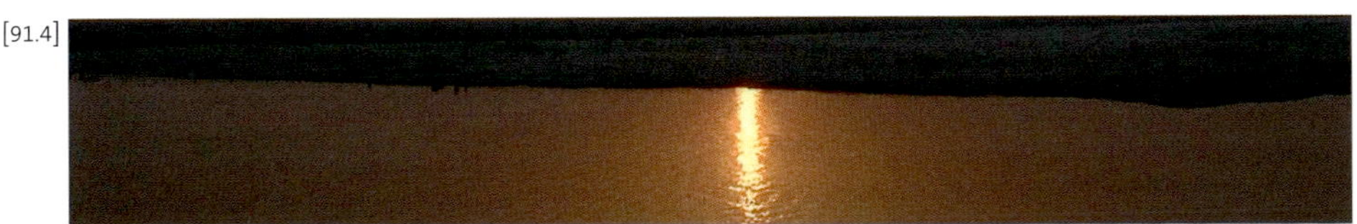

[89] **Water/Stone/Head**
2012 / 4:50 MINUTES / FORMAT HD / COLOUR
CAMERA Sylvia Safdie
EDITING Patrick Andrew Boivin, Sylvia Safdie
AUDIO John Heward, percussion
AUDIO DESIGN Patrick Andrew Boivin

The sound and image of water crashing over a stone are met by John Heward's percussion. Heward's unfocused face emerges, subtly revealing his gestural response to the sound and image of the water.

Morning/Varanasi (Series II)
2012 / FORMAT HD / COLOUR
[91.1] **No. 1** 9:26 MINUTES
[91.2] **No. 2** 13:21 MINUTES
[91.3] **No. 3** 11:35 MINUTES
[91.4] **No. 4** 5:08 MINUTES
CAMERA Sylvia Safdie
EDITING Patrick Andrew Boivin, Sylvia Safdie
AUDIO Silent

During the morning, men are engaged in various activities on the shores of the Ganges in Varanasi, India.

[90] **Morning/Varanasi (Series I, No. 1)**
2012 / 15:40 MINUTES / FORMAT HD / COLOUR
CAMERA Sylvia Safdie
EDITING Patrick Andrew Boivin, Sylvia Safdie
AUDIO Silent

During the morning, a young man sits, a dog wanders, and a man walks in the distance. This footage was filmed on the shores of the Ganges in Varanasi, India.

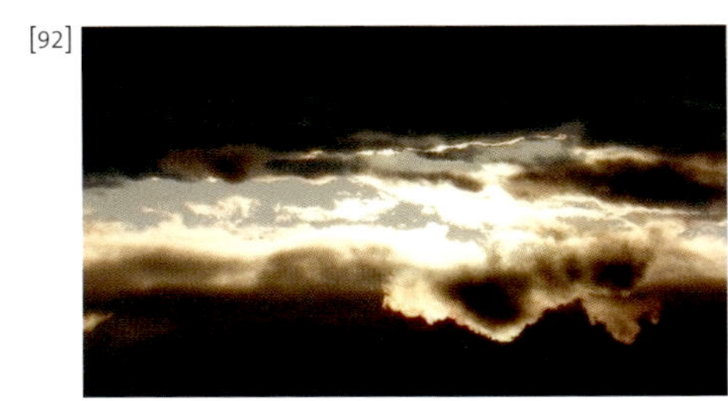

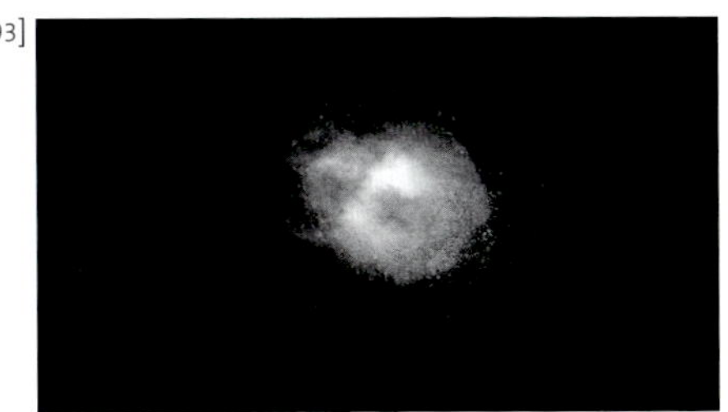

[92] **Time**
2012 / 1:51 MINUTES / FORMAT HD / COLOUR
CAMERA Sylvia Safdie
EDITING Patrick Andrew Boivin, Sylvia Safdie
AUDIO Silent

The image of a setting sun is reversed. The video was recorded at Lake Memphremagog, Quebec.

[93] **Moon/Clouds/Earth**
2012 / 9:46 MINUTES / FORMAT HD
BLACK AND WHITE
CAMERA Sylvia Safdie
EDITING Patrick Andrew Boivin, Sylvia Safdie
AUDIO Silent

In this video, moon, clouds, and earth come together in a work on meditation and transformation.